P9-DDK-768

# MOUNTAINS TO DESERT
## Selected Inyo Readings

compiled by:

**Friends of the Eastern California Museum**
Independence, California

Friends of the Eastern California Museum
Independence, CA 93526

© 1988 by
Friends of the Eastern California Museum

First paperback printing 1988

Library of Congress Cataloging-in-Publication Data

Mountains to desert : selected Inyo readings/
    compiled by Friends of the Eastern California Museum.

    Includes bibliographies and index.
    1. Inyo County (Calif.)—History.
I. Eastern California Museum. Friends.
F868.I6M68 1988
979.4'87—dc19                    88-24595
                                 CIP

ISBN 0-9620913-0-8

Printed in the United States of America

1 2 3 4 5 6 7 8 9

This book is the first publication of the Friends of the Eastern California Museum. While publishing and education are stated purposes of the Friends, a project of this magnitude is easily scheduled for the indefinite future.

The year 1988 marks the 60th Anniversary of the Eastern California Museum. It was decided that the Friends should publish a book to commemorate this event. So, with a commendable goal we naively began this task.

The entire project would have been impossible were it not for the generous financial support of Bruce and Elsie Ivey of Independence. Additional financial support came from the estate of Polly Connable.

Polly, until her death in 1987, had been a longtime resident of the Eastern Sierra. As an avid mountaineer and historian, Polly's association with the Eastern California Museum was a valued asset. We all will miss her.

It is in Polly's memory that we dedicate this book.

# TABLE OF CONTENTS

# ILLUSTRATIONS

# THE
# EASTERN CALIFORNIA
# MUSEUM

by Anna Kelley

Early in 1928 rapid changes occurring in Owens Valley forced a realization that much historical data and material concerning Inyo County would soon be lost unless means of preserving them were found. At the same time, a group of young men were interested in collecting the remains of Indian culture, locating and photographing their petroglyphs and in any way possible recreating the history of a partly vanished way of life. Among these young men were Ralph Bell, Frank Parcher, Charles Forbes, and William Sanford. Frank's mother, Mrs. W. C. Parcher, shared their interest. She also thought that the history of pioneer life in this region should be preserved.

It was her plan that a museum be created to exhibit these varied collections. This resulted in the formation of the Eastern California Museum Association with Mrs. Parcher as first president—a position she held for several years. She strove from the first to develop a broad, comprehensive collection with departments of history, geology, botany, mineralogy, and Indian anthropology. How well she succeeded may be seen by even a casual visit to the museum.

The Eastern California Museum Association was formally organized Sunday evening, May 5, 1928, at the Bishop Branch of the Inyo County Library. The purpose of the organization was to collect, house, protect, preserve, and classify objects and natural landmarks of historic and scientific interest found in Eastern California and adjacent fields.

1

1. Eastern California Museum, 1987. Independence, California. (*Credit: Kathy Barnes.*)

The first officers elected for the organization were Mrs. W. C. Parcher as President, Lawson Brainard as Vice President, and Charles Forbes as Secretary/Treasurer. The othere members of the Board of Directors were Douglas Robinson, William A. Irwin Jr., Bessie T. Best, Frank M. Parcher, and G. Walter Dow. Frank Parcher was appointed to be the museum's first Curator.

The committees created by the Board of Directors were many. They covered all of the "ologies", plus History and Landmarks, Publicity, Research, House and Finance. The committee chairmen were knowledgeable, ambitious, civic-minded people.

Sparked by the enthusiasm of the first officers and committee chairmen, the immediate need of housing was obvious. Search for the means to provide housing began soon after the Association was formed and will continue as long as there is a museum—there is never enough room.

Since the Eastern California Museum Association is sixty years old, and many events have taken place and many supporters have come and gone, it might be well to list the high points in chronological order:

1928   -   May 5. Eastern California Museum Association organized.

1929   -   January 7. Granted use of a room in the basement of the courthouse for storage.
        -   Through hard work and much correspondence to Department of Interior, succeeded in having ten thousand acres of land withdrawn from entry in Eastern California and Western Nevada. This land contained many aboriginal sites, petroglyphs, petrified forests and other Indian artifacts. This order has since been revoked.

1930   -   January. Eastern California Museum Association incorporated.

1931   -   Permanent use of the room in the basement of the Courthouse and a budget of five hundred dollars granted by County Board of Supervisors.

- Annual membership dinners, yearly election of officers, monthly field trips, museum library and a landmarks program. Collection of botanical specimens and participation in a pioneer archaeological survey of Saline Valley.

1940s - Collection of invaluable local family histories.

1950-60 - Second room in Courthouse provided by Board of Supervisors, and a five thousand dollar budget.
- New display cases.
- Washington Hand Press.
- No. 18 Narrow gauge Railroad Locomotive.
- Charcoal Kilns at Cottonwood Creek.
- Herbarium exhibit installed.
- Host to annual meeting of Archaeological Survey Association.
- Research Inyo's complicated history.
- Collections organized, records updated, and increased open hours.

1960-68 - Point Typology Workshop administered by guest scientist, Ruth D. Simpson.
- Mammoth Creek Cave and Crooked Creek Excavation—Ruth D. Simpson served as technical advisor.
- Dr. Louis Leakey speaker at 1965 annual dinner.
- Black Collection of Paiute-Shoshone baskets.
- Membership reached 1300.
- Bottle workshops—fund-raisers.
- G. Walter and Maude Dow donated a large sum of money for construction of a new building on Grant Street. Building dedicated in 1968 to memory of Mr. and Mrs. Dow.
- County Board of Supervisors accepted the new building as a gift and created the Inyo County Museums Department with budget and county staff.
- Commander's House restored.
- "Round About the Museum" column for Inyo Independent.

1968-76 - "Moving Day" to new building.

- Assayer's Office—first building of "Ghost Town" complex.
- Hanna House, Livery Stable, Brewery Office, Pete Mairs' utility shack, stock room and privies added to Ghost Town.
- D.W.P. historic equipment yard.
- Tape of Helen Gunn's music box discs.
- Manzanar exhibit started.

1976 - Bicentennial Variety and Fashion Review sponsored by Independence Garden Club and hosted by Museum.
- Hilderman Estate papers.

1980s - Eastern California Museum Association becomes Eastern California Historical Society.
- Friends of the Eastern California Museum organized.
- Fund-raisers—Christmas Boutique, Western Game Brunch, 1880's Hands-on Work Day, and Bingo.
- Building Fund Campaign.
- Friends of the Eastern California Museum purchased computer for Museum use.
- Ten thousand dollars from Mary Cavitt estate.
- Twenty-five shares of Abbott Laboratories stock donated to Building Fund by Doris Statham.
- George Malcolm butterfly collection.
- Indian baskets, crystal, china, dolls, porcelain figurines, china cabinet, and two small cabinets from Ellen Evans estate.

Through the efforts of loyal supporters and hard work performed by countless volunteers, the Museum has thrived.

\* \* \*

Mary DeDecker takes us back to the Owens Valley prior to the white mans arrival and subsequent "development" of its water resources by the City of Los Angeles. This balanced and healthy ecosystem is compared with what exists today. No one is more qualified than Mary to exhibit these contrasting scenes.

A self taught botanist, more specifically a plant taxonomist, Mary has lived in Independence since 1935. Much of the environmental degradation discussed in her article occurred while Mary was actively engaged in field work in the Owens Valley.

Among Mary's many accomplishments is the discovery of several new plant species, a new variety and an entirely new genus, all within Inyo County.

The author of several books and many articles, Mary is a tireless defender of the many natural values of the Owens Valley.

# OWENS VALLEY, THEN AND NOW

by Mary DeDecker

Owens Valley, as it was first known, was occupied by Paiute Indians. They lived a relatively peaceful life which allowed development of a stable social structure. A newspaper correspondent, on the expedition of Captain J. W. Davidson in 1859, described them as both morally and physically superior to any of their race in California. They had developed a simple form of agriculture in the Bishop, Big Pine, and Independence areas which was an ingenuous way of using the natural resources to advantage. Although they lived on the land, harvesting both natural and their cultivated native foods, they were wise enough to allow for replenishment. No resource was exploited to the point of no return. Above all, they had a high respect for water. They realized that it must never be polluted by waste or dead animal matter. There must have been difficult times, such as extremely long, severe winters, or parching periods of drought, but they knew they must adapt to what came. Their very survival depended upon living within the resources immediately available.

Then the white men arrived. Our first glimpses of the valley are found in accounts of various expeditions passing through. In those days of travel by horseback any new place was judged by its grass and available water. Owens Valley rated high. Its frequent meadows and plentiful bunch grasses impressed them as favorably as did the numerous springs and water courses. Up to that time, the valley had not been exploited in any way. Let us try to visualize what those first parties saw.

The alluvial slopes were probably much as they are today, although some deterioration has occurred. Along the base of the

7

Sierra would have been the Great Basin sagebrush and the large shrubs associated with it. We can assume that deer browsed freely, but were kept under control by coyotes and cougars. Lower on the slopes lesser shrubs mixed with the sagebrush to form a low, grayish scrub cover. Ribbons of riparian growth bordered rushing streams, one from the mouth of each Sierra canyon. The major streamways could be traced by tall ponderosa pine, possibly relics of ages past. Some still survive. (Higher on the mountain slopes its close relative, the Jeffrey pine, is common.) Black poplar came down from the mountains to meet the bright green lance-leaf species and, lower down, the Fremont poplar with toothed leaves. Water birch and various willows filled in between the taller trees. Lush growth of red columbine, streamside paintbrush, rein orchid and tiger lily lined the moist banks. Woodsy places between the trees showed star flower, aspen onion, fritillaria, and other shade-loving flowers. The stream banks had not yet been trampled by fishermen and campers.

The major waterway, however, was the Owens River, meandering down the length of the valley to discharge its waters into the large, bitter lake at the lower end. The river was bordered by bottom lands of lush saltgrass meadows. Tree willows, along with shrubby species, marked its course. Here, too, was a riparian community, but it was composed of plants which could tolerate some alkali. Even though the river was a fresh-water stream, its banks, as it flowed through the valley, were alkaline to some degree. Plants which thrived there included a small-flowered aster, bur marigold, desert buttercup, and a variety of reeds and rushes. Saltgrass was abundant on the river bottom lands. One showy flower which grew there in abundance was the Owens Valley or Coville mallow, *Sidalcea covillei*. So much of its habitat has been destroyed by drying that only remnants of former populations still exist. It is now listed as a rare and endangered species. It was first found by Coville and Funston of the Death Valley Expedition on June 20, 1891. The site was Haiwee Meadows "in the natural alkaline meadow directly in front of the house." In the wet year of 1952 it was reported from the river bottomland north of Lone Pine, where it covered several acres and resembled a large field of shooting stars as viewed from the highway. The floral spikes are 8 to 24 inches tall, the flowers pinkish-lavender. It requires as habitat a fairly wet meadow, more or less alkaline. For a time it was feared extinct, but occasional sites were found which were still moist enough to support it. The plant is a perennial from fleshy roots, so probably was adapted to live through normal periods of drought. Its very limited distribution, however, and the gradual elimination of its moist habitats narrow its chances for survival. Haiwee Meadows have been inundated by the reservoir, the river bottomlands no longer receive annual flooding, and the few remaining populations are gradually being eliminated by draining for roadways or building sites. There is little chance that this beautiful Owens Valley endemic will survive. Its story is symbolic of changing Owens Valley. Another species which may go with it is the lovely white-flowered alkali mariposa, *Calochortus excavatus*. It is the only mariposa which can tolerate alkaline places. Although it is hardy, it must have moisture near the surface. It, too, is an endemic of the area and often occurs with the Coville mallow.

Owens Lake was extremely akaline, so its moist borders supported species with a high tolerance for the concentration of salts which occurred there. Plants known locally as alkali pink, sand spurry, stinkweed, and arrowscale grew nearby, surrounded by an abundance of inkweed. Parry saltbush with stemless, heartshaped leaves probably formed large rounded bushes toward the southeast curve of the shore, just as they are today. Around the lake and extending the entire length of the valley on dry, alkaline soils, the dominant shrub was greasewood, *Sarcobatus vermiculatus*. This is still the most extensive shrub on the valley floor. It is to be highly valued because it occupies a place which would not be filled by other species. It depends on groundwater, but can thrive where the depth to water is as much as 12 feet. It is highly alkali tolerant and it can penetrate layers of heavy clay. Where such conditions exist on the valley floor, it is the last in plant succession. If the groundwater drops below the point of its endurance, the land would be barren of cover. There would be too little precipitation to support even a healthy crop of aggressive weeds, such as Russian thistle, which otherwise could exist there. Characteristic of the greasewood scrub plant community are frequent clay slicks where water ponds form when there is enough rain. These would have been part of that early landscape. The lush alkali sacaton *(Sporobolus airoides)*, the attractive bunchgrass of that community, which the early expeditions found in abundance, has been sadly depleted due to drier conditions and years of overgrazing. A variety of low shrubs were present on the valley floor, probably much the same as they are today.

Most beautiful to behold would have been the saltgrass meadows, vast areas of green in the spring and summer and golden through the fall and winter. These occurred where groundwater came to within eight feet or less from the surface, or where water spread from streams or springs. On the wetter areas, darker green patches of *Juncus* would have shown up in the meadows. Clumps of alkali sacaton would have entered their drier borders. The meadow acreage has been greatly reduced, mostly due to altering the flow of water or by lowering the groundwater level. As the meadows deteriorate, rabbit brush moves in to replace the grass.

Among the most valuable of the early habitats were the marshes and sloughs. Some of these existed on the old oxbows of the river. Others were formed by the flow from springs and in depressions filled by high ground water. These were rich natural ecosystems, important units in the biological chain of life. Lesser forms of life were nurtured here. These, in turn, became food for the higher forms. The dense growth furnished cover and provided nesting places for birds. Flora and fauna were abundant. Of these habitats only traces remain, so few that their function as part of the valley system has been lost. It is considered a waste of water to maintain these basic cradles of the Owens Valley environment. They varied in size from small green islands to extensive sloughs. Ponds of open water were often present. Floating and submersed aquatics were an important part of the food chain. A variety of reeds, rushes, and cattails grew in these wet places, bordered by others which required less moisture.

Early expeditions, looking for sites with adequate grass and water for their horses, were not too well impressed with that part of the valley showing the Mojave Desert influence. It does, however, contribute to the rich variety of species found here. Creosote bush extends northward as far as Mazourka Canyon east of Independence. It is the dominant shrub over much of the Mojave Desert, but it cannot take alkali. In Owens Valley it stays well away from the lake and skirts the alkali flats north of it. It follows the dry slopes and extends into the Inyo Mountain canyons as high as 5400 feet in elevation. Its northerly limit is governed by temperature. Joshua trees, too, are desert plants, but they require more precipitation than creosote bush. In Owens Valley they occur on non-alkali flats and slopes about the southern end.

2. An early photograph of the Owens river near Aberdeen Station showing extensive riparian habitat. (Credit: *Eastern California Museum.*)

Interspersed with the more obvious plant communities would have been transitional areas of varying composition. Species of *Atriplex* (saltbush) would have been well represented then as they are today, but the pattern would have been quite different. Each has a different moisture requirement and a different degree of tolerance to alkali. Parry saltbush *(Atriplex parryi)* can thrive on white alkali flats and on the borders of Owens Lake. Allscale *(Atriplex polycarpa)* can take some alkali, but definitely less than the above. It occurs on the perimeters of alkali places, often where it is very dry. Desert holly *(Atriplex hymenelytra)* occupies a place too hot and dry for the other species and it also has a high tolerance for various salts. On the other hand, Nevada saltbush *(Atriplex torreyi)* requires more moisture than the others. It is found bordering aquatic areas, or in almost pure stands where water percolates near the surface. fourwing saltbush *(Atriplex canescens)* is the largest of all and does best where there is a little extra moisture available. It forms large, rounded masses along roadsides and about springs. Most adaptable of all, and one of the least conspicuous, is shadscale *(Atriplex confertifolia)*. It can tolerate heat, drought, shallow soil, and a wide range of conditions, but is only moderately alkali tolerant. It is the dominant shrub in the shadscale scrub community which is extensive on the alluvial fans and lower slopes of the Inyo Mountains.

The plants of Owens Valley cannot be discussed without mentioning the ever present rabbitbrush. The early explorers would not have seen the yellow fields of rabbitbrush that exist today. The species is a part of many plant communities, but under natural conditions it does not get out of control. It is an extremely aggressive shrub which moves into any situation where the existing vegetation is weakened or removed. This broomlike bush is *Chrysothamnus nauseosus,* which is divided into several common subspecies. Other species of *Chryso-thamnus* are less aggressive. Green rabbitbrush *(Chryso-thamnus teretifolia)* occurs on the alluvial slopes and up into the rocky canyons. A white-flowered species *(Chrysothamnus albidus)* , also a greenish plant, comes in from the Great Basin. It is confined to strongly alkaline places with a relatively high water table and extends southward almost to Big Pine.

The gradual change in the environmental scene can be attributed to man and his activities since the first expeditions. Mining was the impetus which started it all. There was little actual mining on the floor of Owens Valley, but people living in the valley were involved in mining, directly or indirectly. The first settlers worked in the mines or grew produce and raised livestock to support the mining camps. Exploitation was the way of life. The abundant natural resources were here for the taking. Waterfowl on Owens Lake were slaughtered in great numbers, cleaned and packed in barrels and carried to market in the booming mining towns. Gull eggs were gathered on the islands of Mono Lake to satisfy an eager demand. Fortunately, the mining camps did not last long enough to wipe out the gull population then. Its destruction is imminent now, however. Mining activity slowed down and the emphasis changed, but concern for environmental values was slow to come.

The most prolonged activity affecting the land has been grazing by cattle and sheep. Horses and burros have had a lesser influence because their numbers have been less. The need for good grazing practices was not felt by the pioneers. They had more immediate problems. The concept of limiting grazing to the capacity of the land was to come much later. As a result, the native bunch grasses have been greatly reduced or replaced by shrubs in the most impacted areas. There is little trace of the northern grassland which once occupied much of the present sagebrush land in Mono County and extended into Owens Valley. Native bunch grasses simply disappear when under continued stress. Alkali sacaton, which has little competition, and Indian ricegrass, which is extremely hardy and adaptable, have done the best to survive. Impact from grazing is not limited to the use of plants for food. In areas of animal concentration trampling does extensive damage, and any accessible springs and shady spots are subject to trampling and pollution.

The clearing of land and diversion of water for agricultural activities produced changes where they occurred. Land which had supported healthy stands of sagebrush, and land which had been used by Indians for croplands became prime farming communities. Many attempts at farming, however, were on land too alkaline, and perhaps too heavy for raising successful crops. All efforts at agriculture were subject to the unpredictable and extreme weather conditions of Owens Valley. The lack of adequate water distribution systems was a handicap, too, especially in the southern portion of the valley. Most of the farmlands are abandoned now. Most of those which are not too dry have become fields of rabbitbrush. The drier ones are barren wastes.

By far the greatest impact is the result of the acquisition of water by the City of Los Angeles. The diversion of the Owens River near Aberdeen left the river channel dry below that point, and reduced Owens Lake to a dry alkali sink. Purchase of farmlands by Los Angeles to protect its water program resulted in the changes described above. The undeveloped lands acquired, however, remained in a relatively natural state until the last decade. The fact that they were not available for development, and were kept open to public access, has preserved Owens Valley as a unique recreational area. There has been reason for concern during periods of drought when ground water was pumped to maintain the supply to Los Angeles. Owens Valley was always on the short end during such critical periods, but those periods were of limited duration. Extensive environmental damage also occurred during the wet years of the late 1960s when water spreading activities disturbed much of the valley floor south of Tinnemaha. It was after the City of Los Angeles built its second aqueduct and initiated its export plan for that aqueduct in 1970 that the threat of increasing and permanent environmental damage raised fears in the residents of Owens Valley. The purpose of that second aqueduct, it was said, was to take only surplus water. But what was surplus, and by whose definition? Was underground water surplus? Were the flowing springs and wells expendable? Were the marshes and sloughs being maintained by surplus water? What would be the ultimate impact on the native plant communities, and on the ground surface? How would such changes in the natural processes affect the way of life of the people of Owens Valley? In this enlightened age, could arbitrary decisions at the expense of environmental sacrifice be justified? These and many other questions are yet to be answered.

If losses could be measured, among the greatest would have been the loss of Owens River in the south end of the valley. With it went the entire river habitat, its riparian borders and moist bottom lands. In time to come, the loss of Owens Lake may measure considerably greater than it has in the past. Another loss, difficult to measure and not immediately recognized, is the gradual drying of marshes, sloughs and flowing springs. Historically, springs have been highly valued.

Each one was a precious source of water. Now we realize that each one supported a valuable microhabitat. Most of those on the valley floor came from the lower edges of the alluvial slopes, from the edges of the black rock and along earthquake faults. The spring flows ceased abruptly with the increase of pumping activity in the 1970s. Sloughs and marshes, whether spring fed or receiving water from other sources, have gradually disappeared. Their beds have become parched basins, and their vegetation but sad remnants of lush riparian habitats. Some were more valuable than others. Collectively, they were a critical element in the Owens Valley environment. Their loss creates a chain reaction which cannot be overcome. The question now is whether we can, or will, prevent further degradation.

Such have been the changes in Owens Valley. No mention has been made of the mountains on either side, although they are part of the whole and would be included in a comprehensive discussion. Following the same reasoning, the mountain areas cannot be viewed as being independent of the valley. Together, they form a natural unit which has no equal. No other place has so much variation in natural conditions within such a limited area. In the eyes of this observer, the greatest and highest future for Owens Valley would be to serve as a great outdoor laboratory for scientific purposes. It is already popular for field trips by colleges and universities throughout the country. Such a nonconsumptive use, compatible with the present way of life in Owens Valley, has great appeal when compared to the problems faced in other areas. Its economic potential could be surprising.

(This article first published in *Inyo County Museum News Bulletin* —August 1977.)

Roger McGrath's study of the white intrusion into Owens Valley and the resulting battles with the indigenous Paiute Indians first appeared in his 1984 book *Gunfighters, Highwaymen, and Vigilantes*. In this book, McGrath explores the violence and lawlessness of two frontier mining towns: Aurora and Bodie. The discovery of mining riches in the Esmeralda District in the desert mountains north of the Owens Valley, the founding of the town of Aurora, and the growth of this town to a peak population estimated at 5,000, were directly responsible for the settling of the Owens Valley—and for the troubles that followed.

Roger McGrath teaches history at the University of California, Los Angeles.

"No Goodee Cow Man", from *Gunfighters, Highwaymen, & Vigilantes,* by Roger D. McGrath. Copyright 1984 by The Regents of the University of California. Reprinted by permission of University of California Press.

# NO GOODEE COW MAN

by Roger D. McGrath

The Esmeralda strike and the spectacular growth of Aurora generated a tremendous demand for supplies. Merchants from Sacramento and San Francisco responded quickly. So did cattlemen from the southern San Joaquin Valley and the Tejon country of the Tehachapi Mountains. Early in the spring of 1861, they launched the first cattle drives to Aurora. The steers were driven through Walker Pass in the southern Sierra and then up the Owens Valley, finally reaching Aurora by way of Adobe Meadows. The drive was long—some three hundred miles—and rugged, and it took a toll both of men and of animals. Cattlemen soon began to look for ways to take advantage of the Aurora market and yet avoid the long drive. They had not failed to notice that the northern half of the Owens Valley was well suited for grazing cattle and only a short distance from Aurora. During the summer and fall nearly a dozen of them, including Samuel Bishop, Henry Vansickle, the McGee brothers, Allen Van Fleet, and Charles Putnam, established ranches in the valley.[1]

White settlement in the Owens Valley, however, meant encroachment on lands already occupied by Indians. Various bands of "Mono" and "Owens Valley" Paiute made the southern trans-Sierra country their home.[2] Their territory extended from the western reaches of Nevada to the crest of the Sierra, and from Owens Lake to just south of Lake Tahoe. The Washo were neighbors to the north, and the Panamint Shoshone, or Koso, lived to the south. Close linguistic relatives, the Monache, or Western Mono, lived across the divide of the Sierra on the upper reaches of the San Joaquin, Kings, and Kaweah rivers.

17

Before the arrival of the whites and the introduction of the steer, the Paiute of the southern trans-Sierra lived primarily by gathering pine nuts, seeds, berries, and fly larvae, and by digging roots.[3] This latter activity earned them, as it did many other Indian groups in California and the Great Basin, the opprobrious epithet "diggers". Several bands of Owens Valley Paiute dug more than roots; they also dug irrigation ditches and flooded low-lying valley land to increase the growth of seed- and tuber-producing plants which grew there naturally.[4]

Irrigation occurred at ten different sites from Pine Creek on the north to Independence Creek on the south. The most extensive irrigation system was at Bishop Creek where some six square miles of land, known as *pitana patu* to the Paiute, was watered.[5] Paiute women harvested the seeds and bulbs of the wild plants each fall. Since the Paiute only irrigated and harvested—they did not prepare the soil, sow the seed, or cultivate the plants—what they did has been called "irrigation without agriculture".[6] While Paiute women gathered nuts and seeds and dug roots, Paiute men hunted for antelope, deer, bighorn sheep, and jackrabbits and fished for trout. This way of life, in the arid and rocky trans-Sierra country, required a vast territory to support a small number of Paiute. The encroachment of whites, particularly ranchers, would certainly have an almost immediate effect on the ability of the Paiute to hunt and to gather food.

Violent conflict first erupted on range land just southeast of present day Bishop.[7] Al Thompson, a cowboy working for Henry Vansickle, spied a Paiute herding a lone steer off into the brush. Giving no warning, Thompson grabbed his rifle and fired. The Indian fell to the ground dead. A few days later the Paiute evened the score. "Yank" Crossen, an Auroran who had only recently come into the valley to ride herd for Allen Van Fleet, was captured and killed. All that any whites ever saw of him again was his scalp, found at Big Pine.

During the next several weeks Indian conflict with the cowboys and ranchers continued. Prospectors, meanwhile, were safe from attack. The Paiute carefully differentiated between the miners, who seemed to pose little threat and had attacked no Indians, and the cattlemen, who had already killed a Paiute and were drastically altering the Indian way of life by stocking the range lands. "No goodee cow man" became a common expression among the Paiute.[8]

In an attempt to avoid further warfare, a peace conference was held at Samuel Bishop's San Francis Ranch on 31 January 1862.[9] Bishop and ten other ranchers represented the whites, while "Captain George" and "Captain Dick" spoke for several bands of Paiute. Captain George indicated, by drawing two lines on the ground, that the score was even: one Indian—the man shot by Al Thompson—and one white—Yank Crossen—had been killed. There was no reason for more bloodshed. With both the Paiute and the whites in a conciliatory mood, an informal peace treaty was quickly hammered out. The treaty recognized the right of the Indians to continue "their daily avocations" unmolested and the right of the whites to graze their cattle in the valley. Both parties would "live in peace and strive to promote amicably the general interests of both whites and Indians."[10] The treaty was signed by the three Paiute leaders with their marks and by the eleven white representatives with their signatures.

This treaty, like so many others—both official and unofficial—drawn up by whites and presented to Indians, had no chance to succeed. The treaty failed to recognize that the white and Indian ways of life were wholly incompatible, and made peaceful coexistence impossible. For the Paiute to continue "their daily avocations" unmolested, they would need to hunt and gather over every foot of the Owens Valley. To the whites, who did not comprehend that the Paiute were already making maximum use of the valley, the area appeared to be underutilized. Cattle grazing in the valley meant less forage for the indigenous animals, whose numbers would have to decline as the numbers of steers increased, and the destruction of native plants, whose seeds and roots were the staple of the Paiute diet. It would be only a very short time before the Paiute, who had always suffered from a precarious food supply, would begin to feel the effects of white encroachment. The Paiute would then have to prey on cattle and become beef eaters or starve.

This inevitable end was hastened by the severe winter of 1861-1862. Although there was a light snowfall in November, mild weather prevailed until Christmas Eve. Then, as Samuel Youngs of Aurora recorded in his diary, it "commenced snowing fast."[11] Day after day it snowed until the trans-Sierra country was cut off from the rest of the world. Temperatures dropped below zero. Although fires were kept blazing inside Aurora cabins, prospectors wore several layers of clothes when

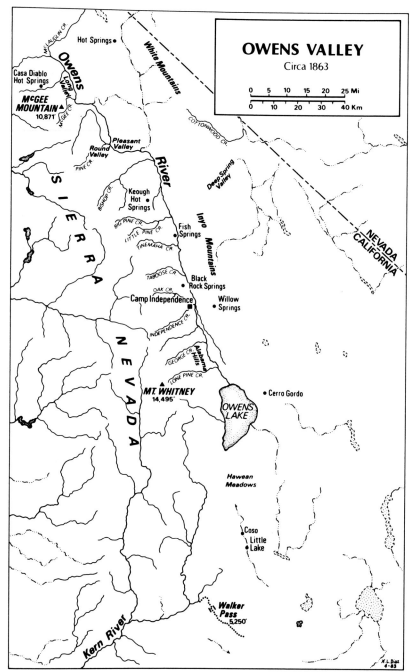

3. MAP "Owens Valley, circa 1863." The Owens Valley contained little more than Camp Independence, cattle ranches, and Paiute in 1863. Its grazing lands were used to raise cattle for the Aurora beef market. *(Credit: University of California Press. Cartography by Noel Diaz.)*

they slept. Upon awakening, they found that the buckets of water and loaves of bread that they had stored inside their cabins had frozen solid. During the second week of January the weather warmed slightly, and the snow became rain. The rain came down in torrents. Adobe cabins turned to mud and collapsed. Esmeralda and Willow gulches overflowed their banks and inundated Aurora. Water stood several inches deep in most buildings. "We have slept each night in our cabin," noted Youngs, "but wet, cold and very bad. Water leaked on my head each night." After a week the rain stopped and snow began to fall again. Within a few days the trans-Sierra was covered with a blanket of snow deeper than before the rain. On 23 January Youngs reported, "We have had but six days since December 24 that it has not stormed more or less—that is 26 days out of 30." A week later he recorded a temperature of fourteen degrees below zero outside his cabin's front door. The stage got through to Aurora only twice during January.

February and March saw a continuation of the Arctic winter with only occasional breaks. March did not go out like a lamb; on the last day of the month a storm left more than a half foot of new snow on the ground. "The coldest April morning I ever knew," wrote Youngs, a native of New York, the next morning. There were some twenty days of snow between the first of April and the twentieth of May when he reported that his cabin was "about dry for the first time since January." The last snow of the season fell on 14 June, and snow was still ten feet deep on north-facing mountain slopes two weeks later.

Aurorans suffered considerable hardship during the winter. They often ran out of supplies of flour and other foodstuffs. Cattle driven in from the Owens Valley saved them from going hungry more than once. The steers also saved the Paiute, not just from hunger, but from starvation. They stole steers throughout the winter, before and after signing the peace treaty with the Owens Valley ranchers. The Paiute must have understood that their thefts would be considered a violation of the treaty, but the severe winter gave them little choice. Either they stole cattle or they starved.

Also playing a role in hastening the outbreak of war was the presence of "Joaquin Jim" in the Owens Valley. A small, compactly built, and agile Western Mono who spoke English and Spanish fluently, Joaquin Jim would make life miserable for the whites.[12]   He had killed at least two white men before coming into the trans-Sierra country, and was greatly feared, if not respected, by whites. The Visalia *Delta* grudgingly admitted that he was "brave as a lion—his one redeeming quality."[13] His expressive, glittering dark eyes—the "eyes of a basilisk," said one rancher—and high forehead perhaps betrayed another quality that whites were forced to admit that Joaquin Jim had in abundance—intelligence.

For a time Joaquin Jim was an outcast among the Owens Valley Paiute, who called him a "shah," or coyote, but he quickly rose to a position of leadership when violent conflict erupted.  He had long despised the white man and now spared no effort in rallying the Paiute for war.  Predictably, he did not attend the peace conference at the San Francis Ranch, nor did any of the Paiute who followed him.

During February 1862 Jesse Summers purchased a small herd of cattle for the Aurora beef market and contracted Barton and Alney McGee to drive the steers to Aurora.  When the McGee brothers made camp at Big Pine Creek, they were visited by Joaquin Jim and several of his men.[14]   According to the McGees, the Indians were surly and demanded food.  "Bart" offered Joaquin Jim a cup of coffee, but the Indian knocked it into the campfire.  Without hesitating a second, Bart leaped for the Indians' guns, which were stacked to one side.  After discharging the weapons, he returned them to the Indians and ordered them out of camp.

The next day the McGees moved the cattle to the San Francis Ranch, and Bart left for Charley Putnam's stone cabin on Independence Creek to recruit drovers.  Although alert to the increasing Paiute hostility, Bart never suspected that he was beginning the ride of his life.  At Fish Springs, about five miles south of Big Pine Creek, a band of Paiute opened fire on him.  Bart, riding one of the fastest horses in the valley, spurred the animal into a gallop and escaped without a scratch.  Despite his harrowing ride, Bart was able to recruit fifteen drovers at Putnam's and return with them without incident to the San Francis Ranch.  Then, just as everyone was settling down for the night, a party of Paiute, waving burning pitch-pine torches set atop long poles, surrounded the ranch buildings.  Dancing around the buildings, the Paiute proclaimed that they could spit out any bullets that might enter their bodies.[15]   The whites, although absorbed in the pyrotechnic spectacle, remained calm, and no violence occurred.

Early the next morning, after an exciting if sleepless night, the cowboys began the cattle drive. Reaching Keough Hot Springs by dusk, the drovers bedded down the herd. Although pickets were posted, Paiute drove off nearly two hundred steers during the night. Three men followed the trail of the stolen beeves until they were stopped by some fifty Paiute. The Indians convinced the cowboys that they had done enough tracking for one day and had best return to the main herd.

The herd was driven on down to Putnam's, although its flanks were continually harassed by Paiute. The next three days passed quietly. Then a small group of Indians were spotted approaching the herd. Bart McGee and several other men, including Allen Van Fleet, ventured out to investigate. They found themselves face-to-face with "Chief" Shoandow and three other Paiute. Shoandow, described by an Auroran as "a large, finely built specimen of the American Indian—independent, proud, generous, and high spirited—a primitive Alexander in disguise," was the leader of a peaceful band of Paiute.[16] It was said that he was honored nearly to the point of worship by his people.

Shoandow told the white men that he and his braves had come to recover three horses which had been stolen from them by whites. Shoandow himself had lost a black mare and a colt, and the tribal shaman, or "medicine man," had lost a small roan. Van Fleet told Shoandow that he might continue the search for the horses if he and his braves would lay their arms aside. The Indians refused. What happened next is debated. One report claimed that the whites fired first and the Indians "without showing any hostile intent . . . were shot down like dogs."[17] Bart McGee and Allen Van Fleet alleged that the fight began when an Indian unleashed an arrow.[18] The results of the fight would seem to indicate that the whites fired first. All four Indians and no whites were killed. Only one white, Van Fleet, was wounded.[19] He was struck in the side by an arrow and carried its obsidian head lodged underneath his ribs for the rest of his life.

Although the whites had suffered only one casualty, this fight would prove very costly for them in the long run. The death of Shoandow so enraged his people that they immediately elected the redoubtable and truculent white-hater Joaquin Jim as their new leader. If Shoandow had lived, as an Auroran later noted, "such a crafty desperado as Joaquin Jim could never have become chief of his tribe."[20]

Whites now began to gather at Charley Putnam's ranch on Independence Creek. Around his stone house they erected a barricade of rocks, old wagons, and logs.[21] Volunteers from Aurora, including Sheriff N. F. Scott who carried a warrant for the arrest of Joaquin Jim, swelled the number of whites to forty-two. Charles Anderson, who had only recently arrived in the valley from Aurora, was elected captain of the defenders, who were armed with rifles, shotguns, and revolvers.

The whites decided that to sit and wait for the Paiute to attack invited disaster. Soon after dusk on 21 March 1862, half of the whites stole out of the fort and headed for the Indian encampment in the nearby Alabama Hills. As the first rays of sunlight reached the valley the next morning, the whites, positioned around the Indian camp, opened fire on the breakfasting Paiute. Although several Paiute were killed by the first volley, most managed to disappear into the clefts and caves of the rocky Alabama Hills.

For several hours the whites poured fire on the Indian position, but they were unwilling to risk an assault, and at one o'clock in the afternoon they broke off the engagement. Battlefield reports indicate that eleven Paiute were killed and a considerably greater number wounded.[22] No whites were killed, and only two were wounded, including Tom Hubbard. He may have been a special target, for he had been with Bart McGee and Allen Van Fleet when Chief Shoandow was gunned down.

Another band of Paiute was having better luck. The Indians found E. S. Taylor, one of the discoverers of Bodie's gold, alone in his cabin at Hot Springs (present-day Benton).[23] When they attacked the cabin, Taylor, half-Indian himself, fought back fiercely and, according to Indian reports, killed several Paiute before he died. His decapitated, arrow-riddled body and his head were later found by a group of passing whites. The head was passed around Aurora and Bodie for years afterward as a grisly souvenir of the Indian attack.

Fighting was now on in earnest. The Owens Valley Paiute called upon their relatives to the north, the Mono Paiute, to come to their aid. They also sent pleas for help to the Western Mono and to various Paiute bands in Nevada. Nevada Paiute had only recently suffered from clashes with whites themselves and were not anxious to support the Owens Valley Paiute. Numaga, a prominent Nevada Paiute leader, counseled his people against war. He spoke English fluently, had traveled in California, and fully appreciated the strength of the whites. Only the year before, he had urged an assembly of Paiute warriors not to attack the whites:

*You would make war upon the whites. I ask you to pause and reflect. The white men are like the stars over your heads. You have wrongs, great wrongs, that rise up like those mountains before you; but can you from the mountain tops reach and blot out those stars? Your enemies are like the sands in the bed of your rivers; when taken away they only give place for more to come and settle there. Could you defeat the whites in Nevada, from over the mountains in California would come to help them an army of white men that would cover your country like a blanket. What hope is there for the Pah-Ute? From where is to come your guns, your powder, your lead, your dried meats to live upon, and hay to feed your ponies with while you carry on this war? Your enemies have all these things, more than they can use. They will come like the sand in a whirlwind and drive you from your homes. You will be forced among the barren rocks of the north, where your ponies will die; where you will see the women and old men starve, and listen to the cries of your children for food. I love my people; let them live; and when their spirits shall be called to the Great Camp in the southern sky, let their bones rest where their fathers were buried.*[24]

Despite Numaga's sobering influence, some Nevada Paiute did join the fight. When several bands of Mono Paiute and one or two of Western Mono arrived in the Owens Valley, total Indian strength reached fifteen hundred to two thousand warriors.[25] Although most of the Indians were armed only with bows and arrows, at least a hundred of them had guns. The Aurora merchant firm of Wingate and Cohn was accused of supplying them with some of their guns and much of their ammunition.[26]

Nevertheless, Aurorans generally supported the beleaguered ranchers. When Al Thompson, the cowboy who had been the

4. An Owens Valley Paiute home. Pictured are (from left to right) unidentified, Hank Baker (on horse), Ollie Kane, Tom Bell, Gladys Harry, George Collins, Teha, Mary Bell, and Jeff Yandell. (*Credit: A. A. Forbes photo, Eastern California Museum.*)

first to kill an Owens Valley Paiute, arrived in town with an urgent plea for assistance, a party of eighteen men, led by John J. Kellogg, a former army captain, was quickly organized.[27] Nearly as soon as the Aurorans reached the valley, they sighted a band of mounted Indians west of the Owens River. The Aurorans prepared themselves for battle and closed in on the Indians. The "Indians" turned out to be a detachment of some thirty whites, led by "Colonel" Mayfield, coming up the valley from Putnam's.

When the two forces united, Mayfield's men related another tale of tragedy. At Big Pine they had come across the bodies of R. Hanson and J. Tallman, who had been killed by Indians.[28] Their corpses had been partially devoured by coyotes. Hanson could only be identified by his teeth. His brother, A. C. Hanson, was one of those riding with Mayfield.

The united parties spent a sleepless night. Paiute, hidden in the rocky hills nearby, howled continually until dawn. At the break of day on 6 April 1862, the citizen militia struck out for Bishop Creek where several bands of Paiute had been sighted. As the whites rode up the valley, they could see Paiute scouts watching their movements. One of the scouts, less cautious than the rest, ventured within rifle range of the white column and was shot dead by Tex Berry. Demonstrating that whites could also mutilate the bodies of their enemies, Dr. E. F. Mitchell of Aurora, the president of the Esmeralda mining district, scalped the dead Paiute and hung the gruesome trophy on his saddle.[29] The incident did not damage Mitchell's career: he later became the president of the Antelope and Real Del Monte mining companies, and in the fall of 1863 Aurorans elected him to the California Assembly.

Near noon the whites reached a large Paiute irrigation ditch just south of Bishop Creek and, appreciating the protection the ditch offered, made camp.[30] A short distance to the north, on the other side of Bishop Creek, were some five hundred Indians led by Joaquin Jim.[31] Not realizing that they were outnumbered (although not outgunned) ten to one, the whites divided their force in two and sallied forth. Kellogg moved his men up along Bishop Creek, and Mayfield flanked him from the south. Mayfield got into trouble first. The Indians opened fire on the head of Mayfield's column, mortally wounding Harrison Morrison. From his vantage point, Kellogg could see that

Mayfield was about to be enveloped, and he ordered Alney McGee to deliver the message to retreat. McGee arrived safely, but his horse dropped dead from bullet wounds.

The whites, advancing on the Indians only minutes before, were now in full retreat. Bart McGee, doubling up, carried the dying Morrison on his horse. Alney McGee protected the slowed riders from the rear, and Cage Pleasant protected them from the front. The McGee brothers happened to be looking at Pleasant, a volunteer from Aurora, when a bullet hole appeared in his coat. Without saying a word, Pleasant stood up in his stirrups and fell dead to the ground. For the moment, his body was left where it lay. A number of men, including A. C. Hanson, ascended a small hill and concentrated enough fire on the Indians for the McGees and the wounded Morrison to reach the ditch. During the action, Hanson avenged his brother's death by killing an Indian who was attempting to stampede the pack animals.

The whites retreated to the ditch and formed a defensive line. Their rifle fire killed two Paiute and held the rest at bay for the remainder of the afternoon. Shortly after dusk, firing from the Indians almost ceased. The whites, for the first time since the beginning of the battle, began to relax. Sheriff Scott of Aurora, still carrying the warrant for the arrest of Joaquin Jim, took time to smoke his pipe. As he lighted it, he carelessly raised his head above the rim of the ditch. A bullet struck him in the forehead, and he rolled to the bottom of the ditch, dead. The sheriff was the last casualty of the "Battle of the Ditch."

When the moon went down, the whites decamped and retreated to Big Pine Creek. Scott and Pleasant had been killed, and Morrison died from his wounds shortly after reaching the Big Pine. The whites also lost some eighteen horses and mules. Indian casualties were estimated at anywhere from five to fifteen dead. If the Paiute had been willing to suffer greater casualties, they no doubt would have been able to overrun the small contingent of beleaguered whites.

Meanwhile, the Indian troubles in the southern trans-Sierra had not gone unnoticed by government officials. On 18 March 1862, Samuel Youngs, who represented Aurora as a member of the Nevada territorial legislature, sent a report on the conflict to Nevada's governor, James Nye.[32] Nye was away in San

Francisco, but Warren Wasson, the Indian agent for Nevada, received the report and then telegraphed the governor:

*Indian difficulties on Owens River confirmed. Hostiles advancing this way. I desire to go and if possible prevent the war from reaching this territory. If a few men poorly armed go against those Indians defeat will follow and a long and bloody war will ensue. If the whites on Owens River had prompt and adequate assistance it could be checked there. I have just returned from Walker River. Piutes alarmed. I await your reply.* [33]

Governor Nye conferred with the commander of the Department of the Pacific, General George Wright, and wired Wasson that the general would order fifty men from Fort Churchill, Nevada, to the scene of action. As was promised, Captain Edwin A. Rowe, commandant of the fort ordered Lieutenant Herman Noble and a detachment of fifty men from Company A, Second Cavalry, California Volunteers, to "Aurora and vicinity."[34] "Upon all occasions," Rowe's orders to Noble continued, "It is desirable that you should consult the Indian Agent, Mr. W. Wasson, who accompanies the expedition for the purpose of restraining the Indians from hostilities. Upon no consideration will you allow your men to engage the Indians without his sanction."

Wasson and his Indian interpreter proceeded from Fort Churchill in advance of the troops.[35] At the Walker River Reservation, Wasson learned that the Paiute feared the outbreak of a general war with the whites. He therefore dispatched Indian messengers to carry a call for peace to all the different bands of Paiute.

On the bitterly cold morning of 1 April 1862, Wasson and the troops arrived in Aurora.[36] The next morning Wasson left, again in advance of the troops, and parleyed with a band of Mono Paiute on the shores of Mono Lake.[37] Although Wasson found the Indians highly excited, he succeeded in quieting them. Taking along a Mono Paiute to act as interpreter with the Owens Valley Paiute, Wasson joined the troops at Adobe Meadows on 4 April. Two days later Wasson and the troops reached the forks of the Owens River. Little did they know that only forty miles to the south at Bishop Creek, the Kellogg-Mayfield men were fighting for their lives.

5. The John Shepherd home on George's Creek. Constructed in 1873, the Shepherd house was a popular stop-over for travelers on the road between Independence and Lone Pine. The Shepherd's were among the earliest homesteaders in the Owens Valley. This site was later the location of the town (and World War II Internment Camp) of Manzanar. (Credit: Eastern California Museum.)

While Wasson and the troops were working their way into the Owens Valley from the north, another force was pushing its way into the valley from the south. General James H. Carleton, commander of the Southern District of California, ordered Lieutenant Colonel George S. Evans of the Second Cavalry, California Volunteers, to the Owens Valley.[38] Leaving Camp Latham (located near present-day West Los Angeles) on 19 March 1862, Colonel Evans and some forty hand-picked men from Companies B, D, E, G, and I crossed the Tehachapi Mountains at Tejon Pass, dropped into the San Joaquin Valley, and then reached the trans-Sierra country by way of the Kern River and Walker Pass. They arrived at Owens Lake, at the southern end of Owens Valley, on 2 April, after a journey of more than three hundred miles.

Although his men and animals were fatigued, Evans pushed on up the valley and reached Putnam's makeshift fort on 4 April. He posted an officer and seven troopers at the "fort" to help protect the score of civilians gathered there, and the next day he continued north. At Big Pine Creek he met the retreating Mayfield-Kellogg party. Most of the party joined Evans, and the civilians and troopers headed for Bishop Creek.

On 7 April, as the Evans command approached the site of the Battle of the Ditch, they spotted a small force of Indians. A scouting party identified the "Indians" as agent Wasson, Lieutenant Noble, and the troopers from Fort Churchill. As ranking officer, Colonel Evans assumed command of the now formidable force and encamped on the spot of the previous day's battle. Cage Pleasant's body, or what remained of it—the Indians had stripped off the clothing and mutilated the corpse—was retrieved, wrapped in a blanket, and buried.[39]

Wasson and Colonel Evans, a battle-hardened veteran of the Mexican War, discussed the growing Indian conflict at length. Wasson argued for a truce, but, as he himself noted, he "found little or no encouragement to make peace with the Indians, their [Colonel Evans and the civilians'] desire being only to exterminate them."[40] With this end in mind, Colonel Evans sent out scouting parties of a half-dozen men each in all directions. About noon on 8 April one of the parties reported that a large number of Indians had gathered in Round Valley.

Two hours later the whites rode into the valley and found themselves surrounded, not by Indians but by blowing snow. Nevertheless, Colonel Evans ordered an advance into the mountains that rimmed the valley. Less than an hour later, Evans, recognizing the futility of a chase in a snowstorm, recalled his men.

Early the next morning, Evans renewed the search for the Paiute. This time the quarry stalked the hunter. While ascending a narrow canyon on the northwest side of Round Valley, an advance party of troopers rode directly into a Paiute ambush. The first volley of bullets killed Sergeant Christopher Gillespie and seriously wounded Corporal John Harris, both of Company A.[41] The main body of men, three hundred yards below at the mouth of the canyon, rushed into action. Lieutenant Noble and his troopers, together with "Colonel" Mayfield and four other civilians, hurried to occupy the southern rim of the canyon, while Colonel Evans and his troopers climbed the north rim. The civilians, except for those who had followed Lieutenant Noble, remained poised at the canyon mouth.

Noble reached his objective, though he probably wished he had not. Indian fire was concentrated on his command from two directions. Mayfield was wounded, and the others were pinned down. The Paiute held the high ground, and a number of excellent rifles, and kept up a severe fire. "Nothing but mountain howitzers," commented one white, "could possibly dislodge the enemy in their mountain fastness."[42]

To remain in position would have been fatal. Lieutenant Noble ordered a retreat. Although the maneuver was well executed, one man was lost, the already wounded Mayfield. While riding a stretcher down the hill, Mayfield was killed by a second bullet. The round had passed between the legs of one of those carrying the stretcher before it struck Mayfield. One man's luck proved to be another's misfortune. Luckier still was John Hubinger, a bugler from Company E, who got cut off and surrounded by Indians. He fought his way out and had nothing more to show for it than a bullet-grazed ear.[43]

Meanwhile, Colonel Evans had found the north rim too steep to climb, and he, like Noble, was forced to retreat down the canyon. The disheartened whites camped that night on Bishop Creek. For the time being, they had to admit defeat.

Moreover, Evans had exhausted his supplies, except for beef obtained from ranchers in the valley, and was forced to retreat down the valley to Putnam's "fort" on Independence Creek and prepare for a return to Camp Latham in Los Angeles. On 13 April, after a two-day layover at Putnam's, Evans and his command broke camp and headed south: Lieutenant Noble and Company A remained behind at the "fort" for a day before heading north for Aurora. Accompanying Evans were dozens of civilians who had decided to quit the Owens Valley. The civilians took some 4,000 steers and 2,500 sheep with them.[44] Although the Paiute were presumably pleased to see the exodus of the whites, they must have regretted the loss of the livestock which they were beginning to depend on for food.

When Evans reached Indian Wells, just to the east of Walker Pass, he parted company with the civilians and their livestock. The civilians turned west and took the established trail through the pass to the Kern River, while Evans continued south in an effort to find a new route to Los Angeles. With relative ease he pioneered a trail through the Antelope Valley, which shortened the distance to Los Angeles by more than seventy miles and saved several days' time. On 28 April he arrived at Camp Latham.[45]

The Owens Valley—in fact most of the southern trans-Sierra—belonged to the Indians in late April, May, and June of 1862. During those months several more violent confrontations between Indians and whites occurred.[46] One pioneer, traveling through the area with his family, livestock, and all his earthly possessions, lost everything but his wife and children to Indians. In another incident, a group of miners en route to Aurora from Visalia were fired upon by a band of Indians, but escaped unhurt. Nor was property safe. Anything left behind by the whites was destroyed. Even a quartz mill in the White Mountains was razed by Indians.

The white residents of the southern trans-Sierra country responded to the Indian attacks by besieging military authorities with letters and petitions that requested the return of the army to the Owens Valley.[47] As a consequence, Colonel Evans had only a brief rest before he was again ordered into the trans-Sierra. Leaving Fort Latham on 11 June with some two hundred men from Companies D, G, and I of the Second Cavalry, he reached the Owens Valley on 24 June.[48] The same day Evans and his troopers surprised a small band of Paiute who were gathering fly larvae on the shores of Owens Lake. Two Paiute were killed, and eleven others, including seven women and two children, were captured and held as hostages. The troopers also captured large quantities of Indian foodstuffs—fly larvae, nuts, seeds, and grasses—and destroyed them. Late the following day Evans and his troopers hurried on to Putnam's. Arriving there on the morning of 26 June they found the citizens' makeshift fort in ruins. Even the stone walls of the cabin had been knocked down. The Indians, said to be in the area and reportedly a thousand strong, were nowhere in sight.

Evans spent the next week scouting the valley, destroying Indian food caches, and attempting to bring the Indians to battle. On 1 July he wrote to army headquarters in San Francisco saying, "The Indians claim the valley as belonging to them, and still insist upon it that no white man shall settle, or, as they term it, sit down in the valley. They say that whites may pass through to and from Aurora if they want to, or they may locate in the hills and work the mines, but must not sit down on the grass patches."[49] Evans said further, however, that if the mines were to be fully developed, the valley, regardless of the Indian right to it, would have to be settled by whites and brought into agricultural production to supply the miners with food. This would mean subduing the Indians, he noted, a task that could not be accomplished quickly: the valley was vast and almost treeless and the Indians could observe the movement of troops "for twenty or thirty miles ahead, and upon their approach they can and will scatter into the hills, where it is impossible to follow them." Evans, arguing that it would be necessary to starve the Indians into submission, concluded:

*These Indians subsist at this season of the year entirely upon the grass seeds and nuts gathered in the valley from the lake up, and the worms gathered at the lake. They gather this food in large quantities during the summer and prepare it for winter use, which together with the piñon nuts gathered in the mountains in the fall of the year, is their only subsistence. Without this food gathered and laid up they cannot possibly subsist through the winter. From the facts set forth above, the nature of these Indians and the surrounding country, it does seem to me that the only way in which they can be chastised and brought to terms is to establish a temporary post, say for one winter, at some point near the center of the valley, from which point send and keep scouts continually ranging through the valley, keep the Indians out of the valley and in the hills, so that they can have no opportunity of gathering and preserving their necessary winter supplies, and they will be compelled to sue for peace before spring and grass come again.*

On the Fourth of July of 1862, Evans selected the site for the post that he had mentioned in his letter.[50] On Oak Creek, two miles north of Putnam's, Evans had a perimeter one mile square marked off and a fifty-foot flagpole erected. Troopers raised the Stars and Stripes and fired a salute, and Evans christened the post, in honor of the day, Camp Independence.

The same day a man named Cox, while on his way to the camp, was suddenly surrounded by a small group of Paiute.[51] They assured Cox that they had no intention of harming him and only wanted to know what Colonel Evans planned to do with the Paiute prisoners. Cox replied that if the Indians harmed no whites, the prisoners would be safe. The Paiute then asked Cox to tell Evans that they wanted peace and were ready to sign a treaty. Only the Indians upriver wanted to fight, they said. The next day several bands of Paiute, led by "Captain George" bearing a flag of truce, headed for the camp.

Meanwhile, there was another force approaching Camp Independence. On 11 May Captain Edwin A. Rowe and Company A, Second Cavalry, left Fort Churchill with orders to establish a camp at Aurora and to open negotiations with the Indians.[52] Three days later Captain Rowe arrived in Aurora and established a camp just outside of town. From there he proceeded with the bulk of his force to Adobe Meadows, where he had a friendly talk with Mannawahe and his band of Mono Paiute. Mannawahe unconvincingly disclaimed any participation in the recent fighting and promised to spread the word to the Owens Valley Paiute that the whites wanted peace. Captain Rowe continued south and made camp just across the Owens River from Camp Independence on 7 July. Evans rode out to meet him but was forced to abandon his horse and swim the Owens River, then at flood stage, to reach Rowe's camp. When Evans arrived at the camp he found that Captain George and some forty other Paiute men were already there.

Both the Indians and the whites quickly agreed to a cessation of hostilities. Captain George said that he was tired of fighting and wanted to be friends with the white man, and that if the whites would not bother him he would not bother them. He further stated that he would send word to all the Indians of the Owens Valley that he had made friends with the whites and that if any Indian stole from the whites he would send him to Colonel Evans for punishment. Captain George returned with Evans to Camp Independence and two days later Evans wrote to army headquarters: "Everything will be quiet hereafter, in my opinion, unless the whites first commit outrages upon the Indians. They are very badly frightened and, I think, are in earnest about wanting peace."[53]

In mid-July Major John M. O'Neill took command of Camp Independence and Companies D, G, and I of the Second Cavalry, when Colonel Evans was called out of the valley on an administrative task. Army headquarters in San Francisco ordered O'Neill to negotiate a peace treaty with the Indians. The treaty must require, said headquarters, that the Indians restore all property taken from whites and that four or five influential Indians and their families surrender themselves and be held hostage at Camp Independence as a guarantee of good faith. Before July was out O'Neill succeeded in negotiating such a treaty with Captain George and Tinemaha, another "great chief." Captain George, Tinemaha, and three other Paiute leaders agreed to serve as hostages.[54]

A few weeks later two Paiute leaders from the northern end of the Owens Valley, Tocobaca and Toyahnook, arrived at Camp Independence and surrendered themselves as hostages. They said that they accepted the peace treaty and claimed that they had only gone to war after white men stole their property, outraged their women, and killed four of their people, including "the old chief of the Monaches." Major O'Neill now held seven Paiute leaders and their families as hostages. Also in his custody were a horse, a Colt revolver, a musket, a Sharps carbine, two double-barreled shotguns, and nine rifles that various Indians had delivered to the camp since the signing of the treaty.[55]

Although several bands of Paiute were still said to be "surly," the rest of the summer passed quietly. Ranchers and miners began a cautious return to the valley. "The Indian troubles have finally ceased to scare the timid or retard our progress, from the fact that a military post has been established on Owens' River," wrote a white resident of the valley. "So those wishing to pay us a visit need have no fears of leaving their scalps."[56]

The principal trouble facing the army during August and September of 1862 was not Indians but lack of supplies. Provisions ordered from Los Angeles never arrived on time, and when they did reach camp they were in insufficient quantities. By September the situation was becoming critical. Some men were barefoot, others were clothed in rags, and all were hungry. Morale was deteriorating badly. On the Saturday night of 13 September a storm hit the area that left the mountains covered in snow and dropped temperatures to freezing in the valley. With his men at the breaking point, O'Neill decided to move his entire command southward, hoping to meet a supply train coming from Los Angeles. He struck camp on Monday morning and headed south. The next day, as he approached Owens Lake, he spotted a supply train of sorts; it was Colonel Evans leading some troopers and a lone freight wagon north. Although not entirely what O'Neill had hoped for, the single wagon was full of provisions. When the two parties met, camp was made on the spot and the men were fed. By the following day the entire force, again under the command of Colonel Evans, was back at Camp Independence.[57]

Colonel Evans now issued a call made by John P. H. Wentworth, Superintendent of Indian Affairs for the Southern District of California, for all the Indian leaders of the Owens Valley to come to Camp Independence.[58] Wentworth, saying he represented the "Great Father at Washington," promised to meet with the "chiefs" on 20 September 1862 and to give them presents and provisions. About a hundred Paiute leaders arrived at the camp at the appointed time, but Wentworth failed to show. After waiting for the agent for ten days, the Paiute became highly indignant and reportedly said, "Whites mucho big lie. No give nothing." Evans, in an attempt to appease the Indians, had his quartermaster begin to give them daily rations of fresh beef.

Superintendent Wentworth finally arrived at Camp Independence in early October and immediately dispatched runners to the different Paiute bands.[59] Wentworth was soon distributing gifts and rations to some four hundred Paiute. He told them of "the folly of endeavoring to oppose the government that was desirous of aiding them" and assured them that whereas "any indication of rebellion would be met with prompt and severe punishment, good behavior would secure its [the government's] fostering care." The Indians, reported Wentworth, were willing to live in peace if the government would protect them and provide a means of support.

On 6 October 1862 a truce was signed, and the Indians celebrated the event with a great dance. Loaded down with gifts and apparently greatly contented, they then dispersed. Captain George remained behind as a hostage to ensure that they would remain peaceful. Wentworth now wrote to William P. Dole, the Commissioner of Indian Affairs, pleading for the official establishment of an Indian reservation in the Owens Valley. Said Wentworth:

*I laid off a reservation of about six townships, bounded by the Big Pine creek on the north, George's creek on the south, Owen's river on the east, and the Sierra on the west. The amount of land (nearly 140,000 acres) will seem large for the number of Indians, (about 2,000,) but it must be remembered that it is only in small spots that it is susceptible of cultivation, the balance being scarcely fit for grazing purposes, and none of it attractive to settlers. Placed on a reservation where the agent's authority is respected by the emigrants, and where they know they are secure from interference and are treated with kindness, experience has demonstrated there is no difficulty in managing the Indian. The troubles in the State have always arisen outside of the reserves.*

*Should the Department agree with me, as I trust it will for I see no other way of keeping these Indians quiet, I hope it will recommend to Congress the immediate appropriation of $30,000 for the purpose of enabling me to establish this reservation. That sum, judiciously expended in the purchase of seed, stock cattle, mules, wagons, ploughs, etc., would place these wretched people beyond the necessity of stealing for a livelihood, and would relieve the Government from any further expense for their support, as well as dispense with the necessity of maintaining an expensive military post in a country where everything has to be hauled a distance of 300 miles over a sandy road, with water only at long intervals, and every obstacle to surmount which is objectionable for a military depot. Already the Government has expended many thousands of dollars in* *sending and keeping troops there to suppress difficulties that would never have occurred had Congress appropriated, a year ago, for this reservation.*

Wentworth further noted that the discovery of gold and silver at Aurora and other spots in the area had quickly transformed a formerly unknown region into a great thoroughfare and precipitated conflict with the Indians. But an Indian war must be avoided, he stressed. The gold and silver that the region produced was sorely needed by the Union, burdened with the Civil War, and an Indian uprising would close mines. "The importance of prompt action by Congress in this matter," concluded Wentworth, "cannot be presented more strongly than in the fact that it can, by a small appropriation, if made at once, secure permanent peace with a people who have shown themselves formidable in war, and save the Government the enormous expense attendant upon an interminable Indian difficulty which will inevitably occur."

Commissioner Dole was not impressed by Wentworth's arguments. Since the proposed Owens Valley reservation could not hold more than two thousand Indians, reasoned Dole, another location should be sought: a location "ample for the wants of all the Indians" of the southern district of California. Secretary of the Interior J. P. Usher agreed with Dole, and Wentworth's recommendations were disapproved.

Meanwhile, with the Indians quieted, Colonel Evans moved Companies D and I from Camp Independence to Visalia, a hotbed of "Jeff Davis traitorism," and a mile north of the town established Camp Babbitt.[60] Company G, about a hundred strong and commanded by Captain Theodore H. Goodman, was left behind to garrison Camp Independence. Goodman spent much of his time supervising the construction of adobe barracks, officers' quarters, stables, a guardhouse, and other camp buildings. He resigned his commission on 31 January 1863 and was replaced by Captain James M. Ropes.[61]

Although there were several isolated incidents of conflict between Indians and whites during the fall and winter, it was not until early spring that a major outbreak of violence occurred.[62] On 1 March 1863, Captain George, after receiving his supply of rations, disappeared from Camp Independence. The next day the Paiute renewed the war with a surprise attack on four prospectors, the brothers Hiram, Albert, and William Ayres, and James McDonald, who were camped along Big Pine Creek. The attack came at dusk while Hiram Ayres was away from camp, chopping wood in the nearby hills. McDonald managed to yell a warning before he was felled by a volley of arrows. William Ayres ran for his life, but was hit by an arrow before he could get out of range. With the arrow stuck in his back, he crawled into a clump of thick underbrush and hid. The Paiute tracked him into the brush and even poked his body with sharpened sticks without discovering him. Albert Ayres escaped unscathed. He had at first attempted to aid McDonald, but McDonald, although punctured by four arrows, was still alive when the Paiute reached him. They refused to kill him quickly, choosing instead to stone him to death.

A band of Paiute led by "Captain Jack" then looted and ransacked the cabin of Henry G. Hanks and his partners of the San Carlos Mining and Exploration Company, based in San Francisco. Everything in the cabin, except for some laboratory equipment, was either destroyed or stolen. Among the missing items were several guns and a store of ammunition. After this attack Hanks, who would later become California's state mineralogist, wrote to his associates in San Francisco:

*I am beginning to change my mind about Indians. I used to think they were a much abused race and that the whites were generally to blame in troubles like this, but now I know to the contrary. Those very Indians who had been entertained at our house were the ones to attack it, and would have murdered us had we been at home.*

*I want you to use all your influence to have the Indian reservation done away with, and to prevent a treaty until the Indians are punished severely. The citizens of this valley are exasperated to the extent that they will not respect any treaty until the Indians are completely conquered and punished. The Indians are a cruel, cowardly, treacherous race. The whites have treated them well, paid them faithfully for all services performed by them, and have used the reservation only after gaining the consent of Captain George, their chief. After living on the charity of whites all winter, having gambled away the blankets and beads given them by the Government, they now, without giving us the slightest warning, pounce down like vultures, rob those who have treated them best, and murdered where they could without danger to themselves. They rush upon their prey in great numbers, like a pack of wolves, and not satisfied with filling the bodies of their victims with glass-pointed arrows, beat them into a pumice with stones. Can we be expected to give such inhuman wretches a chance at us again? We call upon you, the people of California, State and Federal authorities, to have this reservation and this set of wild savages removed to some other point. This valley is the natural thoroughfare through the mountains, and destined by nature to be the seat of a large population.*[63]

Several other cabins were subsequently ransacked, and then another prospector was killed.[64] The Indians, evidently needing lead for bullets, ripped out sections of a pipe that supplied water to Ida, a small mining camp near present day Manzanar. With the pipe destroyed, miners Curtis Bellows and Milton Lambert found it necessary to carry water from a nearby spring to Ida. On 3 March 1863, Bellows and Lambert were returning from the spring when a band of Paiute ambushed them. Bellows pulled out the first arrow that struck him, then a second one killed him. Lambert raced back to Ida and frightened off the Paiute by shouting orders to several imaginary companions.

While these incidents were occurring, Captain Ropes sent out a seven-man scouting party commanded by Lieutenant James C. Doughty to recapture Captain George.[65] Near Black Rock Springs on 3 March 1863, the same day that Bellows was killed, the troopers rode into an ambush. Privates Jabez F. Lovejoy, John Armstrong, George W. Hazen, and George Sowerwine, and Lieutenant Doughty were all hit. Private Sowerwine's horse was shot out from under him, but he doubled up with Lovejoy, and the bloodied scouting party rode furiously back to Camp Independence. That evening Private Lovejoy died of his wounds.

Three days later, Captain Ropes led nearly thirty troopers and several civilian volunteers to Black Rock Springs. When the white force approached the springs, the Paiute, well concealed in craggy lava beds, opened fire. Captain Ropes, knowing that it would be impossible to dislodge them from their natural stronghold, retreated slowly, hoping to draw them out of the lava beds. The Paiute were not fooled by the ruse. They remained in position and derided the whites by "throwing sand in the air and yelling like fiends."[66] Captain Ropes could do nothing but lead an ignominious retreat back to Camp Independence. He realized that the number of men in his command was too small to carry on an effective campaign against the Paiute and requested reinforcements. Consequently, on 11 March 1863, Lieutenant Stephen R. Davis and forty-five men from Company E left Camp Babbitt to aid Captain Ropes.[67]

Meanwhile, early in March Jesse Summers and his wife and daughter, Alney McGee and his mother, and the McGees' "faithful negro" Charley Tyler, left Aurora, bound for Visalia.[68] Unaware that hostilities had been renewed, they traveled leisurely and made camp on the night of 6 March 1863 at the "upper crossing" of the Owens River. The next day they forded the river and traveled on to Big Pine Creek, where circling buzzards attracted them to the stripped, arrow-riddled, and battered corpse of James McDonald. Now alerted in a most gruesome manner to the uprising, they hurried south toward Camp Independence, all the while watching smoke signals rise ominously from the hills below Fish Springs.

Suddenly a band of more than a hundred Paiute swept out of the hills. The whites turned their horses and wagon and headed for the Owens River. At a full gallop the party plunged into the river, only to have the wagon become mired at midstream. With no time to lose, the horses were cut loose and mounted by the women, and they galloped across the river and south toward Camp Independence. By now the Paiute had reached the river and sent a volley of bullets and arrows into the party. Summers and McGee caught horses from the remuda they had been driving and raced for the camp.

The Paiute pursued and shot at the fleeing settlers, but everyone except Charley Tyler reached Camp Independence safely. Mrs. McGee was so stiff that she had to be lifted from her horse and was then unable to stand. Seventeen horses and a wagon—its contents included $600 in cash—had been lost, and Tyler was missing. When Summers and McGee last saw him he was trying to catch one of the horses of the remuda with his lariat. They hoped he had succeeded and had ridden to Aurora.

Tyler had not escaped. He was captured by the Paiute, who considered him a special prize, for he was known to have killed several Indians. Tyler had been a member of the McGee—Van

Fleet party that gunned down Chief Shoandow and three other Paiute, and he had also participated in the Alabama Hills fight and the Battle of the Ditch. The Paiute now made him suffer for his actions. For three days he was tortured, then bound with withes and roasted to death.[69]

To prevent other travelers from being caught unaware, Captain Ropes sent Lieutenant Doughty and a dozen troopers to the upper crossing of the Owens River to warn travelers and post notices of the Paiute uprising. Privates James R. Johnston and William K. Potter of Company G were sent on to alert Aurora. The privates alerted Aurora without incident, but on their return trip they ran into a band of some three hundred Paiute led by Captain George. The Paiute leader, who had known the two cavalrymen at Camp Independence, signaled for them to join the Paiute in a feast. Johnston and Potter, reckoning that they themselves would be the main course, respectfully declined. Spurring their horses, the cavalrymen raced for Camp Independence. The Paiute gave chase and opened fire. A bullet hit Johnston in the hand and another creased his horse's neck, but he and Potter outdistanced the Paiute and reached the camp without further incident.[70]

By now most whites had fortified their cabins and mining camps and were ready for the Indians. Except for some minor incidents, all was quiet during mid-March. Then on the night of 18 March 1863, several ranchers spied a band of Paiute warriors feasting on a stolen steer in a camp on George Creek.[71] The next morning the ranchers counted thirty-seven Paiute as the Indians left camp in single file and headed south. The ranchers, believing that the Paiute intended to intercept the Aurora-Visalia mail carrier, hurried off to Camp Independence.

On hearing the ranchers' report, Captain Ropes dispatched Lieutenant Doughty and twenty troopers, who were joined by a nearly equal number of civilian volunteers, to George Creek. There the white force picked up the Indian trail and followed it south along the western side of the Alabama Hills to a ravine just above Cottonwood Creek. With no warning, a bullet ripped through the hat of one of the whites, leaving a clean hole in the hat but not touching the man's head. The Paiute were well concealed in the rocky ravine and laid down a brisk fire. Lieutenant Doughty deployed his main force as skirmishers and sent Sergeant Ward Huntington and a squad of men charging into the ravine. The charge killed several of the Indians and forced the others to retreat down the ravine toward Owens Lake. The Paiute retreated from position to position until they found themselves backed up against the western shore of the lake. By now sixteen of their number had been killed, and their guns were so dirty that they had to pound the ramrods with stones to force bullets down the gun barrels. It was no longer a contest, and the surviving Paiute sought refuge in the lake. Swimming against a strong headwind, they made little progress. The whites lined up on the shore of the lake and, by the light of a full moon, methodically shot the swimmers to death one by one.

Except for one Paiute who escaped to the west during the fight, all the warriors—thirty-six by count—were slain. The lone survivor was last seen climbing into the Sierra, stopping only to make "derisive signs" to the whites. Corporal Michael McKenna, who was later decorated for bravery for his actions in the fighting, was the only white casualty. He was wounded in the chest when struck by an arrow. Charley Tyler's pistol was found on one of the dead Paiute, and booty taken from the McGee-Summers party, on others.

In response to the continuing warfare, more reinforcements were sent into the Owens Valley. Captain Herman Noble, commanding Company E, Second Cavalry, arrived at Camp Independence on 4 April 1863.[72] Captain Noble was not new to the Owens Valley or to Indian fighting. Only the previous year he had accompanied Indian agent Warren Wasson into the valley, and was second in command to Colonel Evans in the fighting that had occurred in Round Valley.

With the confidence that fresh troops usually bring, Captain Ropes now led 120 troopers of Companies E and G and 35 civilian volunteers in pursuit of a large body of Paiute reported to be some thirty miles north of the camp.[73] On the afternoon of 10 April 1863, the whites made contact with an estimated two hundred Paiute in the Sierra foothills just north of Big Pine Creek. The fighting lasted until nightfall, when, under the cover of darkness, the Paiute were able to withdraw into the mountains. The Paiute suffered several killed and wounded; no whites were killed, and only two were wounded, privates Thomas Spratt of Company G and John Burton of Company E.

6. Camp Independence as it appeared after reconstruction following the devastating 1872 Owens Valley earthquake. Shown are the camp hospital, parade grounds with flagpole, and barracks. *(Credit: National Archives.)*

The wounded troopers were placed in the bed of a wagon, and an eight-man detail was ordered to take them back to Camp Independence. Near Fish Springs the soldiers were ambushed by Captain George and a hundred Paiute. A running battle ensued. One trooper dashed ahead to the camp for reinforcements while the others tried to keep the pursuing Paiute at bay. Arriving just in time to save the detail, the rescue party scattered the Paiute "like a flock of quail."

In the meantime, still more reinforcements were moving toward Camp Independence. On 9 April 1863, the same day that Captain Ropes left for Big Pine Creek, Captain Albert Brown and seventy-one men of Company L, Second Cavalry, passed through Aurora on their way to the Owens Valley.[74] The troopers carried with them a mountain howitzer and an ample supply of shell and canister shot. They also carried fifty Minie-ball muskets for distribution to civilians. Captain Brown told the citizens of Aurora that his orders were to march directly to Camp Independence and not to attack any Indians en route. Nevertheless, if he were attacked, said Captain Brown, he would send for civilian reinforcements from Aurora.

While Captain Brown and Company L were moving toward the valley from Aurora, Captain Moses A. McLaughlin and Company D, Second Cavalry, were moving in from Visalia.[75] Captain McLaughlin left Camp Babbitt on 12 April 1863 and followed the Kern River to Keyesville. There he learned that a large party of Indians was camped near Whiskey Flat (modern Kernville) and that the Indians had killed a white man in Kelsey Canyon and had stolen more than a hundred head of cattle. According to Jose Chico, a local Indian leader who had a farm on the Kern River, the offending Indians were mostly renegades from the Owens Valley. They had come into the Kern River country, he said, to gather recruits and to incite the local Indians to war against the white man.

Taking Chico along as a guide and interpreter, McLaughlin set out for the Indian camp. He reached the camp at dawn on 19 April and took the Indians by surprise. Allowing the old men and boys and those Indians that Chico could vouch for to remain behind, McLaughlin marched the others, thirty-five by count, out of the camp. The marching Indians evidently soon realized the fate that awaited them and tried to make a fight of it. Having no weapons but the knives that some of them had concealed on their persons and the sticks and stones which others grabbed from the ground, the Indians could offer little resistance and were quickly slaughtered. Most were shot to death; a few were run through with sabers. "This extreme punishment, though I regret it, was necessary," said McLaughlin, "and I feel certain that a few such examples will soon crush the Indians and finish the war in this and adjacent valleys. It is now a well-established fact that no treaty can be entered into with these Indians. They care nothing for pledges given, and have imagined that they could live better by war than peace."

Whites generally agreed with Captain McLaughlin and accepted the slaughter as a wartime necessity. "This act," commented a correspondent for the Visalia *Delta*, "the harshness of which at first view appeared astounding, is generally approved of by the friends of the Union who are gradually waking up to the necessity of energy in war, whether it be against the secesh or Indians."[76]

Captain McLaughlin arrived at Camp Independence on 24 April 1863 and, as senior officer, assumed command. The day after his arrival at the camp, McLaughlin led a three-day reconnaissance in force. This was an indication of things to come. Under Captain McLaughlin's aggressive and resourceful command, the troopers would see plenty of action during the next month. McLaughlin also used a novel strategy. Colonel Evans had operated only in the daytime and had his men chase the Indians from the valley, up the canyons, and into the mountains. McLaughlin reversed the action. He had his men ascend the mountains at night and secrete themselves until daylight. Then they moved down the canyons, surprising the Indians and flushing them into the valley. The strategy was an enormous success.

On 3 May Lieutenant Francis McKenna and thirty men of Company G routed a group of Paiute in the Inyo Mountains, killing several and driving the rest into troopers under the command of Lieutenant George D. French stationed in the valley below.[77] French's men killed another of the Paiute and mortally wounded three. Captain Noble led Company E on a patrol that resulted in the capture of thirty Indians at Big Pine Creek on 11 May. A few days later Captain McLaughlin and another patrol destroyed the camp of Joaquin Jim, but Jim and his men escaped into the mountains. Company L, under the command of Captain Brown, was in the field for the entire month of May and destroyed some three hundred bushels of pine nuts and seeds that the Indians had cached near Bishop Creek. Sergeant Henry C. Church and four men of Company L surprised a band of fourteen Paiute near the headwaters of the Owens River and killed four of them. Even civilian parties were now besting the Indians. Alney McGee and H. Hurley, leading a group to Aurora, killed three Indians in a fight in mid-May.[78]

With over a hundred men killed and many others wounded or taken prisoner, and with hundreds of bushels of seed destroyed, the Paiute were, for the time being, well-beaten. Sergeant Daniel McLaughlin of Company D met with Captain George and led him into Camp Independence on 22 May 1863.[79] When Captain George had left the fort in March his face was plump and round; now it was sunken and hollow. "The Indians," as the Visalia *Delta* aptly put it, "are hard up for food."[80] No food meant no war, and day after day Indians came to Camp Independence and surrendered. Captain George's band was followed by those of "Captain Dick" and Tinemaha.[81] By June there were some five hundred Indians in camp and by July the number had swelled to nearly a thousand.

Not all whites, however, were ready to accept peace. Two Indian messengers who were sent to bring in the Paiute of the White Mountains were fired on by some miners. The messengers never returned and probably became renegades who preyed on prospectors.[82] In another incident a small band of Paiute on their way to Camp Independence to surrender was attacked by a group of miners. Three of the Indians, including a young girl, were killed and scalped. One of the miners, Frank Whetson, was arrested by Lieutenant French and placed in irons. Whetson spent the next few months imprisoned at Camp Independence and Fort Tejon. Said Captain Ropes:

*Of the Indians who escaped from this attack most of them made their way to the mountains, where they now are and where they will remain for all that anyone can do to drive them out. Never again can any of them be induced to place any faith in the promises of white men, and if another outbreak occurs it will be far the most desperate we have ever seen. I should have mentioned that the last party of Indians mentioned also bore a white flag, traveled openly in the road in daylight, and that their purpose was known to everyone. But for such ruffians as those who fired upon them, unarmed as they were, there would not today be a hostile Indian in the entire country; and those who may hereafter suffer will have Mr. Whetson and others of like ilk to thank for it.*[83]

There were those who believed that Whetson and his fellow prospectors were justified. Milo Page, a prospector who participated in the war, noted that the band of Paiute that Whetson fired on was the same one that killed four of Whetson's partners—Hall, Turner, Shepherd, and White—a few months earlier. Recovered from the dead Indians were Hall's rifle and Turner's coat.[84] The Visalia *Delta*, although noting that "the Indians had on articles of dress known to belong to Whites who had been murdered," deplored the killing of the Indians and urged restraint: "We know that it must be very trying to the self-control of any one to let an Indian pass under such circumstances, but yet it ought to be done, as a different course endangers the lives of the entire community."[85]

Just like some whites who were not ready to call it quits, there were those Indians who refused to surrender. Joaquin Jim's band of Paiute remained at large and continued to prey on the unsuspecting traveler or prospector. About the middle of June one of the most prominent citizens of Visalia, Thomas M. Heston, was killed by Paiute somewhere between Adobe Meadows and Aurora.[86] Similar attacks, usually attributed to Joaquin Jim, continued to plague the valley. In late June, Captain McLaughlin with ninety soldiers and twenty-six Indians, including Captain George, trailed Joaquin Jim and his band of warriors through Round Valley and over 12,400 foot high Italy Pass into the western Sierra.[87] The chase continued for another week before Joaquin Jim's trail turned cold.

On 11 July 1863, Captains McLaughlin, Noble, and Ropes with a detachment of seventy cavalrymen from Companies D, E, and G and twenty-two foot soldiers from the Fourth Infantry, California Volunteers, left Camp Independence with some 900 Indians, bound for the San Sebastian Reservation near Fort Tejon.[88] Travel was slow, and it was not until 22 July that the Indians, about 50 of whom slipped away en route, were delivered to agent John Wentworth. Wentworth was angry because Congress had not approved his request of the previous year for an Owens River reservation and $30,000 in relief funds. At that time the Commissioner of Indian Affairs, William P. Dole, had disapproved of the Owens Valley as a location for an Indian reservation, and Representative Aaron A. Sargent had stated to Congress that the amount of money requested was excessive and that there were not 500 Indians in the entire valley. Wentworth now reported to the Bureau of Indian Affairs that the 850 Indians delivered to the reservation probably represented only about one-third of the total. He further contended that:

*the government has expended nearly ten times the amount asked for in that report in trying to suppress the present Indian War. Had Congress promptly made that appropriation, no Indian War would have been waged, and the country would have been saved more than two hundred and fifty thousand dollars to its treasury, the lives of many of its valuable citizens, and many of the poor, ignorant, misguided Indians, to whom the government have promised protection would to-day, instead of being dead, be living and tilling the soil of their native valley and through their own willing hands, obtaining an honest and well earned livelihood.*

*These Indians, like all others of their race, are very exacting, and a promise to them unfulfilled they look upon as a just cause for war. Therefore it is of the utmost importance that Congress awaken to the necessity of giving, in future, heed and consideration to the reports of its agents upon the condition and wants of the Indians under their respective charges.*[89]

Agent Wentworth now concluded his report by asserting that, because of mining activity in the region, the Owens Valley was "entirely impracticable" for an Indian reservation and that "the Indian and white race can never live peacefully in close proximity to each other."

Wentworth apparently failed to see the contradiction in his own report. If his conclusions were true, then little good would have come from the establishment of a reservation in the valley during the winter of 1862-1863 unless whites could have been kept out of the area. Prospectors and ranchers were already there, however, and more were coming. The United States government had never fought with much vigor against encroachment by whites on lands reserved to Indians, and it is unlikely that the Owens Valley would have been an exception. Wherever whites had demanded Indian land, sooner or later the Indians were forced to cede their holdings.[90]

Wentworth also failed to note that the Paiute uprising came after they had received gifts and rations throughout the winter. Captain George's band of Paiute, for example, who had left Camp Independence loaded down with blankets and food, became one of the most active warrior bands in the spring. Wentworth apparently forgot that it was the Indians, not the whites, who renewed hostilities as soon as spring arrived. Moreover, there is no evidence that the Paiute conceived of themselves as potential yeoman farmers who would soon be "tilling the soil of their native valley."

The Paiute of the trans-Sierra country were primarily hunters and gatherers. Although there were bands of Paiute in the Owens Valley who irrigated wild plants, even those bands cannot be considered agricultural. Furthermore, it was the job of the women, not the men, to gather nuts and seeds and to dig roots. That the Paiute men would have voluntarily abandoned their manner of living and become farmers is unlikely. They were certainly proud of what they were and, as events proved, were willing to fight to protect their way of life.

Finally, Wentworth neglected to mention that the most aggressive, or perhaps the most freedom-loving, band of Paiute, the one led by Joaquin Jim, did not attend the peace conference of October 1862 at Camp Independence and was party to no agreements. Considering all of these circumstances, it is unlikely, even if Wentworth's recommendations had been followed, that an Indian war could have been avoided—unless, of course, the United States government would have been willing to keep whites out of the Owens Valley.

On 17 July 1863, Captain McLaughlin received orders to abandon Camp Independence and to reoccupy Fort Tejon.[91] Two weeks later he led Companies D and G out of the Owens Valley (Company L had left at the end of May, and Company E at the end of June.)[92] Sporadic Indian attacks continued during the summer of 1863. Many of these were attributed to Joaquin Jim who, with the abandonment of Camp Independence, now considered himself overlord of the southern trans-Sierra. He even marked his principal territory, Round Valley, with a war banner of scarlet, trimmed with raven feathers. A few other bands of Paiute were also active, and it was still dangerous for whites to travel alone.

In August, Stephen Orjada was ambushed by Indians as he rode from Keyesville to Walker's Basin.[93] One round carried away two fingers of his left hand, and several others barely missed him. Orjada spurred his mule, but the stubborn beast, "with the perversity for which that animal is fabled," refused to move. He dismounted and outran the Indians to safety. At about the same time, nine prospectors in Little Round Valley held off an attack by a large band of Paiute, two of whom were killed.[94] A few weeks later two prospectors from Aurora, Mark Cornish and W. L. Moore, killed two Paiute while repulsing an attack on the southeast edge of Adobe Meadows.[95] The prospectors were chased back to Aurora, but arrived safely. Still another two Paiute, reputed to be members of Joaquin Jim's band, were killed by miners in the White Mountains.[96] Even without having to contend with the Second Cavalry, the Indians were faring badly. Their luck was about to change.

In early September four horse-mounted prospectors found themselves in Round Valley—Joaquin Jim's territory—as they followed Pine Creek into the Sierra in search of timber.[97] The prospectors, members of a church group from San Francisco, had crossed into the trans-Sierra, in the belief that goodwill and generosity would win the friendship of the Indians. Now, despite having been warned by other whites of Indian hostility and despite signs of Indians, they began working their way up a steep trail toward a timber-covered ridge. When they were only twenty-five yards from their destination, the quiet of the eastern Sierra was shattered by the roar of a dozen rifles. "My God, I'm shot!" cried Silas Parker as he fell from his saddle. Two bullets had ripped through his chest.

Edward Ericson, Edmund Long, and Ezra Merriam grabbed their rifles and jumped to the ground. With bullets kicking up the dirt around them, they ran to cover behind outcroppings of rock that bordered the trail. The Paiute had laid a neat ambush: they were in front and on both flanks of the prospectors. Although the Paiute rifle fire was intense, Ericson tried to assist the wounded Parker, who lay helpless in the middle of the trail. As soon as Ericson exposed himself, a round tore into his thigh. Merriam could see the blood streaming out of Ericson's leg and tried to move to another position to better cover his partner. Merriam did not get far. He missed his step and tumbled down a steep hillside to the edge of Pine Creek.

7. Joe Bowers, an Owens Valley Paiute, was employed by the soldiers at Camp Independence in the 1870s. This photo was taken after 1904. *(Credit: A. A. Forbes photo, Eastern California Museum.)*

Working his way through the riparian undergrowth, Merriam finally hid in a dense clump of chaparral. He could hear rifle fire from above, but for two hours he saw no Paiute. Just when he thought he might be safe, seven Paiute appeared on the opposite bank of the creek. They motioned to others on his side of the creek and pointed to where he was concealed. Merriam sprang to his feet and raced pell-mell down the canyon. The Paiute whooped and gave chase.

For a time Merriam was able to outrun his pursuers, but gradually they began to gain on him. In desperation, he plunged into the creek. The current swept him downstream faster than the Paiute could run, but after a half mile he was carried over a waterfall and was slammed into the creek bottom. He found himself caught between two rocks, and struggle though he might, he could not free himself. With his lungs screaming for air, Merriam gave one final push. He broke free and popped to the surface. Pausing only to gulp in some air, he resubmerged and swam to shore. He discovered a small ledge of rock that jutted out from the shore just above the surface of the water. Merriam sank under the ledge until he was well hidden, leaving only his nose above the surface.

The Paiute were now swarming over both banks of the creek. They scanned Merriam's hiding spot from the opposite bank. They stood on the rock ledge under which he lay. They found his hat, which had washed ashore. Never once did they enter the stream themselves. For three hours the Paiute sat and waited and watched, and for three hours Merriam lay still and silent under the ledge. By now he had a new enemy: chilled to the bone, he was beginning to freeze to death. To move meant certain and possibly cruel death at the hands of the Paiute. Not to move meant certain death from exposure.

Suddenly the Paiute stood up and headed back upstream. Merriam relaxed but still remained hidden for another half hour before he let the current carry him downstream. He floated quietly along until he caught hold of a protruding branch. With great difficulty, he pulled himself ashore and slowly and painfully regained full use of his limbs. He hid in a canebrake until nightfall and then cautiously made his way down into the Owens Valley.

Once Merriam reached the valley, word of the attack spread rapidly. George K. Phillips, a veteran prospector from Aurora, organized a force of thirty men and established a base camp in Round Valley. Merriam guided the force to the scene of the ambush, where the stripped and bullet-riddled bodies of Edward Ericson and Edmund Long were found. Signs indicated that the two prospectors had been dragged along the trail by ropes tied around their necks. The body of Silas Parker was never found. The whites conjectured that Parker was still alive when captured and was taken to another location for torture.

The bodies of Ericson and Long were placed in shallow graves and covered with pine branches, soil, and rocks. A member of the force eloquently described what happened next:

*One man said: "Come, boys, let's go; we can do no more for the poor fellows." Then in a lower and tremulous voice he added: "God give his soul a better show than this." I have listened to long prayers in grand cathedrals, where the sunlight poured in through stained glass windows and fell on pews of carved oak, but I never heard so fervent, so touching a prayer as this, far away in this mountain land, among the pines, under the shadow of the giant Sierras, where the river, deep in the wild and rocky canyon below, murmured the requiem of the dead; where the blue sky, widespread, extends from mountain range to mountain range, over mile upon mile of valley land and wooded hills. We left them, sadly and silently, and went up to our comrades on the hill.[98]*

The whites examined the scene of the ambush and then followed tracks to a Paiute camp, where they found dozens of baskets of piñon nuts, but no Paiute. They also found the bridle to Merriam's horse, and Ericson's boots and hat. A blood-splattered bullet hole in the hat told the story of Ericson's end. Each man packed as many pinon nuts as he could carry, and the rest were burned. The whites concluded that further pursuit of the Paiute would be futile and returned to the valley.

In October some five hundred Paiute, nearly half of whom were warriors, assembled at a point twenty-five miles southeast of Aurora for a great fall feast and "pine nut dances."[99] The Paiute, led by Joaquin Jim and "Captain Tom," had unknowingly camped directly in the path of a twenty-man survey team running California's eastern boundary. The surveyors made presents to the Paiute leaders, distributed food, and explained, through an interpreter, their intentions. The Paiute in reply demanded that the whites leave their arms in camp when they went out to survey. This less than subtle stratagem caused the surveyors to pack up their equipment and what was left of their provisions and head back to Aurora posthaste.

During the winter of 1863-1864 the Paiute, as in the previous winter, were relatively quiet. Nothing more than minor incidents were reported. Captain McLaughlin with a detachment of fifteen men arrived at Camp Independence in early December, but spent only a week in the valley before returning to Camp Babbitt.[100] The Paiute, in contrast to their actions in 1862 and 1863, mounted no spring offensive in 1864. But during the summer they were seen moving their women and children into the mountains, and the whites reasoned that they were contemplating a new campaign. Toward the end of July, James G. Anderson, a prospector from Aurora, was shot to death by Indians in his cabin along the Walker River.[101] Then another white was wounded, and a horse trader was killed and his livestock stolen.[102]

Reacting to these events, the whites formed two companies of militia after their pleas for military assistance went unheeded.[103] The militia companies visited the various Paiute camps and let it be known that if the Paiute continued killing and stealing, they would be punished without mercy. The warnings apparently had an effect; no more incidents occurred until late in the fall.

Early in November 1864, a Paiute man and woman wandered into the mining camp of A. W. Crow, Byrnes, and Mathews, three prospectors from Aurora.[104] The miners had been working their Deep Springs Valley claim, the Cinderella, since summer. They had been on friendly terms with the local Paiute and had no reason to view these two arrivals with suspicion. Mathews was cooking dinner at the time. Crow was operating the windlass to their shaft, and Byrnes was seventy feet below ground digging at the shaft bottom.

The woman asked Mathews for something to eat, and as he turned to fetch the food, the Paiute man shot him in the head. The pistol ball entered Mathews's temple and exited through his lower jaw. The Paiute left him for dead. At the same time, other Paiute opened fire on Crow, killing him instantly. Byrnes, at the bottom of the shaft, was wounded in both arms but not killed. The Paiute, not yet satisfied, hurled several hundred pounds of rock into the shaft. Byrnes somehow managed to protect himself with his shovel and then wisely played dead. Convinced that Byrnes was dead, the Paiute ransacked the camp and left.

Mathews, although horribly wounded, began to stir. Struggling to his feet, he crept over to the mine shaft, where he saw the dead form of Crow and listened for movement below. Byrnes was playing dead and trying not to make a sound, and Mathews's wound prevented him from calling to Byrnes. Moreover, the Paiute had stolen the windlass rope. Mathews, reckoning that Byrnes must have been killed, set out for the Owens Valley.

For two days Mathews, a man in his late fifties who had come to California in 1831 aboard a hide-and-tallow ship, pushed himself through the White Mountains, suffering terribly from his wound and lack of water. On the third day of his ordeal and nearing death from dehydration, he reached the Owens River and was greeted by cold, limpid water from the Sierra Nevada. Mathews could not drink a drop. His throat was so clotted with blood that swallowing was impossible. With great anguish, he decided that he might as well try to ford the Owens and push on to the settlements. He stepped into the river and promptly slipped on a rock and fell into the water. It was a lucky fall. The clot in his throat was broken loose, and he painfully drank his fill. A cowboy later spotted Mathews and carried him to a ranch near Big Pine. There Mathews slowly regained his health, if not his voice, with regular feedings administered through a cow's horn. A party of men was dispatched to the Cinderella mine, and Byrnes, who had almost given up hope after five days of suffering at the bottom of the shaft, was rescued.

Meanwhile, the band of Paiute responsible for the attack at the Cinderella mine raided another mine some ten miles away.[105] The miners there held the Indians at bay long enough to saddle horses and gallop madly out of camp. The Indians gave chase, but after a running fight of forty miles the whites escaped. Joaquin Jim was said to have been the leader of the Indians.

8. Ranchers quickly displaced the Paiute in the Owens Valley. Pictured here are wranglers on the Robinson ranch east of Independence. Photo is facing east, with the Inyo Mountains in the background. *(Credit: Eastern California Museum.)*

Despite these attacks the whites took no organized action against the Paiute. All was again quiet until the very end of the year. About an hour before sunrise on 31 December 1864, Mary McGuire and her six-year-old son, Johnny, and two workmen, were awakened by the noise and the light of the fire that was burning the roof of the McGuires' cabin.[106] The cabin had been built by Mary's husband, John McGuire, at Hawean Meadows (now covered by Haiwee Reservoir) as a way station on the road from Visalia to Aurora. McGuire was now away on business in Bend City, but Thomas Flanigan and Daniel Newman, two men he had hired to build an irrigation ditch, were at the cabin. They ran outside to extinguish the fire, supposing that it had occurred by accident. To their surprise, they were greeted by a hail of arrows and were driven back into the cabin.

Mary McGuire, her son, and the men now began to knock off the roof shingles from inside the cabin and to douse the flames with brine from barrels of corned beef. They had almost succeeded in controlling the fire when the Indians threw new brands onto the roof. The heat now became so intense that it was impossible for them to remain inside. The men urged Mary McGuire to take the only choice left and attempt with them to dash past the Indians. "It is of no use," she is said to have replied, "nothing can save us." Unable to persuade Mary McGuire to join them, the men dashed out of the cabin and ran for their lives. Flanigan's hat was shot off his head, and Newman was struck in the forehead by an arrow, but both men managed to reach Little Lake, some eighteen miles to the south. They were both exhausted, and Newman was near collapse from loss of blood.

In the meantime, two riders traveling from Aurora to Visalia spotted the smoke rising from the McGuire way station. They raced to the station and found Mary McGuire riddled by fourteen arrows and near death. Beside her lay her dead son, Johnny. He had been hit by six arrows, his arm had been broken, and his forehead had been bashed in by a club. The boy also had had his teeth pounded out to prevent him, as the Paiute believed, from returning after death as a wild animal who might attack an unsuspecting Indian. Mary McGuire, wounded though she was, had somehow managed to pull every one of the arrows out of her son. The two of them had evidently put up a stout defense; an ax was found alongside her body, and the boy had a stone tightly clenched in his fist, indicating that, as one settler termed it, "he died grit."

Express riders soon carried the news to the Owens Valley, Visalia, and Aurora. The whites of these areas were enraged by the killing of Mary McGuire and her son. The McGuire way station had become a landmark, and the family was liked by all. H. T. Reed, a pioneer of the southern trans-Sierra and an occasional correspondent for the Visalia *Delta*, wrote:

*Both Mr. and Mrs. McGuire had done more for the "Poor Indian" than they were able, often denied themselves to feed them. Her loss is deeply felt by all, and no one who has ever stopped there will fail to remember the hearty welcome and the happy face of bright, intelligent little Johnny and his noble mother. They have erected a monument in the hearts of all who knew them by their many acts of disinterested kindness, sympathy and love; and a tear is to-day coursing its way down the cheek of many a Pioneer in sympathy for the husband and father who is so cruelly bereft of all; and in memory of the loved ones so cruelly murdered.*[107]

The militia companies, known as the Home Guard, now swung into action. Their cry was for extermination. A member of the Guard from Lone Pine wrote to Colonel L. W. Ransom at Camp Babbitt:

*For some time past we have been compelled to let the Indians do as they please. If a white man kills an Indian he must leave the country or be imprisoned. I think things have reached the point, that either the white people must leave this Valley or the Indians killed off, or in some other way got rid of. We have fed them all Summer, and it is a pretty hard thing now, because we are unable to do it any longer on account of County Taxes, high price of living, and altogether are unable to do it any longer to have our throats cut and butchered. Only last week an Indian drew his knife on my wife because she would not let him take possession of the kitchen and give him sugar in his coffee. The bodies of the killed [Mary McGuire and her son] were brought to this place (Lone Pine) and buried. "Poor Indian" is played out with this settler.*[108]

The militia followed the trail of the Indians from the smoldering ruins of the McGuire cabin to a camp on the eastern shore of Owens Lake. At daybreak on 5 January 1865 the whites attacked. The Indians were taken by complete surprise—they had as usual not posted sentries—and some thirty-five of them, including women and children, were killed.[109] John McGuire himself got some measure of revenge by killing two Paiute men.[110] Only two girls and a boy were spared.

Soon after this slaughter, seventeen Paiute were killed near Taboose ranch in the foothills of the eastern Sierra.[111] In several other scattered incidents Paiute were killed, including two who had evidently taken part in the Cinderella mine attack. These latter two were first captured—one of them with A. W. Crow's gun on him (Crow was the prospector killed at the Cinderella mine)—and put under guard at Lone Pine. A local settler wrote the night of the capture that the Indians "will hardly see the sun rise tomorrow."[112] He was right.

Ironically, now that the Indians of the southern trans-Sierra had been dealt these blows, the army returned. On 13 January 1865, Captain John G. Kelly, a former Pony Express rider who had won his army commission in a poker game with Nevada governor James Nye, arrived at Bishop Creek with Company C, First Nevada Infantry, and on 1 April began the reoccupation of Camp Independence.[113] Violent conflict between Indians and whites was nearly over. There would only be a few more incidents during 1865.

On 28 February 1865, J. N. Rogers, an Owens Valley rancher who had participated in the slaughter of the Indians at Owens Lake in January, was attacked by a band of Indians as he drove his wagon loaded with hay by Hell's Gate, four miles north of McGuire's way station.[114] Rogers took off on foot, reasoning that the Indians were more interested in his horses and hay than in him. Several of the Indians rushed for his wagon, but most of them followed him. He managed to hold the Indians at bay by pausing now and then to shoot at them with his revolver. Wounded a half-dozen times by arrows and nearly exhausted from loss of blood, Rogers reached Little Lake six hours later.

The very next day two prospectors from Aurora, Robert Rabe and Isaac Stewart, were killed by Paiute near Walker Lake.[115] According to the report of a friendly Indian, the men were taken by complete surprise. Rabe was lighting a campfire when he was shot in the back and killed, and Stewart was scouting the route the prospectors would take the next morning, when the Paiute swept down on him. The four horses the prospectors had with them were probably the cause of the attack, although the *Esmeralda Union* noted that Stewart had flogged an Indian some time earlier, and this may have inspired the Indians to seek revenge.

During the summer of 1865 Indians burned the Willow Springs, Lotta, and Union mills and wounded one miner.[116] This was the last gasp of Paiute resistance. Sometime during the winter of 1865-1866, Joaquin Jim died near the Casa Diablo geysers in Long Valley. His death was evidently a natural one, although one report had him killed the previous winter by other Indians.[117] Without the forceful leadership of the redoubtable firebrand, the Paiute had little hope of ever again launching a major or even a minor offensive against the whites. Disturbances generally ceased in the trans-Sierra country, although isolated incidents were reported in remote mountain areas for another two years.

John Shipe, a prospector and trapper who had perhaps gone a little mad, continued to hunt down and kill Paiute who had fled to the mountains.[118] Shipe had been one of those with Frank Whetson when the white men killed and scalped three Paiute who were on their way to Camp Independence to surrender in July 1863. The white men had claimed at that time that the killings were retribution for four of their partners who had been killed by Paiute. Shipe continued the apparent vendetta against the Paiute until his death in 1867. Squads of soldiers were frequently sent to arrest him, but they were never successful.

Camp Independence was occupied until the summer of 1877, when it was abandoned for good. Captain Noble and Company E, Second Cavalry, California Volunteers replaced Captain Kelly and Company C, First Nevada Infantry, during November 1865.[119] Captain Noble and his outfit remained there until May 1866, when they were replaced by regulars who had served under General Philip Sheridan. These hardened veterans of the Civil War had the last two known clashes with the Indians. In August 1866 they killed several warriors on the eastern side of Owens Lake and took many prisoners, and in March 1867 they routed a band of Indians who had attacked miners at Coso.

Conflict between Indians and whites in the southern trans-Sierra cost the lives of no less than two hundred Indians and thirty whites; perhaps another hundred Indians and whites were wounded. Nearly a thousand Indians were removed to reservations. The conflict paralleled the rise and decline of Aurora. The first killings occurred in 1861, full-scale warfare in 1862 and 1863, a rapid tapering off of conflict in 1864, and a final few sparks in 1865 and 1866.

The cattle drives to Aurora first aroused Paiute curiosity, and then the stocking of the range land of the Owens Valley ignited the war. The Paiute initially attacked only the cattlemen, but soon turned on prospectors as well. Aurora was the outfitting center and point of departure for these prospectors who, after the Esmeralda strike, were roaming the southern trans-Sierra in ever greater numbers. The whites' activities of cattle grazing and mining were not compatible with the Paiute way of life. Conflict could have been avoided only if whites had been kept out of the region or if the Indians would have voluntarily abandoned their customary way of life and become a reservation-settled agricultural people.

Indian agents Warren Wasson and John P. H. Wentworth thought that the Paiute should and could become farmers. The Paiute, however, were a hunting and gathering people, and food gathering was the job of the women, not the men. That men from Joaquin Jim's band, or any other band for that matter, would have voluntarily become farmers toiling behind plows was a less than realistic assumption; that they *should* have done so was nothing more than ethnocentricism and paternalism on the part of Wasson and Wentworth. For their part, the Paiute, though they did not accept the philosophy of the Indian agents, did accept the agents' gifts and rations as tribute and must have thought that the white man was either cowed, terribly gullible, or stupid.

The warfare that occurred in the trans-Sierra country was not unlike that which occurred elsewhere in California and the American West.[120] The Paiute fought as individual bands with only an occasional coordinated effort. They had little sense of strategy and no logistical support to sustain a protracted fight against the white invaders. The Paiute could possibly have held back the white advance for years if they could have developed an overall plan of defense, unity of command, and a system of supply. Expecting the Paiute to have made such developments, however, is as unrealistic as expecting them to have voluntarily become farmers. The various bands of Paiute were fiercely independent and only rarely came together for a common purpose. The intelligent and resourceful Joaquin Jim came as close as anyone to being a commanding general, but even his influence seldom extended beyond his own band.

The Paiute were superb at laying ambushes and hit-and-run raiding, but they attacked only when they had a significant advantage and little chance of losses. Individual whites or small groups of whites were prized targets. Citizen militia and the United States Army were generally to be avoided. The Paiute evidently did not believe that it was courageous or glorious to die in battle. Their purpose was to kill their enemy, but only if they could do so without harm to themselves. The Battle of the Ditch was just one of several examples in which the Paiute could have overrun and annihilated the whites if they had been willing to suffer a substantial number of casualties.

The Paiute were nearly always outgunned. They did have some guns, but not nearly enough to arm more than a small number of their men. Moreover, the guns were mostly old, smooth-bore muzzle loaders.[121] One trooper who served in the Owens Valley war with the Second Cavalry noted that arrows fired by the Indians often had more force than the lead balls of the muzzle loaders.[122] This was probably caused by improper charging. The Paiute did not have an adequate supply of gunpowder. Nor did they have enough lead to make bullets, as evidenced by the theft of lead pipe from the mining camp of Ida. Moreover, the Paiute did not regularly clean their firearms. In one battle their guns became so fouled that they had to force bullets down the gun barrels by pounding the ramrods with stones.

Perhaps more important for the Paiute than lack of unity, strategy, and weaponry was lack of food. Since their food supply depended on hunting and gathering in the less than bountiful trans-Sierra country, the Paiute could not cache enough food to wage a long war against the white invaders. The whites, especially the United States Army, quickly learned that destroying Paiute food caches was tantamount to destroying the

Paiute themselves, proving once again that it is easier to starve a fierce enemy into submission than to fight him. This led to the so-called surrender of Captain George and others after spring and summer raids. The Paiute would then live off the white man's rations during the fall and winter, only to renew warfare with the coming of spring. When they had exhausted their food supplies, they would return to Camp Independence and again make "peace." Many whites found it impossible to accept this cyclical status of the Indians, and some, such as Frank Whetson and his partners, shot down Paiute who were under a flag of truce.

Although the Paiute never intentionally took prisoners, a white captured alive was a great prize because he could then be tortured. Ironically, the most famous torture victim was not a white but a black, Charley Tyler, who was tortured for three days and then roasted to death. Almost all white corpses were found stripped of clothing and mutilated. Scalps were taken, and in a few instances whites reciprocated in kind. Torture was not something the Indians reserved for the whites. Long before any whites set foot in California, Paiute and other Indians had practiced torture.[123]

The war saw possibly the first manifestation of the Ghost Dance. The group of Paiute that danced around the cabins and sheds of the San Francis Ranch and proclaimed that they could spit out any bullets that might enter their bodies were performing a ritual that would eventually spread to the Sioux on the northern Plains. Wodziwob, the tribal shaman of the Mono Lake Paiute, was probably responsible for the demonstration at the San Francis Ranch. It is no accident that one of his followers, Tavibo, was the father of Wovoka—the Indian messiah and leader of the Ghost Dance during the late 1880's and 1890's.[124]

The Second Cavalry, California Volunteers, bore the brunt of the fighting for the United States Army. The outfit consisted entirely of volunteers from California and Nevada and, like other Civil War units, had a large number of Irish immigrants and first-generation Irish-Americans. These men were encouraged to enlist by promises of active service in the East. Instead, they served their country chasing Indians in the southern trans-Sierra. Although they considered it less than glorious duty and were paid only seven dollars a month, desertions were surprisingly few.

Just as surprising, the officers proved highly capable. Captain Moses A. McLaughlin was an able and aggressive commander who quickly turned the tide against the Indians. His ruthless slaughter of the Indian prisoners at Whiskey Flat was characteristic of the man who crossed into the trans-Sierra with only one purpose in mind: eliminate the Indian menace. Within a couple of months he had nearly accomplished that goal. Indian raids were only sporadic affairs after McLaughlin's stay at Camp Independence, and the war for the Owens Valley was over.

Citizen militia also played a significant role in the fighting. The first volunteer company was raised in Aurora and included Sheriff N. F. Scott, who died in the Battle of the Ditch. In nearly every fight civilians aided the military, and in the final major confrontation it was two Owens Valley civilian militia companies that routed the Paiute. The civilians, many of whom had had friends or loved ones killed or wounded in Indian attacks, proved more ruthless than the military. Whereas the army often took Indian prisoners and, with only one exception, treated the captives humanely, the civilians rarely did so. On several occasions civilians shot down Paiute women and children, although the army restricted its targets to men.

Since the whites were trespassers in Paiute territory, ultimate responsibility for the conflict lay with the whites. The whites were, in effect, invading foreign territory. From the perspective of the whites, however, there appeared to be ample room for settlement. There were no Paiute farms, no ranches, no mines, no industry, no roads or bridges, no permanent settlements. Paiute were only occasionally sighted and then only in small groups. The land generally appeared to the whites as if it were uninhabited or only very sparsely settled. The whites did not comprehend that the Paiute were already, as required by their way of life, utilizing the land to its fullest capacity. Nor did the whites comprehend that stocking the range lands with cattle would force the Paiute to either abandon their way of life or fight against white encroachment. Most Paiute chose to fight.

NOTES:

1. San Francisco *Daily Evening Post*, 22 Nov. 1879; *Inyo Register*, 11 Feb. 1904, 15 Jan. 1914. Especially useful for the conflict between the Indians and the whites in the Owens Valley are the accounts of J. W. A. Wright, published in the *Daily Evening Post* on 22 and 29 November 1879, and those of W. A. Chalfant, which began appearing

in the *Inyo Register* shortly after the turn of the century and were later included in his minor classic, *The Story of Inyo*. The accounts of both men are slightly flawed by occasional errors and omissions but are generally accurate and, most important, make use of several manuscript collections that have since been destroyed or lost.

2. For territorial boundaries and linguistic area, see Robert F. Heizer and Albert B. Elsasser, *The Natural World of the California Indians*, esp. pp. 5, 12, 19, and 29; and A. L. Kroeber, *Handbook of the Indians of California*, esp. pp. 574-92. Kroeber refers to the Paiute of the Mono Lake area and the Owens Valley as the Eastern Mono. For an in-depth look at the Paiute, including identification of the various bands of Owens Valley Paiute, see Julian H. Steward and Erminie Wheeler-Voegelin, *The Northern Paiute Indians*, esp. pp. 103-23.

3. For a description of the eating habits and cooking methods of the Owens Valley and Mono Paiute, see Steward and Wheeler-Voegelin, *Northern Paiute Indians*, pp. 115-18; C. Hart Merriam, *Studies of the California Indians*, pp. 117-22; Kroeber, *Handbook of Indians of California*, pp. 591-92; and Harry W. Lawton et al., "Agriculture among the Paiute of Owens Valley."

4. Lawton, "Agriculture among the Paiute of Owens Valley," pp. 13-50.

5. The irrigation system at *pitana patu* consisted of a dam on Bishop Creek and two main irrigation ditches. One ditch, some two miles long, led to wild-plant-producing land on the northern side of the creek, and the other, more than three miles in length, led to similar ground on the creek's south side.

6. See Julian H. Steward, "Irrigation Without Agriculture." Lawton and others argue that the work the Paiute did—irrigating and harvesting—was enough to say that they "practiced agriculture."

7. San Francisco *Daily Evening Post*, 22 Nov. 1879; *Inyo Register*, 18 Feb. 1904.

8. *Daily Evening Post*, 22 Nov. 1879.

9. *Daily Evening Post*, 22 Nov. 1879; *Inyo Register*, 18 Feb. 1904, 15 Jan. 1914.

10. *Inyo Register*, 18 Feb. 1904, 15 Jan. 1914.

11. Samuel Youngs's Journal, 25 Dec. 1862.

12. San Francisco *Daily Evening Post*, 22 Nov. 1879; Visalia *Delta*, 16 April 1863; *Inyo Register*, 20 Sept. 1906.

13. Visalia *Delta*, 16 April 1863.

14. San Francisco *Daily Evening Post*, 22 Nov. 1879; *Inyo Register*, 18 Feb. 1904, 22 Jan. 1914. Jesse Summers is called James Summers by the *Aurora Times* and the Visalia *Delta*.

15. *Inyo Register*, 22 Jan. 1914. It is no accident that there are similarities here with the Indian Ghost Dance and Ghost Shirt beliefs of the late 1880s. Wovoka, the leader of the Ghost Dance during the

late 1880s, was himself a Mono Paiute from the Walker River country. His father, Tavibo, was a shaman and a follower of Wodziwob, the tribal shaman of the Mono Paiute during the 1850s and 1860s. Wodziwob may have been responsible for the Paiute demonstration at the San Francis Ranch. His beliefs certainly influenced Tavibo and Wovoka. Wodziwob told his people that they could bring the dead back by performing a ritualistic dance—later called the Ghost Dance—and he prophesied a frightening upheaval in which God would appear on earth and transform it into a paradise. See Edward C. Johnson, *Walker River Paiutes: A Tribal History*, pp. 41-57; and James Mooney, *The Ghost-Dance Religion and the Sioux Outbreak of 1890*. Mooney's classic work was originally published as Part 2 of the *Fourteenth Annual Report of the Bureau of Ethnology to the Secretary of the Smithsonian Institution*, 1892-93 (Washington, 1896).

16. San Francisco *Daily Evening Post*, 22 Nov. 1879.
17. *Daily Evening Post*, 22 Nov. 1879; see also Department of War, *The War of the Rebellion: A Compilation of the Official Records of the Union and Confederate Armies*, vol. 50, part I, pp. 966-67.
18. *Inyo Register*, 18 Feb. 1904, 22 Jan. 1914.
19. W. A. Chalfant says that Tom Hubbard was also wounded, but it is obvious that Chalfant confused this fight with a fight in the Alabama Hills in which Hubbard was in fact wounded. Compare the San Francisco *Daily Evening Post*, 22 Nov. 1879, the *Inyo Register*, 18 and 25 Feb. 1904, and W. A. Chalfant, *The Story of Inyo*, pp. 152-53.
20. San Francisco *Daily Evening Post*, 22 Nov. 1879.
21. *Daily Evening Post*, 22 Nov. 1879; *Inyo Register*, 22 Jan. 1914.
22. *Daily Evening Post*, 22 Nov. 1879; *Inyo Register*, 25 Feb. 1904.
23. *Daily Evening Post*, 22 Nov. 1879; *Inyo Register*, 18 Feb. 1904, 22 Jan. 1914; Joseph Wasson, *Account of the Important Revival of Mining Interests in the Bodie and Esmeralda Districts*, p. 6.
24. Myron Angel, ed., *History of Nevada*, p. 151.
25. San Francisco *Daily Evening Post*, 22 Nov. 1879; *Inyo Register*, 18 Feb. 1904, 22 Jan. 1914.
26. *Inyo Register*, 25 Feb. 1904, 22 Jan. 1914.
27. *Inyo Register*, 25 Feb. 1904, 22 Jan. 1914; Angel, *History of Nevada*, p. 166.
28. See n. 27; *Daily Evening Post*, 22 Nov. 1879; *War of the Rebellion*, vol. 50, part I, p. 46.
29. *Inyo Register*, 22 Jan. 1914.
30. This was the southern irrigation ditch at *pitana patu*.
31. Estimates of Indian strength varied from as low as 400 or 500 to as high as 1,500. See the San Francisco *Daily Evening Post*, 22 Nov.

1879; *Inyo Register*, 25 Feb. 1904; Angel, *History of Nevada*, p. 166; *War of the Rebellion*, vol. 50, part I, p. 47.

32. Samuel Youngs's Journal, 18 March 1862.
33. Official Report of Indian Agent Warren Wasson to Governor James W. Nye, 20 April 1862, as quoted in Angel, *History of Nevada*, p. 166.
34. Angel, p. 166. The Second Cavalry, California Volunteers, was organized and mustered into service at Camp Alert, San Francisco, on 30 October 1861. The regiment served throughout the Far West during the Civil War and was mustered out of service at Camp Union, Sacramento, in April 1866.
35. Angel, p. 166.
36. Samuel Youngs's Journal, 1 April 1862.
37. Wasson's Report in Angel, *History of Nevada*, p. 166.
38. For the initial excursion of Evans and the Second Cavalry into the Owens Valley see the *War of the Rebellion*, vol. 50, part I, pp. 46-49, 934-36, 939, 966-67, 972, 1025-26; and the San Francisco *Daily Evening Post*, 22 Nov. 1879.
39. Pleasant Valley, a few miles northwest of present-day Bishop, was named in his honor.
40. Wasson's Report in Angel, *History of Nevada*, p. 167.
41. Angel, p. 167; San Francisco *Daily Evening Post*, 22 Nov. 1879; California, *Records of California Men in the War of the Rebellion, 1861 to 1867*, pp. 202, 205, 874. Harris's wounds proved so serious that he was discharged for disability on 16 Sept. 1862.
42. San Francisco *Daily Evening Post*, 22 Nov. 1879.
43. *Records of California Men*, p. 235; *Inyo Register*, 3 March 1904, 29 Jan. 1914.
44. Wasson's Report in Angel, *History of Nevada*, p. 167.
45. *War of the Rebellion*, vol. 50, part I, pp. 48-49.
46. Visalia *Delta*, 17 July 1862.
47. *War of the Rebellion*, vol. 50, part I, pp. 1025-26, 1047.
48. *War of the Rebellion*, vol. 50, part I, pp. 145-46.
49. *War of the Rebellion*, vol. 50, part I, p. 146.
50. *War of the Rebellion*, vol. 50, part I, p. 147; San Francisco *Daily Evening Post*, 22 Nov. 1879.
51. Visalia *Delta*, 17 July 1862.
52. *War of the Rebellion*, vol. 50, part I, pp. 148-49; San Francisco *Daily Evening Post*, 22 Nov. 1879.
53. *War of the Rebellion*, vol. 50, part I, p. 149.
54. *War of the Rebellion*, vol. 50, part II, p. 75. George and Tinemaha creeks in the Owens Valley were named after the Paiute leaders. Captain George's Paiute name was Tosahoidobah. See *War of the Rebellion*, vol. 50, part I, p. 213.
55. *War of the Rebellion*, vol. 50, part II, pp. 91-92.

56. Visalia *Delta*, 25 Sept. 1862.
57. *War of the Rebellion*, vol. 50, part I, pp. 149-50; part II, p. 122.
58. *War of the Rebellion*, vol. 50, part I, pp. 151-52.
59. The following account is drawn from Department of the Interior, *Report of the Commissioner of Indian Affairs for the Year 1863*, pp. 105-7.
60. *War of the Rebellion*, vol. 50, part I, pp. 152-153; part II, p. 139; Visalia *Delta*, 27 November 1862.
61. *Report of the Adjutant-General of the State of California, from May 1st, 1864 to November 30th, 1865*, p. 500.
62. Visalia *Delta*, 12 March 1863; *Inyo Register*, 10 March 1904.
63. Henry G. Hanks manuscript collection (destroyed in the San Francisco fire of 1906) as quoted in the *Inyo Register*, 10 March 1904.
64. Visalia *Delta*, 12 March 1863; San Francisco *Daily Evening Post*, 22 Nov. 1879; *Inyo Register*, 12 Feb. 1914.
65. See n. 64; *Records of California Men*, pp. 255, 877; *Report of the Adjutant-General of the State of California, from May 1st, 1864, to November 30th, 1865*, p. 547.
66. *Inyo Register*, 10 March 1904.
67. *War of the Rebellion*, vol. 50, part II, pp. 346-47; Visalia *Delta*, 12 March 1863.
68. *Aurora Times* (date unknown) as reprinted in the Visalia *Delta*, 16 April 1863; *Inyo Register*, 10 March 1904, 12 Feb. 1914; San Francisco *Daily Evening Post*, 22 Nov. 1879.
69. Visalia *Delta*, 25 Jan. 1865; San Francisco *Daily Evening Post*, 22 Nov. 1879. Charley's Butte, not far from the intake for the Los Angeles Aqueduct, was named in his honor.
70. *Inyo Register*, 20 March 1904, 19 Feb. 1914; *Report of the Adjutant-General of the State of California, from May 1st, 1864, to November 30th, 1865*, p. 547.
71. Visalia *Delta*, 2 April 1863; San Francisco *Daily Evening Post*, 22 Nov. 1879; *Inyo Register*, 19 Feb. 1914.
72. *Records of California Men*, p. 181.
73. *Records of California Men*, p. 181; San Francisco *Daily Evening Post*, 22 Nov. 1879; *Inyo Register*, 10 March 1904, 19 Feb. 1914.
74. *Esmeralda Star*, 11 April 1863, as reprinted in the Visalia *Delta*, 23 April 1863.
75. Visalia *Delta*, 23 April 1863; *Records of California Men*, p. 181; *War of the Rebellion*, vol. 50, part I, pp. 208-10.
76. Visalia *Delta*, 23 April 1863.
77. The following military actions were reported in *Records of California Men*, pp. 181-82, and *War of the Rebellion*, vol. 50, part I, pp. 210-12; part II, pp. 414-423.
78. *Inyo Register*, 26 Feb. 1914.

79. *Records of California Men*, p. 181; *War of the Rebellion*, vol. 50, part I, pp. 209-10; Visalia *Delta*, 4 June 1863.

80. Visalia *Delta*, 28 May 1863.

81. Visalia *Delta*, 25 June 1863.

82. *Esmeralda Star*, 30 July 1863, as reprinted in *Report of the Commissioner of Indian Affairs for the Year 1863*, p. 100.

83. Commissioner's *Report*, p. 100.

84. *Inyo Register*, 20 Sept. 1906; Visalia *Delta*, 23 July 1863.

85. Visalia *Delta*, 23 July 1863.

86. Visalia *Delta*, 2 July 1863.

87. Visalia *Delta*, 25 June 1863; San Francisco *Daily Evening Post*, 22 Nov. 1879.

88. *War of the Rebellion*, vol. 50, part II, pp. 535-36; *Records of California Men*, p. 182; *Report of the Commissioner of Indian Affairs for the Year 1863*, pp. 99-100; Visalia *Delta*, 23 July 1863.

89. *Report of the Commissioner of Indian Affairs for the Year 1863*, p. 99.

90. For a survey of Indian treaties and the inevitable Indian loss of their lands, see, e.g., Helen Hunt Jackson, *A Century of Dishonor*, Charles C. Royce, *Indian Land Cessions in the United States;* Edward H. Spicer, *A Short History of the Indians of the United States.*

91. *Report of the Commissioner of Indian Affairs for the Year 1863*, p. 100; *War of the Rebellion*, vol. 50, part II, pp. 515-16, 535. Chalfant says that Captain McLaughlin without authorization sold Camp Independence to Warren Mathews and was later courtmartialed and dismissed from the service for the action. McLaughlin was courtmartialed and dismissed from the service early in 1864, but the cause of the dismissal was the misuse of government goods at Fort Tejon. McLaughlin was later cleared of any wrongdoing and his military privileges were fully restored. See the service record of Captain Moses A. McLaughlin, Company D, Second Cavalry, California Volunteers; *Records of California Men*, p. 225; *War of the Rebellion*, vol. 50, part II, p. 544; Visalia *Delta*, 17 Dec. 1863, 4 Feb. 1864; *Inyo Register*, 17 March 1904, 26 Feb. 1914.

92. *Records of California Men*, pp. 190, 191, 194.

93. Visalia *Delta*, 27 August 1863.

94. *Inyo Register*, 5 March 1914.

95. *Inyo Register*, 5 March 1914; San Francisco *Daily Evening Post*, 22 Nov. 1879.

96. *Inyo Register*, 5 March 1914.

97. Visalia *Delta*, 24 Sept. 1863; San Francisco *Daily Evening Post*, 22 Nov. 1879; Ezra D. Merriam's personal account in the Henry G. Hanks manuscript collection as quoted in the *Inyo Register*, 5 March 1914.

98.  Henry G. Hanks manuscript collection as quoted in the *Inyo Register*, 5 March 1914.

99.  *Appendix to Journals of Senate and Assembly of the Fifteenth Session of the Legislature of the State of California*, "Annual Report of the Surveyor-General for the Year 1863," p. 40.

100. *War of the Rebellion*, vol. 50, part II, p. 699; Visalia *Delta*, 17 Dec. 1863.

101. *Esmeralda Union*, 5 August 1864.

102. San Francisco *Daily Evening Post*, 22 Nov. 1879; *Inyo Register*, 31 March 1904.

103. See n.102 and *War of the Rebellion*, vol. 50, part II, pp. 989-90, 1017.

104. *Esmeralda Union*, 21 Nov. 1864; Visalia *Delta*, 30 Nov. 1864; *Inyo Register*, 31 March 1904.

105. *Esmeralda Union*, 21 Nov. 1864.

106. Sources for the following account are the Visalia *Delta*, 11, 18, and 25 Jan. 1865, and the *Esmeralda Union*, 7 Jan. 1865.

107. Visalia *Delta*, 18 Jan. 1865.

108. Visalia *Delta*, 11 Jan. 1865.

109. *Esmeralda Union*, 18 Jan. 1865.

110. *Inyo Register*, 26 March 1914.

111. San Francisco *Daily Evening Post*, 22 Nov. 1879.

112. Visalia *Delta*, 11 Jan. 1865.

113. San Francisco *Daily Evening Post*, 22 Nov. 1879.

114. Visalia *Delta*, 15 March 1865.

115. *Esmeralda Union*, 11 March 1865; Angel, *History of Nevada*, pp. 169-70.

116. San Francisco *Daily Evening Post*, 22 Nov. 1879.

117. *Daily Evening Post*, 22 Nov. 1879; *Esmeralda Union*, 7 Jan. 1865.

118. *Daily Evening Post*, 22 Nov. 1879; *Inyo Register*, 20 Sept. 1906.

119. *Records of California Men*, p. 191.

120. See, e.g., Keith A. Murray, *The Modocs and Their War;* Lafayette H. Bunnell, *Discovery of the Yosemite and the Indian War of 1851;* C. Gregory Crampton, ed., *The Mariposa Indian War, 1850-1851;* Paul I. Wellman, *The Indian Wars of the West;* Carl C. Rister, *Border Command: General Phil Sheridan in the West;* George A. Custer, *My Life on the Plains;* John G. Bourke, *On the Border with Crook;* Robert M. Utley and Wilcomb E. Washburn, *The Indian Wars;* Don Russell, "How Many Indians Were Killed."

121. *Inyo Register*, 20 Sept. 1906.

122. *Inyo Register*, 22 Feb. 1900.

123. Kroeber, *Handbook of the Indians of California,* esp. pp. 400, 468-69, 633, 843-44. Torture did not play the important role among California Indians that it played among Indians in other regions of North America. See, e.g., Anthony F. C. Wallace, *The Death and Rebirth of the Seneca,* esp. pp. 103-7, and Richard Irving Dodge, *The Hunting Grounds of the Great West,* esp. p. 422.

124. In 1885 Wovoka, Jack Wilson to the white ranchers of the Walker River country, began having visions of a cataclysm that would cover the earth with a new layer of soil, sweet grass, and great herds of buffalo. Whites would be buried under the new soil; Indians who performed the Ghost Dance would be lifted into the sky and suspended there until the cataclysm was over; dead Indian warriors would be brought back to life. By 1890 Wovoka had become, for the Indians, the Messiah, and the Ghost Dance and the wearing of Ghost Shirts, to repel bullets, had spread to the Sioux on the northern Plains. The United States Army thought the Ghost Dance a threat to security and made moves to suppress it, which eventually led to the Wounded Knee massacre. See note 15 of this chapter.

The allure of the wall of granite bordering the western edge of the Owens Valley has long been recorded. Here, with Anna Mills ascent of Mt. Whitney in 1878, we have the first recorded attempt to put a woman on the summit of the highest peak in the continental United States.

Leonard Daughenbaugh is an instructor of Sierra Mountaineering subjects for the University of California. His history of Sierra Mountaineering from 1827 to 1933 is scheduled to be published by Padre Publications.

"On Top of Her World: Anna Mill's Ascent of Mt. Whitney" by Leonard Daughenbaugh. *California History,* Winter, 1985. Reprinted by permission of the California Historical Society.

# ON TOP OF HER WORLD
## Anna Mills' Ascent
## of
## Mt. Whitney

by Leonard Daughenbaugh

For mountaineering men and women, California's Sierra Nevada has posed a unique allure. Boasting a cluster of the highest mountain peaks in the lower forty-eight United States and virtually unexplored until little more than a century ago, this 400-mile long mountain range has challenged nineteenth and twentieth century climbers to test the depth of their physical strength and mental courage.

Native Americans living on the eastern and western approaches to the Sierra were, undoubtedly, the first to travel and climb in the range, but only legends remain to describe the important part it played in their religious and ceremonial lives. For example, legend has it that the Indian maiden Tee-hee-neh rappelled to the base of the Lost Arrow spire on lodgepole saplings joined together with deer thongs to recover the lifeless body of her despondent lover, Kos-soo-kah.[1]

Portuguese sailor Juan Cabrillo gave the name "las sierras nevadas" (the snowy range) to a group of mountains he observed while sailing down the coast of California in 1542. Since he could not have seen the true Sierra from the coast, the first Europeans to see the range were members of Captain Pedro Fages' party in 1772. In 1776, members of the Anza expedition to San Francisco Bay also viewed the range. They called it, "una gran sierra nevada," and thus was the Sierra Nevada named.[2]

Serious exploration of the forty-to-eighty mile wide range waited almost another century, however, until the California legislature directed State Geologist Josiah Whitney to "make an accurate and complete Geological Survey of the state, and to furnish in his report of the same, proper maps and diagrams thereof. . . ."[3]

The Whitney Survey team entered the Yosemite area in the season of 1863, and the next year moved south to the areas of the Kings, Kern, and San Joaquin rivers. During the summer of 1864, survey members William Brewer and James Gardner made the first ascent of 13,570-foot Mount Brewer (named after William Brewer, the chief assistant of the survey), a peak they thought to be the highest in the Sierra. From that point, however, the men discovered that they were:

. . . *not on the highest peak, although we were a thousand feet higher than we anticipated any peaks were. The view was yet wilder than we have ever seen before. Such a landscape! A hundred peaks in sight over thirteen thousand feet—many very sharp—deep canyons, cliffs in every direction almost rivaling Yosemite, sharp ridges almost inaccessible to man, on which human foot has never trod—all combined to produce a view the sublimity of which is rarely equaled, one which few are privileged to behold.* [4]

It was a mountaineer's dream. The three highest peaks were named, in descending order of altitude, Mount Whitney (after the leader of the survey), Mount Williamson (after Major Robert S. Williamson of the U.S. Engineers who was in charge of the Pacific Railroad Survey), and Mount Tyndall (after John Tyndall, an English physicist, philosopher, and mountaineer). After this first sighting, two other members of the survey, Clarence King, who would become the first head of the U.S. Geological Survey, and Dick Cotter, the survey's packer, unsuccessfully attempted to ascend the highest peak, 14,494-foot Mount Whitney.[5]

In 1873, three fishermen from the nearby town of Lone Pine, Charley Begole, Johnny Lucas, and Al Johnson, claimed to have made the first ascent of Mount Whitney, which they named "Fisherman's Peak." After considerable controversy during the same year about who really made the first ascent and what the peak's official name should be, the "Immortal Three," as the fishermen became known, received credit, but Mount Whitney remained the peak's official name.

Following the Whitney Survey, most of the Sierra still remained unexplored, and most of the peaks remained unclimbed. Sufficient time was probably the prime requirement for a serious Sierra mountaineer in this era because there were no automobiles and no roads into the mountains. Excursions frequently took weeks or months and covered hundreds of miles. Most Sierra mountaineers of this early period were professors, teachers, lawyers, or other professional people who could arrange long summer vacations.

Most mountaineers traveled in groups with the assistance of pack animals because of the weight of provisions and equipment. An exception to this rule was John Muir, who usually traveled alone and took only what he could carry with him. During his first attempt to climb Mount Whitney in 1873, he spent the night below the summit dancing in his shirt sleeves to keep from freezing. Of that night, he later said, "The view of the stars and of the dawn on the desert was abundant compensation for all that."[6]   Returning to his base in Independence, he started again on foot two days later and on the third day reached the summit.

In Muir's day, specialized equipment, if it was even carried, consisted of hob-nailed boots and perhaps an ice-axe. A climbing rope might also be used, but, unlike today's nylon ropes that stretch considerably before breaking (and thereby absorb the shock of a fall), ropes were made of hemp which simply breaks under stress. These hemp ropes might also have been utilized to lead the animals and tie equipment on their backs. The main function of the rope was psychological protection. For example, when King and Cotter were returning from their first ascent of Mount Tyndall in 1864, Cotter climbed out of sight and lowered the rope to King, saying, "Don't be afraid to bear your weight." After a difficult climb, King reached Cotter, who was:

*sitting upon a smooth, roof-like slope where the least pull would have dragged him over the brink. He had no brace for his feet, nor hold for his hands, but had seated himself calmly, with a rope tied around his breast, knowing that my only safety lay in being able to make the climb entirely unaided; certain that the least waver in his tone would have disheartened me, and perhaps made it impossible. . . . To coolly seat one's self in the door of death, and silently listen for the fatal summons . . . requires as sublime a type of courage as I know.* [7]

Climbing rope could have other uses. Stanford University professor Bolten Coit Brown first ascended Mount Clarence King's summit spire with the aid of his ingenuity and his rope. This ascent has been labeled "the finest Sierra climb of the nineteenth century." [8] His account:

*Poised on a narrow ledge, I noosed the rope and lassoed a horn of rock projecting over the edge of the smooth-faced precipice overhead. But the pull on the rope toppled the rock bodily over, nearly hitting me, who could not dodge. So I took out the noose, and having tied a big knot in the rope-end, I threw it repeatedly until this caught in a crack. Then I climbed the rope. I did not dally with the job either . . . The ugliest place of all was exactly at the last rock, only a few feet from the top. With great caution, and as much deliberation as I had used speed below, I finally looped the rope over an all too slight projection, along the upper edge of the side face of the topmost block, and compelled myself to put one foot in it and lift myself, and so stand, dangling in that precarious sling, until I could set my arms over the top and squirm over.* [9]

While the Sierra is large and the number of nineteenth-century mountaineers was small, smaller still was the number of female mountaineers. The nineteenth-century woman mountaineer needed not only courage with which to face the unknown, but inner strength to go against social convention. Some male mountaineers were more liberal than the times, but as Helen Gompertz LeConte, one of the most proficient and active mountaineers of her time, recalled, this increased the pressure on women to perform:

*No greater difficulty had we met than an incredibly steep trail into the canyon, but now the angry, foam-flecked river made the men look grave, and the women silently shiver at the thought of daring to cross it. I say 'silently,' for we were old campers and knew better than to cry before we were hurt. Besides, there was a pride and sense of responsibility in the fact that we were looked upon as comrades by the men, and we must in no wise fall below the standard by increasing their anxieties.* [10]

9.  Mt. Whitney.  Taken from near Whitney Portal.
    *(Credit:  Eastern California Museum.)*

There were many things that made it difficult for pioneering female mountaineers to be on an equal basis with men. Most men, for many reasons, felt that women should be treated differently, even in the mountains. For example, on the first Sierra Club Outing in 1901, it was recommended that: "Women should have one durable waist [blouse] for tramping and one light one for wearing around camp. The skirt can be short, not more than halfway from knee to ankle, and under these can be worn shorter dark-colored bloomers."[11] Men had no clothing regulations. Yet, considering the society as a whole, these restrictions were very libertarian. During the second Sierra Club Outing in 1902, Mrs. LeConte reported: "Having for many seasons withstood the surprised gaze of the gaily gowned hotel guests all by myself, I was delighted to have the tables turned and see short skirts and hob-nailed boots look askance at trailing garments."[12]

Twenty-three years prior to the first Sierra Club Outing, pioneering woman mountaineer Anna Mills joined a party from Porterville in Tulare County whose primary goal was to climb Mount Whitney. The group's secondary goal was to put the first women on the summit of the highest peak in the continental United States. Through Mills' fortitude, and that of her three other female companions, both of these goals were realized. Although they probably did not realize it at the time, these four were the first women on record to climb above 14,000 feet in the United States.

Well-known during her lifetime, Anna Mills is an obscure figure today. Most of what is known appears in her obituary, which reads: "Born in New York in 1854, she moved to California in 1877, where she worked as a school teacher in various schools throughout Tulare County, and took a prominent part in all educational matters throughout her life. She married Robert Johnston and helped raise a stepson, Fred. She traveled extensively and frequently gave of her store of knowledge in lectures before clubs, literary entertainments, and benefits in many towns of the valley. She was very active in the Order of the Eastern Star and was a member of the board of directors of the Visalia Music Club and was responsible in a large degree for the success of the organization."[13] Her outstanding collection of Indian baskets is still maintained in the Tulare County Library. She was also the first vice-president of the short-lived Mt. Whitney Club, the main purpose of which was "to aid in making Mt. Whitney—the crown of the Sierra—and the adjacent mountain region better known to the world." Membership was restricted to individuals who had climbed Mount Whitney.[14]

In 1881, three years after Anna Mills' ascent, a party led by William Wallace, who would become a superior court judge, spent the night on the summit of Mount Whitney. Sharing the peak with them were members of the Langley Party, which included William Crapo, who had also been the guide who led the Mills party.[15] James W. A. Wright, a member of the Wallace party, relates: "Mr. Crapo so impressed us with his account of the heroic perseverances of Miss Mills to make the ascent, she being partially crippled, that we named a peak Mount Mills in her honor."[16] Wallace continues: "It was undecided which peak to name for her, but the final selection was a long, high peak just south of Loomis Cañon and about four miles south of Mt. Guyot."[17]

At the present time, [1985, ed.] an effort is being made to have this peak officially named Mount Anna Mills, since there is already a Mount Mills located in the Abbot group farther north. A decision by the National and State Boards on Geographic Names is pending.

The following account by Anna Mills of her ascent of Mount Whitney appeared in 1902 in the *Mt. Whitney Club Journal*, the official publication of the Mt. Whitney Club.

While it can be argued that people climb mountains for many different reasons, it appears, that there may be one major reason. It was described in 1900 by Lincoln Hutchinson, a member of a party which intended to make the first ascent of Matterhorn Peak in the Sierra. When they arrived in the unknown area, they had to decide which of two peaks was the Matterhorn and, also, which peak they should climb. Hutchinson reports: "After a long council of war, our decision was made. We had come for glory; our attack should be directed against the peak which was highest and apparently the most difficult of ascent."[18]

There are, however, two different types of glory. One is external and gives an individual recognition from others; the other is internal and gives an individual recognition from within.

10. Climbers on the summit of Mt. Whitney. An 1893 publication described the three
day journey from Lone Pine: "Every summer parties, in which are girls and married
women, go up from the valley. An early breakfast is had, and then a start is made
for the summit of Whitney . . . Women can climb to the summit in four hours, and
young men in much less time." *(Credit: Eastern California Museum.)*

For this reason, most mountaineers—and Anna Mills was no exception—write their accounts in a flowery, flamboyant style in an attempt to convey to their readers the glory, along with the pure joy and exhilaration, of mountaineering.

\* \* \*

The summer of 1878 is memorable to many of the old settlers as one of excursions to the various mountain resorts of Tulare County. While it was yet winter a party from Porterville and vicinity was formed and plans were made during the next few months. As no ladies had yet made the ascent of the real Mt. Whitney, we determined to be the first to stand on its lofty summit. So anxious was I to begin climbing, that I left Porterville two weeks ahead of the party, going as far as Dillon's Mill. There I spent two weeks peering into Nature's beauties, enjoying the invigorating mountain air and the breath of the pines, which seemed to put new blood into my veins, and nothing in the way of climbing or walking did I consider too difficult to undertake.

One pleasant afternoon in early July, the Porterville party, consisting of Judge R. C. Redd and wife, and two sons, George and Robert, Miss Hope Broughton, Miss Mary Martin, N. B. Martin, and Henry E. Ford, arrived at the mill. Soon all was in readiness, and we started on our journey, traveling four miles through a dense forest of redwood, pine, and fir, when we camped on a little stream. Resuming our journey in the morning, we traveled in an easterly direction through a wild and picturesque country. Higher, higher up we went, and soon began the ascent of Chisel Mountain, one of the loftiest peaks in that section. The ascent required considerable time, and called into requisition the strength of both man and beast.

The surpassing beauty of the view from that peak will always remain with me. In front, and seemingly at our feet, lay Tulare Valley, with its broad lake stretched out before us. The course of Tulare River, Deer Creek, Outside Creek, and various other streams, with their valleys dotted with grain-fields, orchards, and vineyards, could plainly be traced. On either side and behind us peak after peak towered one above the other, some composed of barren rocks and crowned in snow, while others were clothed in living green from base to summit.

We continued our course over a rough mountain-side without any trail, and descended a steep and rocky cliff into a pretty little valley, where we remained two days, feasting on trout. We traveled from here without any trail, over precipitous mountains, down to Little Kern, along which we journeyed for many miles, sometimes high on the mountain-side and sometimes along the margin of the stream. During the day we saw a deer, but did not succeed in getting him. The sun was still high in the heavens when we reached the sheep-camp of Martin Click, who presented us with a fat mutton ready dressed. (I might add that several years later, Mr. Click married the belle of our party, Miss Hope Broughton.) Crossing Little Kern, we camped for the night on the edge of a flower-decked meadow, hid away amid barren hills. Getting an early start, we crossed a long mountain range with trail scarcely visible. This is the dividing ridge between Little and Big Kern.

Our next camping-place was Trout Meadows, where we spent several pleasant days resting, hunting, and fishing. After making a short side trip to Big Kern Flat on Big Kern River, we pursued a northerly course for about two miles, when we struck the Hockett trail. We were headed for Kern Lakes—and such a rough, rocky, and precipitous trail as we had to pass over! The scenery is grand, and has only to be seen to be appreciated. Lofty mountain-peaks in every direction tower thousands of feet towards the blue heavens, seeming to say that there is something still grander beyond. While wending our way high upon the mountain-side, we saw far below a precipice, over which the water madly rushed, seeking repose in a granite basin a hundred feet below. And Big Kern, with its wealth of ice-cold water, dashing and foaming over its rocky bed, leaping cataracts, bounding through gaps and gorges, madly pressed its way to the valley below. Words fail to express the joy we felt when we reached the summit and looked down upon Little Kern Lake, a miniature of beauty, nestled so closely to the base of the mountain, as if seeking protection. For a long time we watched the varied reflections in its quiet water, forgetting for the time the dangerous trail to be traversed before reaching it. As the mountain was so steep, for the first time we dismounted, considering ourselves safer on foot than on horseback. It was not necessary, however, to do much walking. We just slid.

The little lake is circular in form, and at that time its border was free from tules. The larger lake was oblong, and presented an unsightly appearance, many dead trees and rotten logs lying in its limpid waters. On this lake were several small boats, each manned by two fishermen, who were supplying the Owens River country with trout. We camped at the lower end of Runkle's pasture, near a soda spring, about two and one-half miles above the lakes. We found there over thirty people from various parts of Inyo County—as jolly a crowd as one would wish to meet. Pleasant indeed were the evenings spent around the campfire, and the excursions made to the various points of interest. Parties making hurried trips to Mt. Whitney and vicinity lose half the pleasure of the outing by not making these side excursions, as many of the most interesting places are off from the main trails. We visited the falls of Volcano (or Whitney) Creek. The lower, about a mile east of our camp at the spring, consists of two falls, the first leap being about eighty feet, and the second sixty, terminating in a fine spray, which swayed to and fro in the breeze like an immense white veil. The constant fall of water has worn into the rock a basin, where we found curiously shaped pieces of wood and bark, worn as smooth as glass by the action of the water. The upper fall, a mile still farther east, or a little north of east, is still grander than the lower, having an unbroken descent of over a hundred feet. Between these two falls we caught the largest trout, some of them measuring fifteen inches. Right here I wish to express my sentiments regarding what I consider an act of vandalism perpetrated by the Board of Supervisors of Tulare County in 1883, in granting a franchise allowing the diversion of the waters of this most beautiful stream into Ramshaw Creek, thereby ruining falls which in many respects rival those of Yosemite. This stream was the real home of the golden trout, and between the falls they grew to an enormous size, reaching a length of from fourteen to sixteen inches. But along comes the water-shark, and, aided and abetted by a Board of Supervisors, destroys that which lovers of the beautiful have come thousands of miles to see, and the destruction of which benefits few.

William Crapo, of Cerro Gordo, to whom Clarence King gives the honor of being the first man to stand on the summit of Mt. Whitney, was so delighted to learn that we ladies were going to undertake what was then considered a most hazardous climb, that he offered his services as guide, saying that he wished to have the honor of leading the first party of ladies to the top of the United States.

11. This pack train on the Mt. Whitney trail is typical of those used to travel in the Sierra Nevada. Although pack animals are no longer allowed on the Mt. Whitney trail, they are still one of the most popular methods of travel in the mountains of eastern California. *(Credit: F. C. Harvey photo, Eastern California Museum.)*

On the morning of August 1st, in company with Luther Anderson, of Porterville, Kit Carson Johnson, and "Prof. Crapo," as we called him, amid cheers of "Godspeed" from the crowd at the spring, we were off for Mt. Whitney. Following the Hockett trail, we forded the river and climbed a steep and very high mountain. After crossing the summit, we traveled with difficulty over angular lava rocks for quite a distance, when we came to Whitney Creek. Continuing our journey, we crossed a branch of this creek on a natural bridge some ten or twelve feet wide. A little farther on, after attaining the summit, we passed what seemed to be an extinct volcano having a funnel-shaped edge. The whole country shows the effect of volcanic action, several of the mountains being extinct volcanoes. Leaving the Hockett trail near a cinder mountain, and turning to the left, we continued our course in a northeasterly direction up Whitney Creek, over rough and nearly impassable mountains, through dense forests of tamarack. This stream literally swarmed with golden trout. So numerous were they that we could almost catch them with our hands. Still following the creek for some distance, we turned to the right, passing up a mountain of no great altitude, and began the descent into a most singular-looking valley. My feelings when it flashed into view would be hard to describe. Here the scene changed from grand to sublime; here appeared the loftiest mountains we had yet seen.

This desert, or vast plain of sand, called by some an extinct or dry lake, is locked in on all sides by rock-ribbed mountains whose peaks mount upward among the clouds. One could imagine himself descending into the valley of death and having the gates closed after him.[19] We crossed another mountain and lake-bed of like character, leaving old Mt. Whitney, or Sheep Mountain, several miles to the right, and descended into a meadow, where we camped for the night.

Soon after sunrise on the following morning we were pressing our way over a boggy meadow and along the stream upon which we camped the night before. Then, turning north, we wended our way up a steep and rocky mountain without any trail. It was with difficulty that we gained the summit, having to pass over places where the space between us and eternity could be measured by inches. Still pressing our way over mountains and through boggy meadows, we came to an impassable wall of rock, and were obliged to turn back. We then descended a cliff to the edge of a most beautiful lake, the waters of which were so clear that objects could be plainly seen on the bottom. Added to this were the reflections of the pink-tipped peaks and cloud-flecked sky, making a scene of rare beauty. Although quite deep, none of the lakes or streams in that locality contain any fish. Slowly we followed the margin of this lake for quite a distance, admiring the beautiful pictures in its quiet waters, then climbed a rocky cliff, making camp about a quarter of a mile from the summit on the opposite side. We were then in full view and about a mile south of what some call Fisherman's Peak, but what Clarence King describes as Mt. Whitney. In appearance it is oblong, having a gap on either side between it and other mountains of nearly equal magnitude.

A short distance east of our camp was a ledge of rocks over one hundred feet high. Along the ridge can be distinctly traced the effect of glacial action, the rocky slopes in many places being worn as smooth as a mirror. Here the books of Nature are open, and on every page is written the handiwork of the Infinite. Here is presented a world of food for thought, and it can be truly said "the half has never yet been told."

Just before reaching camp my horse took a notion to jump over a small stream, very unexpectedly to me, and my back was so severely injured that I could hardly step without experiencing severe pain. Having been lame from early childhood, everybody said it would be utterly impossible for me to climb to the summit of Mt. Whitney. But I was not easily discouraged, and had always held to the idea that I could do what other people could—my surplus of determination making up for what I lacked in the power of locomotion. But now at the eleventh hour, with the Mecca to which I had so long been journeying in full view, to have such a calamity befall me was more than I could bear, and I gave vent to my feelings in tears. Like Moses, I had gotten where I could see the promised land, but the chances for getting there were indeed few. For a long time success or failure seemed to hang in the balance. Never before had I experienced such a profound feeling of disappointment. In that hour of anguish I remembered my sins, and carefully walking to an obscure place, away up there so near heaven, where none but God could hear, I knelt, facing the great mountain, and prayed—prayed as I had not for years; prayed with the spirit and the understanding also. When I had finished the mountaintop seemed closer, and I returned to camp with a much lighter heart.

12. The men of the early survey teams—such as this one pictured in front of the Big Pine Hotel in 1891— were among the first to explore the Sierra Nevada peaks. *(Credit: Eastern California Museum.)*

I did not care for supper, neither did I care to join the party in a game of snowball on a huge snow-bank nearby.  Rest was what I wanted; so I retired early, and Mrs. Redd bathed my back with "Seven Seals, or Golden Wonder."[20]  I thought if a little was good a good deal would be better, and insisted on "gettin' plenty while I was gettin'."  During the night I learned where the "Golden Wonder" came in.  Such a blister!  The wonder to me was that I had any back left.  At peep of day I was up and glad to find that the pain had nearly gone.  Eating a hurried breakfast, I started alone, soon after five o'clock, for Guitar Lake, where I was to rest and wait for the other members of the party.  Climbing over those rocks was no easy task—and how my back did smart and burn!  But I didn't mind such trifles when there was so much at stake; my heart was set on something higher, and nothing short of the highest point would satisfy me.  I would reach that and die if need be.

By the time the crowd arrived I was somewhat rested, and we began the ascent of what is called the "Devil's Ladder," which is nearly perpendicular for a distance of about a quarter of a mile, and from forty to fifty feet wide.  Emerging from this, we paused to rest and drink in the far-sighted view.  Nestled close to the base of the opposite mountains were many pretty lakelets, and the peaks which before looked so high began to assume smaller proportions.  The shapes of the rocks, too, were changed; instead of being oval, like those in the crevices below, they were angular in shape, many of them being very large.  Up over these we had to crawl, or leap from one to another.  The exertion of climbing, together with the lightness of the air, made breathing difficult.  We passed over the snow-belt, about an eighth of a mile through, with ease, and from there on had no trouble in gaining the summit.

Walking over to the monument, we planted the Stars and Stripes on its topmost point (I doubt if "Old Glory" ever waved from a grander flagstaff); then we sang the "Star-Spangled Banner" and "Nearer, My God, to Thee."  The acoustic properties being so perfect, we sang with ease, notwithstanding the lightness of the air.

The supreme joy I felt when I realized that my prayer had been answered, and that I was at last really standing on the summit of Mt. Whitney, knew no bounds.  For the time being I forgot that I ever was tired; one glance was enough to compensate for all the trials of the trip. The day was perfect, and so were the surroundings. How strange it seemed to be standing on the highest point in the United States, and looking off for a distance of seventy miles down into Death Valley, the lowest point! How strange, too, it seemed, after spending so many weeks in the mountains, to look up and see nothing but the blue-vaulted heavens! Oh, what an inspiration it was to look from that magnificent peak on the grand panorama of mountains, reaching from beyond the Yosemite to San Bernardino! Range after range in every direction, peak on peak, comprising almost limitless forms, rise one above the other, each striving for the mastery. Stepping near the eastern edge, I looked down a sheer descent of three thousand feet on a small lakelet, partially covered with snow and ice. Still farther east lay Owens River Valley, with its sparkling lake, winding river, and golden fields of grain. Every road and trail could be plainly seen, and, looking through the glasses, we could see the buildings at Lone Pine and Independence.

After feasting for several hours on the glory of our surroundings, we returned to the monument, where we examined the records of Clarence King, Lieutenant Wheeler and party,[21] and others. We found recorded there the names of several people from Inyo County and a number from the Eastern States, but only one Tularean—Frank Knowles, who accompanied King on his first trip. We also found several pieces of silver money, but I have heard it hinted that none of it has been seen since our party left! After placing our record in the monument, we very reluctantly took a last lingering look, then descended the mountain, reaching camp just before sunset.

Early the following morning we turned our faces homeward, traveling over an unknown route, rough in the extreme, towards the headwaters of Kern River. Before the sun was very high we came in sight of the river about four miles below us, but how to get there was the puzzling question. It seemed almost impossible. But we were accustomed to overcoming difficulties, and did not propose to give up at this stage of the game. All hands dismounted and took it on foot down the mountain, over rocks, through brush, and up cliffs, which seemed impassable for an animal (or an Anna Mills) to travel over. After trying several routes, and being compelled each time to turn back on account of precipitous bluffs and impassable streams, we at last found a pass and descended to the river, where we camped for the night.

13. Residents of the Owens Valley have traveled the mountain trails for recreation from the days of the earliest homesteaders. Here, on a pack trip in Cottonwood Canyon, are Bert and Ora Johnson, and Mary Johnson Dearborn—children of A. H. Johnson who was a member of the first party to reach the summit of Mt. Whitney in 1873. Also pictured are Henry Dearborn, Veda and Willie Miller, Amelia and Mercy Johnson. (*Credit: Eastern California Museum.*)

We made the rest of our trip home by way of Kern River
Cañon, Soda Springs, and Dillon's Mill, arriving at Porterville
on the evening of August 9th.

To me it seems that the grandest mountain scenery in this
State is Kern River Cañon.

In conclusion, let me say that since my visit to Mt.
Whitney, nearly a quarter of a century ago, it has been my
privilege to visit the various mountain regions in this country
from the Atlantic to the Pacific and from Alaska to the Rio
Grande, and to scale the volcanic mountains of Hawaii. I have
also crossed the watershed of the Bavarian Alps, traversed the
Austrian Tyrol, visited the German, Italian, and Swiss Alps, and
gazed with admiration on the beauties of the Matterhorn and
Jungfrau. Yet I can candidly say that I have never seen, nor do I
ever expect to see, a picture so varied, so sublime, so awe-
inspiring, as that seen from the summit of Mt. Whitney on the
third day of August 1878.[22]

## NOTES

1. David Brower and Richard Leonard, "A Climber's Guide to the High
   Sierra, Part IV, Yosemite Valley," *Sierra Club Bulletin*, February
   1940, p. 41.
2. Francis P. Farquhar, *History of the Sierra Nevada* (Berkeley:
   University of California Press, 1966), p. 15.
3. Josiah Whitney, *Geological Survey of California* (1865), Volume 1,
   Geology, p. ix.
4. William H. Brewer, *Up and Down California* (Berkeley: University of
   California Press, 1966), pp. 524-525.
5. Geologist Clarence King, immediately upon arriving in California,
   joined the Whitney Survey as a volunteer. The ascent of Mount
   Whitney became an obsession with him. The day after Brewer and
   Hoffmann first observed Mount Whitney, King and the party's packer,
   Dick Cotter, set out to make the first ascent but climbed Mount
   Tyndall instead. Later the same season, King made his second
   attempt, also unsuccessful. In 1871, he came back to Mount Whitney
   for a third attempt. This time, he believed he had made the first
   ascent. Bad weather and heavy clouds prevented him from seeing that,
   instead of Mount Whitney, he had made the first ascent of what would
   later be named Mount Langley. On his fourth and final attempt in
   1873, he succeeded, but he was too late to be the first. He left the
   following record on the summit: "September 19, 1873. This peak,
   Mt. Whitney, was on this day climbed by Clarence King, U.S.

Geologist, and Frank Knowles, of Tule River. On September 1st, in New York, I first learned that Mount Whitney of 1871 was not the highest peak. Storms and clouds prevented me from recognizing it, or I should have come here then. All honor to those who came here before me." Lieutenant George M. Wheeler, *Wheeler Survey Geographical Report. U.S. Geographical Surveys West of the 100th Meridian*, I(1889), p. 100.

6.  John Muir, "A Rival of the Yosemite," *Century Illustrated Monthly Magazine*, November 1891, p. 93.

7.  Clarence King, *Mountaineering in the Sierra Nevada* (Boston: James R. Osgood and Company, 1872), quoted in University of Nebraska reprint, 1970, pp. 90-91.

8.  Steve Roper, *Climber's Guide to the High Sierra* (San Francisco: Sierra Club Books, 1976), p. 247.

9.  Bolton Coit Brown, "Wanderings in the High Sierra Between Mt. King and Mt. Williamson". Part II, *Sierra Club Bulletin*, May 1897, p. 96.

10. Helen Gompertz LeConte, "High Water in Tehipite," *Sunset*, September 1902, p. 326.

11. Farquhar, op. cit., p. 228.

12. Helen Gompertz LeConte, "The Sierra Club in the Kings River Canyon," *Sunset*, July 1903, p. 251.

13. Obituary, "Mrs. Anna Mills Johnston Sinks Into Eternal Slumber Today," *Visalia Times-Delta*, June 25, 1921.

14. "Organization of the Mt. Whitney Club and List of Members," *Mt. Whitney Club Journal*, Volume I, Number 1, p. 37.

15. William Crapo was a local resident who made the claim that he and Abe Leyda were the first non-Native Americans to ascend Mount Whitney. When Clarence King finally reached the summit in 1873, he substantiated Crapo's claim but reported Crapo had made the ascent in the company of a Mr. Hunter. The claims and counter-claims made in this dispute constitute one of the more fascinating accounts in Sierra history. It is now generally believed that Crapo made the second ascent rather than the first. He was also a member of the third ascent team that was organized to obtain an accurate altitude measurement of Mount Whitney.

    In addition to guiding Anna Mills' party, Crapo was the guide for Samuel Pierpont Langley's party that was organized to observe and quantify the quality and quantity of the heat sent to the earth by the sun.

16. J. W. A. Wright, "In the High Sierras. The Grand View from the Summit of Mount Whitney," *San Francisco Daily Evening Post*, November 3, 1881.

17. W. W. Elliott, *A Guide to the Grand and Sublime Scenery in the Sierra Nevada in the Region about Mount Whitney* (San Francisco: Elliott and Co., 1883), p. 43-45.

18. Lincoln Hutchinson, "The Ascent of 'Matterhorn Peak'," *Sierra Club Bulletin*, May 1900, p. 16.

19. In his own account of the trip, Judge Redd added to Miss Mill's description: "Of one thing I am satisfied: Neither of these can be the mountain that Satan took the Savior upon, nor this the country he showed him when he wished him to fall down and worship him; or, if it is, I don't blame him for not accepting the offer." Judge R. C. Redd, "Trip to Mr. Whitney, Kern River, Upper and Lower Lakes," *Visalia Times-Delta*, September 20, 1878.

20. "Seven Seals" liniment was used for various aches and pains.

21. Lieutenant George M. Wheeler was a member of the U.S. Army Engineers. He was in charge of a government survey that operated in the Sierra from 1875 until 1878. During 1875, members of the survey made two separate ascents of Mount Whitney, and, by triangulation, made the most accurate estimation of the altitude of Mount Whitney that had ever been made, 14,471 feet above sea level.

22. Anna Mills Johnston, "A Trip to Mt. Whitney in 1878," *Mt. Whitney Club Journal*, Volume I, Number 1, May 1902, pp. 18-28.

Bighorn or mountain sheep have captured the attention of man for longer than we will ever know. Early rock art in the Owens Valley shows that the bighorn was important to people thousands of years ago.

Today, the bighorn symbolizes wilderness and strength in our society. The arrival of the white man was catastrophic to most of California's bighorn populations. Only recently have we become aware of this and set out to make things right.

John Wehausen received his undergraduate degree from the University of California at Berkeley, his Masters Degree at the University of California at Davis and his Doctorate in Wildlife Management at the University of Michigan. His specialty was Sierra bighorn sheep and his academic studies involved over four years of field research.

Since graduation Dr. Wehausen has spent three years studying the bighorn sheep of the White Mountains and two years studying the Inyo Mountains wild sheep populations. In 1984 he began studies of the bighorn sheep in the Eastern Mojave Desert mountain ranges. Throughout this period Dr. Wehausen has continued monitoring the bighorn sheep of the Sierra Nevada.

John works as an independent researcher, solely on wild sheep, under funding from the California Department of Fish and Game, U.S. Forest Service, The University of California White Mountain Research Station and private granting institutions.

Dr. Wehausen initiated the Sierra re-introduction program, which at printing has resulted in three new populations of Sierra bighorn sheep.

# THE HISTORICAL DISTRIBUTION OF MOUNTAIN SHEEP IN THE OWENS VALLEY REGION

by John D. Wehausen

Any interest in the restoration of native wildlife populations quickly brings one up against the question of their distribution before the influences of European man set into motion a pattern of wildlife decimation. This is not such a problem for species that by themselves readily explore and colonize unoccupied suitable habitat. Mountain sheep do not fit that mold. Their populations frequently occur in disjunct pockets where habitat characteristics are suitable, and, with the exception of some wandering rams, dispersal out of these pockets is quite slow.

The major decimation of mountain sheep populations in the Eastern Sierra began with the influx of miners to the Sierra Nevada beginning in 1849. These miners ate any meat that was convenient, including mountain sheep; and market hunting that arose to supply mining camps and towns probably caused the elimination of some populations that were locally vulnerable when concentrated on small winter ranges. Mountain sheep meat was listed on an early restaurant menu from Bodie.

Undoubtedly the most severe impact came with the grazing of domestic livestock. Livestock grazing in California began with cattle in low-lying ranges, primarily the Central Valley. Severe droughts caused livestock operators to seek summer pastures in the Sierra Nevada, where cattle grazing began about 1861. Cattle were quickly replaced by domestic sheep, because the latter could be grazed over more rugged high country. Stocking rates became rapidly excessive, with hundreds of thousands of domestic sheep grazed annually in the high country of the Sierra Nevada. Severe destruction from overgrazing on the Kern Plateau was already documented in 1873 by Clarence King. There developed an annual grazing circuit that Mary Austin's delightful book, *The Flock,* chronicles. It began in the Central Valley in winter, crossed Tehachapi and Walker Passes in early spring, headed through the Mojave Desert and Owens Valley to high country summer pastures, then returned to the Central Valley in fall. Prior to the 1890s, most of the summer grazing was in the Sierra Nevada. During the decade of the 1890s, this grazing was largely eliminated with the creation of Yosemite and Sequoia National Parks and the forest reserves, later to become national forests and additional park lands. Although most shepherds violated the new grazing restrictions at all opportunities, grazing on these lands was essentially eliminated by the turn of the century. This probably resulted in some shifts of grazing pressure to the east slope of the Sierra Nevada, where most ranges of the native mountain sheep occurred, as well as to ranges further east, such as the White Mountains. An estimated 40-50 thousand domestic sheep were grazed in the White Mountains each summer during the early decades of this century.

The impacts of the domestic sheep grazing on the native sheep were threefold. First, where their ranges overlapped, the domestic sheep denuded the forage. Second, the sheepherders were known to shoot the native sheep as competitors with their stock when the opportunity presented itself. Finally, and most importantly, major diseases were introduced to the native sheep, to which they had little resistance. One major such disease was scabies, which was reported to decimate the native sheep population inhabiting the Great Western Divide in the Sierra Nevada in the 1870s. Introduction of pathogenic bacteria and viruses causing pneumonia had perhaps the largest impact. Die-offs of mountain sheep herds following contact with domestic sheep continue to be documented.

Early records concerning mountain sheep populations are indeed few; thus, some populations undoubtedly disappeared without record of their existence. In some cases, the only hint

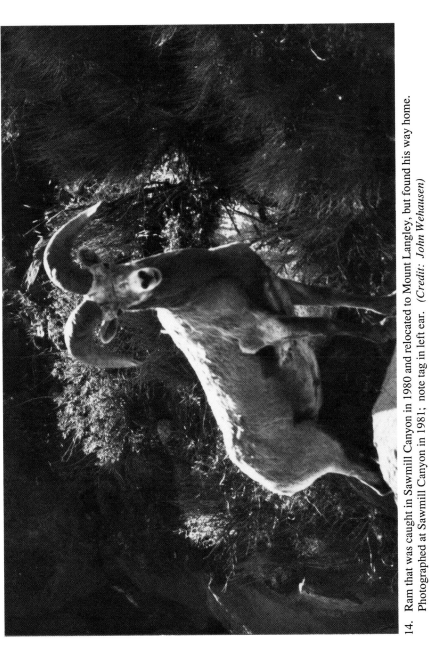

14. Ram that was caught in Sawmill Canyon in 1980 and relocated to Mount Langley, but found his way home. Photographed at Sawmill Canyon in 1981; note tag in left ear. *(Credit: John Wehausen)*

we have that native sheep were once there is old weathered remains of skulls picked up many years later. Since these are invariably only from rams, which can sometimes wander widely, they have the potential to be misleading. Game wardens and land management agency personnel that might have recorded important information on early distribution of native sheep were not present in the Owens Valley region before about 1910. John Muir, however, was a keen naturalist who kept detailed journals of his observations in this area beginning in 1868. Yet, even he only records seeing mountain sheep on a single occasion in the Sierra Nevada, in the vicinity of Mount Darwin. Particularly noteworthy is that, in all the time he spent in the high country of the Yosemite area, he never recorded seeing any native sheep there, although he documented that they existed. This probably speaks to the earliness of their decimation in that area.

Our best information on early distribution of native sheep is for those populations that persisted into this century, and comes from information recorded by the first game warden, Ed Ober, who lived in Big Pine, and annual fish and game reports of what was then the Mono National Forest. Ed Ober took a particular interest in the native sheep of this region, and recorded his finding, beginning in 1911. Mention of mountain sheep populations in national forest annual reports began in 1921.

Native sheep populations in the Yosemite region of the Sierra Nevada extended north to the Sonora Pass area, but probably not continuously. This whole region may have had only two populations, one that wintered in the Lee Vining and Lundy Canyon area, where they were reintroduced in 1986, and one wintering just north of the Sonora Pass Road where Highway 395 passes through the Walker River Gorge. The only records further north in the Sierra Nevada are for a population that occupied the Truckee River Canyon.

South of Yosemite, a population occupied the area of McGee and Convict Creeks. In 1911, local residents there told an assistant from the Museum of Vertebrate Zoology of the University of California at Berkeley that the mountain sheep in that region left the Sierra in winter. It is probable that they crossed over the rocky region of the Bishop Tuff immediately north of Tom's Place to winter in the Owens River Gorge because of the deep snow in that region of the Sierra Nevada.

In the Bishop area, there were mountain sheep in the Wheeler Ridge—Mount Morgan area, where they have since been reintroduced in 1979. Mount Tom had a population that extended south along the crest to at least Mount Emerson and persisted to about 1940. It is possible that under extreme snow conditions, these may have crossed the flats of the Buttermilk area to Grouse Mountain. There are no substantial records of a population inhabiting the area of the South Fork of Bishop Creek. Suitable contiguous winter range appears lacking in this area. However, it is possible that one of the early populations to be lost occurred there, and included a long migration route between high country summer range and winter range on the east side of Coyote Flat in the area from Shannon Canyon to Rawson Creek above Keough Hot Springs.

Further south, the next population wintered in Taboose Creek and neighboring drainages on either side, and probably summered as far north as the Palisades. There is considerable early mention of mountain sheep wintering in drainages east of Mount Baxter. This is the largest of the two native populations that survived to the present, and currently serves as transplant stock for reintroductions. Its summer range extends as far south as Kearsarge Pass. The next known population to its south occurs on Mount Williamson and is the other surviving native population. Observations by Norman Clyde of sheep on Mount Russell suggest that the range of this population may have once extended somewhat further south than it currently does.

Just south of Mount Whitney, a population in the Lone Pine Peak—Mount Langley area disappeared sometime after 1950. It was reestablished with transplants in 1980 and 1982. The most southern Sierran population in the Owens Valley region occupied the area of Olancha and Cartago Canyons, and probably canyons to their north. At least two more populations occurred further south in the Sierra Nevada, one just north of Walker Pass, and one just north of Tehachapi Pass. At the very south end of the Owens Valley, the Coso Mountains contained a mountain sheep population that disappeared about the middle of this century.

On the east side of Owens Valley, both the White and Inyo Mountains contained mountain sheep populations. In the White Mountains, the earliest historical accounts discussed populations occupying the Cottonwood Basin and Wyman Canyon areas on

15. Mixed group of bighorn in spring south of Sawmill Canyon. (*Credit: John Wehausen*)

the east side of the range. Slightly later accounts mentioned native sheep in the northern White Mountains between White Mountain Peak and Montgomery Peak. This latter northern section is where they have survived to present. Early historical references do not specify any occupation of west side canyons south of the White Mountain Peak area, although they specify sheep use of the peaks at the top of Paiute Canyon. Paiute, Silver, and Black Marble Canyons all provide suitable habitat and probably contained populations. Early decimation may have precluded their documentation in the early records.

These early records stated that the sheep occupying Wyman Canyon utilized the low-lying rocky hills on the north side of Deep Springs Valley at times in winter. Another population occupied the spur of the Inyo Mountains on the south side of Deep Springs Valley, sometimes called the Soldier Pass Range. This was a common area to observe mountain sheep in the 1950s; but the population disappeared about 1970.

Further south on the east side of the Inyo Mountains, the earliest records mention an abundance of mountain sheep on Waucoba Mountain and in the vicinity of Willow and Paiute Canyons. Waucoba Mountain was undoubtedly an area used only by rams, and apparently is still occasionally visited by that sex. Records further south are sparse. Early distribution appears to have extended south along the east side of the range to the area of Daisy and San Lucas Canyons. In recent years, ewes have occasionally been observed as far south as Craig Canyon, but the population at this end appears to be exceedingly sparse. A viable population currently hangs on in the Willow Creek area, but is itself quite sparse compared with early reports. With the exception of wandering rams, there are no records to indicate that any mountain sheep populations ever inhabited the west side of the Inyo Mountains. This is surprising given seemingly adequate habitat there, especially south from Keynot Peak. Perhaps west side populations disappeared before the turn of the century in association with the very active mining in this range at that time.

In summary, the mountain ranges surrounding the Owens Valley, including the entire White Mountains and the Sierra Nevada from Olancha to Yosemite, historically probably supported about twenty populations of mountain sheep. Of these, only four survived to the present. Furthermore, the loss

16. Three bighorn in the Sawmill Canyon herd. (*Credit: John Wehausen*)

of most of these populations is not just a phenomenon of the distant past, but has continued throughout this century. Reintroductions will help reverse this trend, but prevention of further losses is equally important.

## PERTINENT LITERATURE

Austin, Mary, *The Flock,* Houghton, Mifflin and Co. New York, 1906.

Foreyt, W. J. and D. A. Jessup, *Fatal Pneumonia of Bighorn Sheep Following Association with Domestic Sheep,* Journal of Wildlife Diseases, 1982, 18:163-168.

Goodson, N. J., *Effects of Domestic Sheep Grazing on Bighorn Sheep Populations; A Review,* Proceedings Biennial Symposium, Northern Wild Sheep and Goat Conference, 1982, 3:287-313.

Jones, F. L., *A Survey of the Sierra Nevada Bighorn,* Sierra Club Bulletin, 1950, 35:29-76.

Muir, John, *The Mountains of California,* The Century Co., New York, 1894.

_ _ _ _, *Among the Animals of the Yosemite,* Atlantic Monthly, 1898, 82:617-631.

Ober, E., *The Mountain Sheep of California,* California Fish and Game, 1931, 17:27-39.

Wehausen, J. D., *Sierra Nevada Bighorn Sheep: History and Population Ecology,* Ph.D. Dissertation, University of Michigan, Ann Arbor, 1980, 240pp.

_ _ _ _, *Bighorn Sheep in the White Mountains: Past and Recent History,* Pages 180-182 in C. A. Hall and D. J. Young, eds., *Natural History of the White-Inyo Range, Eastern California and Western Nevada and High Altitude Physiology,* University of California, White Mountain Research Station, 1896.

Wolfe, L. M. (ed.), *John of the Mountains; The Unpublished Journals of John Muir,* The University of Wisconsin Press, 1979, 459pp.

Opening day of fishing season is one of the busiest events in the Eastern Sierra. Every year thousands of anglers flock to our streams and lakes to try their luck at this popular recreational activity. In this article, Tom Lipp discusses the history of fish in Inyo County from the ice age lakes to the modern day fish hatcheries.

Tom Lipp is a Fish and Game Warden for the California Department of Fish and Game, and a past Chairman of the Friends of the Eastern California Museum. He has also written for *Tuva,* a publication of the Eastern California Museum.

# FISH AND HATCHERIES OF INYO COUNTY

by Tom Lipp

It comes as an enormous surprise to most people that there are no trout native to Inyo County. The abundance and variety of trout now found in the waters of Inyo County are the result of introductions which began in the 1870s.

The true native fishes of the Owens River Valley have almost disappeared. Only through aggressive measures have small populations remained. The pupfish, dace, sucker and chub are the Owens Valley's only remaining natives.

The native fishes are the vestigial representatives of the species which occurred in the great pluvial periods, the last of which ended with the last Ice Age, about 11,000 years ago.

During these wet periods the Owens River Valley was a part of the enormous Death Valley Lake System. This chain of lakes began with what is now Mono Lake in the north and drained south through what is now Long Valley (Crowley Lake) then south to Owens Lake. Waters continued south past Little Lake, where evidence of its passing may be seen at Fossil Falls, to now dry China Lake. The waters of this great system flowed to Searles Lake (near the present day town of Trona) then into the Panamint Valley. Finally the waters flowed over Wingate Pass and to their terminus, Lake Manly in Death Valley. Lake Manly, at its greatest size, was about 70 miles long and covered some 270 square miles.

17. One of the two trucks purchased for construction of the Mt. Whitney fish hatchery. A 1916 Federal, it was used to haul trout from the hatchery to the railroad after the construction was complete. (Credit: Mt. Whitney Fish Hatchery)

With the ending of the Ice Age, gradual warming resulted in recession of the lakes until only vestigial waters remain.

The fishes of the pluvial lake system adapted to their new conditions or perished. The adaptation in some cases is remarkable. The pupfish, a tenacious remnant, evolved into different species located in separate areas of the now defunct lake system.

The preservation of our remaining native fishes in the Owens River Valley is critical. Fortunately the public awareness and will to do so is strong.

Probably the first trout were brought into Inyo County by A. W. Robinson, a resident of Independence. The trout came from Bubbs Creek via Kearsarge Pass. Robinson, assisted by Sonny Wallace, planted these trout in Little Pine Creek (Independence Creek). Robinson also brought trout from Bubbs Creek on another occasion which were planted in Eight Mile Creek (Sawmill Creek). These plants took place in the mid 1870s. Robinson never lived to appreciate the importance of his efforts as he was killed in a gunfight on the streets of Darwin on Christmas Day, 1882.[1]

The best known early trout plant occurred in 1876, when golden trout were brought from Mulkey Creek, a small tributary to the South Fork of the Kern River. These fish were carried to the Eastern Sierra and planted in Cottonwood Creek. The men involved in this operation were Col. Sherman V. Stevens, A. C. Stevens, and Thomas George.

The golden trout were caught with hook and line and carried in a coffee pot over Hockett trail (Trail Pass). They were released in Cottonwood Creek about one mile above Col. Stevens' sawmill. The men left Mulkey Creek with 13 trout. One died in transit and the remaining 12 were successfully planted.[2]

Roy Hunter, a third generation member of the pioneer Hunter family, remembers his grandfather telling him that Manuel Silva brought golden trout from Golden Trout Creek to Mulkey Creek. At a later date, but prior to Col. Stevens introduction, Silva carried trout from Mulkey Creek and planted them in Cottonwood Creek.[3]

The golden trout found in Mulkey Creek and the Cottonwood drainage are *Salmo roosevelti*, the species native to Golden Trout Creek. The species found in the South Fork of the Kern River are *Salmo aguabonita*.[4]

Mulkey Creek does not flow above ground all the way to the South Fork of the Kern River, but is in that drainage. This evidence lends credence to the supposition that man transported golden trout from Golden Trout Creek to Mulkey Creek. That man was probably Manuel Silva.

In 1891 M. P. Hand, E. H. Edwards, Manuel Silva, James Moffett, and B. H. Dutcher transplanted about 100 golden trout from Cottonwood Creek to the Cottonwood Lakes. This plant is well documented as B. H. Dutcher was with a U.S. Biological Survey team which was visiting the area.[5]

Undoubtedly many other "private" introductions were made by locals during this early period. Phil Kehoe is credited with the release of about 700 small catfish into Fish Slough in 1887. The fish had been taken from an irrigation ditch at the home of J. R. Elred near Bishop.[6]

The first state fish hatchery to be built in Inyo County was the Mt. Whitney Hatchery, which is still in operation, located about 4 miles north of Independence.

There was great rivalry and political infighting in determining where this hatchery should be located. Between Inyo County and San Bernardino County the argument centered around the difference in the population of the two areas. Within Inyo County the contest was between the towns of Lone Pine and Independence. Lone Pine wished to locate the new hatchery on nearby Tuttle Creek. Independence sought selection of their chosen site on Oak Creek. California Fish and Game Commissioner M. J. Connell of Los Angeles said that the area which could make the "best business arrangement" would be selected.

Judge Dehy of Independence called a public meeting at the Courthouse and encouraged all civic minded persons to attend. With the assistance of County Supervisor and former sheriff George W. Naylor and A. W. Eibeshutz, a local merchant, the Judge raised $1,850 in less than one hour.[7]

18. A photo of the Mt. Whitney Fish Hatchery just completed in early 1917. *(Credit: Eastern California Museum)*

Of this, $1,500 was used to purchase a 40 acre tract on Oak Creek from A. N. Bell. This property was donated to the State of California for construction of the hatchery. Another $500 was pledged to the Fish and Game Commission to construct a road from the hatchery to El Camino Sierra—the State Highway running north and south through the Owens River Valley.

This business arrangement along with the persistent work of Carl J. Walters, a rancher at Fort Independence, was instrumental in the eventual selection of the present site on Oak Creek.

Construction of the Mt. Whitney Fish Hatchery began in late March of 1916 with the goal of completing the project in time to take eggs from Rae Lakes trout for propagation in the spring of 1917. H. V. Grant, Superintendent of Construction for the State Department of Engineering was in charge of construction. Initial cost was estimated at $30,000; final cost was reported to be $60,000.[8] Some things never change.

Design of the hatchery was done principally by Charles Dean of the State Department of Engineering. His guidelines from Fish and Game Commissioner M. J. Connell were that the structure match the mountains and should last forever.

The walls are constructed of native granite rock and reinforced with steel and are between two and three feet thick. They were guaranteed "not to crumble until the mountains shall fall". About 3,500 tons of boulders, all found within a quarter mile of the site, were used in construction. A notable feature is that none of the stones were cut, but "sorted to fit". The Spanish tile roof was made in Lincoln, a small town near Sacramento, where red soil of the desired tint was found. The interior wood was natural finish Oregon ash.

Mt. Whitney Fish Hatchery was completed in early 1917, on schedule I might add. Some things do change. The first Superintendent, Frank A. Shebley, supervising 5-7 men, hatched the first trout in that year from eggs collected at Rae Lakes. The eggs were transported from the collecting station at Rae Lakes via Oak Creek Pass (now Baxter Pass) by mule train to the Mt. Whitney Hatchery. After the 1927 spawning season eggs were no longer collected at Rae Lakes due to declining egg production.

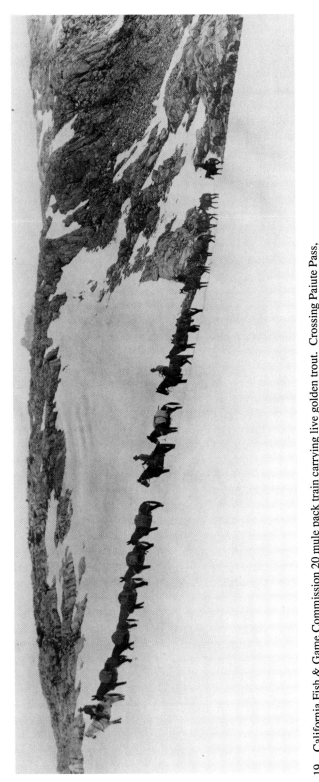

19. California Fish & Game Commission 20 mule pack train carrying live golden trout. Crossing Paiute Pass, elevation 11,400 feet, snow was 60 feet deep. July 26, 1914. *(Credit: Mt. Whitney Fish Hatchery)*

The spawning season of 1918 saw the first collection of golden trout eggs from the Cottonwood Lakes. These eggs were successfully hatched at Mt. Whitney and the fingerlings planted in local waters. This program continues to this day and has provided golden trout for planting throughout California and much of the West. As egg collection occurs in the spring, bitter cold and heavy snow is not uncommon. Weather, combined with the 11,000 foot elevation, make this a most rigorous assignment.

At the Black Rock Rearing Ponds, built in 1941 north of Independence, about 750,000 fingerling trout are raised annually to a catchable size of about three fish to the pound. These trout are then planted into Sierra lakes and streams as part of the California Department of Fish and Game's catchable trout program. Trout at Black Rock were raised in large earthen ponds until 1984 when the whirling disease outbreak precluded this technique. Now all fish are raised in concrete raceways.

Fish Springs Hatchery, built in 1952 near Big Pine, is another rearing facility. All the trout are raised in concrete raceways. There are eight series of these raceways, each 10 feet wide, 42 inches deep and 1,000 feet long. Annually, Fish Springs raises 100,000 fingerlings and 500,000 subcatchables for planting. The bulk of Fish Springs production is the 1,400,000 catchable trout raised for planting. Total planting weight of trout raised annually at Fish Springs is an incredible 473,500 pounds.

The next time someone talks about the native trout they caught in Inyo County, you should be able to speak with authority to this common misconception. In the words of the noted fisheries biologist Phil Pister, "Fishing in Inyo County ain't what it used to be—and never was".

NOTES
1. *Inyo Independent,* March 17, 1977.
2. Evermann, Barton Warren; *The Golden Trout of the Southern High Sierras,* Bulletin of the Bureau of Fisheries, 1905-1.
3. Hunter, Roy; Personal Comment, 1988.
4. Moyle, Peter, *Inland Fishes of California.*
5. Curtis, Brian; Stanford University, Master of Arts Thesis, *The Golden Trout of Cottonwood Lakes,* 1934.
6. *Inyo Register-Independent,* May 27, 1984.

7. *Inyo Independent,* December 3, 1915.
8. Ibid, December 15, 1915.


BIBLIOGRAPHY
Curtis, Brian, *The Golden Trout of Cottonwood Lakes,* Stanford University, 1934.
Moyle, P. B., *Inland Fishes of California,* U.C. Press, 1976.
Pister, E. P., *Desert Fishes and Their Habitats,* Transactions of the Amercan Fisheries Society 103, (1974): 531-540.

As in much of the arid west, the control and distribution of water has been the dominant force influencing the history of the Owens Valley. In Part I of "The Politics of California Water: Owens Valley and the Los Angeles Aqueduct, 1900-1927", William L. Kahrl explores the complex political maneuvering behind the acquisition of water rights in the Owens Valley by the city of Los Angeles for the construction of the Los Angeles Aqueduct.

William L. Kahrl has many years experience exploring water issues in California. He served as Director of Research in Governor Brown's Office of Planning and Research, project director for the *California Water Atlas,* and is the author of the widely acclaimed book, *Water and Power.*

"The Politics of California Water: Owens Valley and the Los Angeles Aqueduct, 1900-1927" by William L. Kahrl. *California Historical Quarterly,* Vol 55, No. 1 (Spring, 1976). Reprinted by permission of the California Historical Society.

# THE POLITICS OF CALIFORNIA WATER
Owens Valley
and the
Los Angeles Aqueduct, 1900-1927
Part I

by William L. Kahrl

## I. The Politics of Appropriation

More than gold and oil, railroad and freeway construction, the film and aerospace industries, water distribution has shaped the development of California's cities and countryside. Nowhere is the vital significance of water more obvious than in Los Angeles, which today imports more than 80 per cent of its water supply from sources lying hundreds of miles beyond its legal boundaries. Los Angeles grew in the nineteenth century despite its lack of sewers and schools, a coastal city without a port, its growth fed by booster advertising and its development founded on prospects for the future rather than on actual demand. By the turn of the century, however, the rigid limits of the city's indigenous water supply had already begun to circumscribe the business community's prospects for continued growth and expansion. And so, with money, guns, and a unity of purpose with what they identified as the public interest, the bankers and businessmen of Los Angeles determined to seize the water resources of the Owens Valley 240 miles to the northeast. And, by correcting God's design for their community with the construction of the Los Angeles Aqueduct, they laid the foundations for the modern metropolis.

Depending upon the popular proclivities of the times, the complex and dramatic story of Los Angeles, the Owens Valley, and the building of the aqueduct has been used variously as a

117

demonstration of the evils of municipal ownership of utilities, as an example of the nastiness of Los Angeles in general and of the *Los Angeles Times* in particular, and, most recently in the widely successful film *Chinatown*, as a setting for an examination of the multiple levels of human corruption.[1] Certainly, the story is rich in the interplay of personality and event, for it boasts a cast of characters ranging from Teddy Roosevelt to the KKK and includes moments of triumph, bitter betrayal, armed conflict, and numerous harrowing escapes from disaster. The popular memory of these events, however, has been shaped largely by a controversy over questions of municipal corruption. In addition, primary research materials, such as the letters and personal memoirs of the principal actors, are lacking, with the result that formal histories of these events have tended to side either with Los Angeles or the Owens Valley, arguing their cases on one another's authority.[2]

This study, however, focuses upon the politics of the controversy, including the way in which the aqueduct was promoted to the Los Angeles electorate, and, in the second article of this series, the governmental response to the conflict which ensued. From this perspective, the problem of corruption is transformed to reveal a conflict not between the public and private sectors but between competing public interests.

The initial problem which Los Angeles confronted in its determination to develop a new source of water was that at the end of the nineteenth century the city did not even have control of its existing water resources. Until the twentieth century, water development in California was almost exclusively an activity of private enterprise.[3] Private water companies proliferated wherever the rights to an existing streamflow could be secured and the water sold to nearby towns. Confidence in the free enterprise system ran particularly strong in nineteenth-century Los Angeles where private companies provided the full range of utility services upon which the community depended—gas, electricity, communications, and all forms of public transportation. In 1868, the city granted a thirty-year lease on its water supply to the Los Angeles Water Company. In exchange the company developed a distribution system which it operated at considerable profit to itself. Public dissatisfaction with rates and the quality of service, however, increased as the term of the lease drew near.[4]

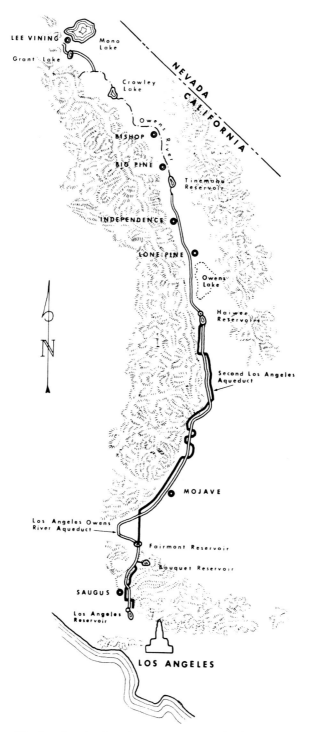

20. Los Angeles Aqueduct system map. *(Credit: Los Angeles Department of Water and Power.)*

Amendments to the city charter in 1889 affirmed the city's authority to operate its own water system, and the Republican party platform of 1896 called for municipal ownership on the promise that the city could provide water at ten per cent of the company's charges.[5] The chairman of the Republican City Central Committee that year was the former superintendent of the private water company, Fred Eaton, a native Angeleno and son of a forty-niner who had helped found Pasadena. In 1898, Eaton was elected mayor on a municipal ownership platform from which he attacked his former employer for the fire hazards presented by the company's reliance on small diameter water mains.

After the expiration of the lease in 1898, Los Angeles had to fight in the courts for four years to force the company to withdraw, and the city ultimately paid $2 million to buy back its own water system. Bonds for this purchase were approved in August, 1901, and the city assumed control the following February through a seven-member elective Board of Water Commissioners. Progress on the development of the system was delayed another year, however, until in the elections of February, 1903, the city charter was amended again to prohibit the granting of another lease and to insulate the Board of Water Commissioners from politics by requiring that all positions on the board be appointed by the mayor subject to confirmation by the city council.[6]

Initially, the move for municipal ownership of the city water system was presented simply as a means of securing more efficient service at lower rates. The unspoken related issue of urban expansion, however, possessed a far greater importance for the city's future. In 1868, the city had leased its water rights to private enterprise because the development of an efficient distribution system was believed to be too great a burden for the city treasury to bear. By 1900, the situation had reversed. The costs involved in securing and transporting a new source of water to Los Angeles lay beyond the reach of private capital. The availability of the far greater resources of municipal finance was a necessary first step toward the construction of a new water project.

Henry Huntington, masterbuilder and first among financial giants in the Los Angeles business community, had already recognized these altered conditions when his unsuccessful efforts to fund construction of a harbor at San Pedro forced him to turn to the federal government for assistance. Once the city had organized itself to operate its own water system, Huntington in 1904 lent his support to a water development scheme which Fred Eaton had been attempting to promote ever since he resigned from the Los Angeles Water Company in 1886. Although grand designs abounded in the early 1900's for bringing water to the expanding cities of Southern California, Eaton enjoyed a special advantage in advocating his own plan for Los Angeles because of his experience in the field, his prominence in the community as a former mayor, his leadership in the battle over municipal ownership, and his close personal relationship with the superintendent of the new municipal water system, William Mulholland.

Mulholland in turn owed much of his success to Eaton's friendship. A former merchant seaman and itinerant knife-sharpener, Mulholland had taken a job digging ditches for the water company upon his arrival in Los Angeles in 1878. Although he lacked any formal training as an engineer, Mulholland rose so rapidly through the ranks of Eaton's staff that when Eaton left the company eight years later to seek public office, Mulholland took over as his successor, a position he retained through the transfer to municipal ownership.[7] Thus it was to a protege that Eaton took his plan, and Mulholland, in September, 1904, readily agreed to accompany his mentor on a buckboard journey to the Owens Valley, a slender, ten-by-one-hundred-mile depression between the Sierra Nevada on the west and White Mountains and Inyo Range on the east in Inyo and Mono counties. There, Eaton claimed, lay a water supply capable of supporting a city ten times the current size of Los Angeles.

The agricultural communities of the Owens Valley at this time were just emerging from the frontier landscape of chaparral, cactus, and sagebrush.[8] More than 60,000 acres were already under irrigation, and the area's agricultural products of hard grains, apples, corn, and honey were among the finest displayed each year at the state fair.[9] With the opening of mining camps in southeastern Nevada, the Owens Valley looked forward to the prospect of expanding prosperity as one of the prime agricultural and mining regions of the state.

21. City of Los Angeles as seen from the Plaza area, (circa 1880).
(Credit: Los Angeles Department of Water and Power.)

Los Angeles was not the only public entity to recognize the potential of the valley for water development. Fully a year before Mulholland's first visit, the federal government's newly created National Reclamation Service had entered the valley eager to establish a demonstration model of systematic irrigation. The Reclamation Service's plans called for doubling the total irrigated acreage within the valley, and by the time of Mulholland's visit, the local farmers had already signed over their water storage rights for the new project and agreed to the removal of more than 500,000 acres of the valley from entry for settlement under the Homestead Act.[10]

Mulholland's initial problem, then, was one of convincing the federal government to withdraw its interest in favor of the interests of Los Angeles. Fortunately, the Chief of Southwest Operations for the Reclamation Service, J. B. Lippincott, was himself a resident of Los Angeles and a leader with Eaton in the campaign for the successful bond issue with which the city bought back its water supply. On September 17, 1904, Lippincott advised the Department of Interior of Los Angeles' interest in the Owens Valley, and in a meeting with city representatives in November, Lippincott recommended to his immediate superior, F. H. Newell, Chief Engineer for the Reclamation Service, that Los Angeles be provided with all of the maps and technical studies the service had prepared on the valley. In February, 1905, Lippincott and Newell worked out a plan for Los Angeles to reimburse the service for its work, and Lippincott privately arranged to provide Mulholland with a detailed report on the available water supply in Southern California. Thus, in the months which followed—and unbeknownst to the Owens Valley ranchers—the efforts of the federal engineers gradually shifted from the development of an irrigation project for agricultural development of the Owens Valley to the design of an aqueduct for Los Angeles.[11]

Eaton himself presented Mulholland with a more delicate problem, for Eaton's earlier advocacy of municipal ownership of the city water system had been tied to his own scheme for private exploitation of the Owens Valley water. Realizing that the Los Angeles Water Company lacked both the means and the desire to undertake a project requiring capital of such magnitude, he had joined Huntington and other members of the business community in recognizing municipalization as a necessary first step toward the development of a new water source for the city. Municipalization in Eaton's view, however, served only to open a source of capital for the construction of the mammoth project and to guarantee a market for the private enterprise Eaton had been promoting for years. Eaton intended that the water itself should remain in private hands and be made available to Los Angeles in an initial lot of 15,000 miner's inches at an annual rate of $100 and inch.[12] And, while Mulholland returned to the city to meet with the members of the water board after his first visit to the valley in September 1904, Eaton raced East to consult with Dillon and Hubbard, bond attorneys in New York, in yet another fruitless attempt to form a private consortium for the purchase of water rights in the Owens Valley.[13]

Mulholland, however, believed in a more radical view of public ownership of water, and he regarded as folly an arrangement which would render the city's water supply and the operations of his agency captive to the interests of private owners and the rates they might demand. Accordingly, he skillfully maneuvered to use the Reclamation Service to resolve this conflict with Eaton. Rather than pressing his case with Eaton directly, Mulholland deployed Lippincott of the Reclamation Service to confront Eaton with the essential condition that the Reclamation Service would not withdraw its interest in the Owens Valley unless the Los Angeles project were "public owned from one end to the other"[14] In return Mulholland sweetened the bitterness of defeat for his old friend and mentor with a very favorable deal on the key property in Long Valley at the headwaters of the Owens River on which Eaton held an option.

Under the terms of this agreement, finalized in May, 1905, Los Angeles agreed to pay Eaton $450,000 for the water rights and an easement allowing the eventual construction of a small reservoir on the 12,000 acre ranch Eaton had purchased for $500,000. If Los Angeles failed to exercise its option by the end of that year, the price would go up to $475,000, and if for any reason the project were not built, all the land would revert to Eaton. Eaton retained control of the rest of the property, more than 10,000 acres, together with 500 head of cattle valued at $7-10 a head. Eaton would thus be paid the entire purchase price of the property at Long Valley, 90-95 per cent in cash and the balance in livestock, while still retaining control of more than 80 per cent of the land. In addition, it was recognized that as the ranchers downstream were forced out of business by the project, they would have no choice but to sell their cattle at reduced prices to Eaton who would be the sole surviving rancher in the valley.[15]

For the time being, Eaton seemed to be as happy dreaming about an eventual cattle empire as he had been about a possible water empire, and he promptly set about acquiring options on the downstream water rights for transfer to the city of Los Angeles, as he and Mulholland had agreed. Using the Reclamation Service maps provided by Lippincott and outfitting himself with credentials which appeared to identify him as an agent of the federal government, Eaton encountered little resistance from the unsuspecting farmers who thought they were aiding reclamation for the valley rather than giving up their water to Los Angeles.[16]

All of these negotiations, purchases, and plans were carried out in strictest secrecy due to the fears of Los Angeles officials that publicity about the project would escalate prices on the properties they needed. Accordingly, a pledge was secured from all the Los Angeles newspapers that no mention would be made of the city water board's activities in relation to the Owens Valley. Nevertheless, Eaton's massive purchases and transfers of title to the city could not fail to be noticed at the valley land office, and embarrassing questions began to be raised about the real intentions of the Reclamation Service and its putative agent, Fred Eaton.

Faced with the threat of disclosure, the service headquarters staff in Washington, D.C., resolved: "We cannot clear the skirts of the Reclamation Service too quickly or completely."[17] They decided, therefore, to call a panel of engineers to meet on neutral ground in San Francisco to review the Reclamation Service's plans and then to issue a report announcing that the proposed federal project was not as attractive as it had first seemed and, by default, that the aqueduct was a more worthy endeavor.

At the hearing in July, 1905, Lippincott of the Reclamation Service testified that the claims of Los Angeles to the Owens River water were superior to those of the reclamation project, and he recommended that the service therefore should do all it could to aid the city.[18] This graceful transfer was fouled, however, by the appearance at the hearing of J. C. Clausen, the Reclamation Service engineer who designed the Owens Valley project. Clausen had been sent to Yuma during the period that the service was trying to plan a way to bow out of the valley, but he was not a man to play anyone's fool. When the hearing was called, he returned to testify about the Valley's assets for his irrigation project: abundant water power, fertile soil, genial climate, and the availability of agricultural markets in nearby Tonopah and Goldfield. Moreover, he demonstrated, it was economical. The Reclamation Service had twenty-eight projects on its drawing boards at that time, some ranging as high in cost as $86 an acre. The Owens Valley project was budgeted at $21.58 an acre as compared with an average price for all twenty-eight of $30.97 an acre.[19]

Clausen's embarrassing testimony encouraged the review panel to issue a report favoring the federal government's project "unless the men who had bought key property for Los Angeles had made it impractical."[20] This report was not released, however, until July 28, 1905, the very day that Mulholland and Eaton concluded the final series of purchases which did, in fact, render the federal project impractical.

With the appearance of this all-important caveat in the Reclamation Service's published report, the *Los Angeles Times* next morning breached the voluntary wall of silence which had hitherto surrounded the project with its own massive report on the city's plans to bring the Owens River to a vast reservoir in the San Fernando Valley. In characteristic exalted prose, it proclaimed: "The cable that has held the San Fernando Valley vassal for ten centuries to the arid demon is about to be severed by the magic scimitar of modern engineering skill."[21]

The *Times'* sudden revelation, however, had unfortunate consequences for a number of the aqueduct's principal supporters which were entirely unintended by the publisher of the *Times*, Harrison Gray Otis. The appearance of the *Times'* report that morning left Fred Eaton unprepared and trapped amidst an angry crowd of Owens Valley ranchers whom he just barely succeeded in staring down. An investigation of Lippincott's role in the affair began immediately and produced the not very surprising discovery that he had been drawing a salary from the city of Los Angeles while simultaneously working for the federal government. Lippincott's prospects of continued employment with the Reclamation Service were not improved by the fact that the *Times*, in its first report on the project, injudiciously commended him for his "valuable assistance" in "looking after" Fred Eaton's purchases and for his help in arranging an initial survey of the route for the aqueduct by federal engineers. The *Times* concluded, "Without Mr. Lippincott's interest and cooperation, it is declared that the plan never would have gone through. . . . Any other government engineer, a non-resident of Los Angeles and not familiar with the needs of this section, undoubtedly would have gone ahead with nothing more than the mere reclamation of arid lands in view."[22] Damned by such avid praise, Lippincott was forced to resign the following May and moved directly to a post high in Mulholland's staff.

Newell similarly suffered from special commendation by the water board when on June 5, 1905, it passed an official resolution thanking him for his "valuable assistance". The resolution was promptly withdrawn when its potential effect upon Newell's career was realized, and Newell managed to remain on the federal payroll until a House investigation of his conflicting activities forced his suspension in 1913.[23] Clausen, meanwhile, resigned from the Reclamation Service and worked intermittently thereafter as a consulting engineer for the Owens Valley ranchers.

More important for the long-term prospects of the Los Angeles project, by breaking the gentleman's agreement among the other editors and scooping every other paper in town, Otis stirred the wrath of William Randolph Hearst, who, in 1903, had established the *Los Angeles Examiner,* the seventh in his expanding empire. The older newspapers in town, Otis' *Times* most prominently among them, shared the booster gospel of the business community; in the 1870's, for example, they had turned their pages into publicity broadsides for the first great land boom and distributed them in the hotels and business establishments of the East.[24] Hearst's press, however, was of the muck-racking persuasion, and while the other papers rallied in uniform praise of the proposed aqueduct, the *Examiner's* reports on the issue started out with suspicion and rapidly deteriorated into hostility.

The *Examiner's* initial line of inquiry focused sharply on the awesome haste with which the water board and city council were proceeding to get the project underway. On August 14, 1905, barely two weeks after the citizens of Los Angeles had learned for the first time of the planned aqueduct, the city council called for a $1.5 million bond election to pay the costs of preliminary surveys and acquisition; the election was to be held three weeks later on September 7. The people were thus being asked to give initial approval to a project which was expected to cost $23 million before they had even seen a map of the proposed aqueduct.[25]

Meeting the attack, Mulholland attempted at first to drown all questions in a flood of statistics which, as they proliferated, became increasingly contradictory. The *Examiner* lept on the inconsistencies, pointing out that Mulholland could not even give a definite figure for the amount of water that Los Angeles would receive from the project. Mulholland, in turn, produced the voluminous reports prepared by the Reclamation Service to demonstrate that technical studies of the Owens River had been made, at least by someone.[26]

Mulholland's other efforts to explain his inordinate haste met with no better reception on the editorial pages of the *Examiner*. When Mulholland, for example, warned that private investors would take over the development of the aqueduct if the city failed to act promptly, the *Examiner* pointed out that Eaton had been trying for years to interest a private investor in the project without success and that the federal government's interest in the valley would prohibit a private takeover at this point. Similarly, when Mulholland maintained that the bond issue had to be passed to meet the first $50,000 installment, due October 1 on Eaton's property at Long Valley, the *Examiner* argued that committing $1.5 million in public funds for the sake of $50,000 was patently absurd.[27]

Mulholland ultimately resorted to exaggerations of the city's need for water as a way of encouraging voters to approve his bonds, and, in the weeks before the election, the *Times* began to print almost daily predictions of the dire consequences which would be visited on Los Angeles if the aqueduct were not built. One of the most persistent stories apparently fabricated as a part of this scare campaign involved the so-called drought which descended on Southern California at a time variously cited as 1892 or 1895 and which reportedly persisted until 1904. Modern historians still refer to this drought, although it seems to have originated with Mulholland in the election of 1905. For example, Erwin Cooper's *Aqueduct Empire* recalls on Mulholland's authority that the average rainfall in Los Angeles from 1895 to 1904 dropped to only six inches per year;[28] in fact, national weather bureau records reveal that Los Angeles' annual precipitation in this period averaged 11.52 inches.[29] Similarly, Remi Nadeau in his history of the Los Angeles Aqueduct reports that Mulholland first traveled to the Owens Valley in September, 1904, because that summer's "water famine" had set the city "reeling."[30] In fact, Los Angeles in 1904 received a perfectly average rainfall of 11.88 inches, and in August, the city experienced a record downpour for that month which was not even approached in the entire forty-year period from 1891 to 1930.[31]

Los Angeles did experience two successive years of rainfall below nine inches in 1898 and 1899, but over the next four years the levels of precipitation steadily increased, and in 1905, rainfall totaled 19.19 inches. In the sixteen years from 1890 to 1905, rainfall in Los Angeles averaged 13.00 inches a year, an amount not appreciably less than the 13.69-inch average annual rainfall in the corresponding, contemporary period from 1958 to 1973.[32] Alternatively, in the twenty-four-year period from 1890 to 1913, the year the aqueduct was completed, the average annual rainfall in Los Angeles of 13.84 inches actually exceeded the 13.46-inch average for the corresponding period from 1950 to 1973.

Nevertheless, Mulholland declared that the shortage existed, imposed strict measures to prevent waste by the citizenry, and predicted that the city's existing water supply could not support more than its present population of 200,000.[33] The reliability of this claim can be assessed by observing that before the aqueduct was completed, the population of the area more than tripled without the city experiencing a water shortage of any kind. To suggest that Mulholland's figures were calculated from whole cloth is not to say that Los Angeles' need for water was not real but rather that it was a need conditioned almost entirely upon the business community's prospect of massive growth and expansion in the years ahead.

The *Examiner,* meanwhile, continued digging for a more creditable reason behind the city's rush to judgment at the polls. Although the *Examiner* had long supported the idea of a water project for Los Angeles, they had maintained from the outset, "There must be no politics and no graft."[34] Their first question for Mulholland when he announced the project was whether the possibility existed for graft. "None at all," Mulholland answered. "The only man who could graft is Fred Eaton, and I know that he never made a dirty dollar in his life and never will."[35] When the resolution to call an election sailed through the city council on August 14, the only dissenting councilman, A. D. Houghton, himself the product of the political reform movement led by J. R. Haynes and J. B. Irvine, observed ominously, "It almost looks as if some of these men [the other council members] whose character and integrity are above reproach, had been let in on this deal three or four months ago, had purchased arid lands, and are in haste to have them made valuable by this water project."[36] The *Examiner* picked up the insinuation of corruption and played it coyly on the editorial page, observing of the city council, "They are all men who, like Jim Fisk's legislators, 'do not stir around for nothing.' ...They are the same men who obey the behests of the trolley and gas monopolies. How far is the water project allied with the interests which control their actions?"[37]

The reference to the monopolies was a cut at a favorite *Examiner* adversary, Henry Huntington. Before the aqueduct story broke, the *Examiner* was campaigning against Huntington and the city council for lax municipal ordinances which permitted the unsafe operation of Huntington's trolley cars to claim several hundred casualties among the citizenry each year. Huntington's active support of the aqueduct bond issue quickened the *Examiner's* suspicions for several reasons. In the first place, while the other local power companies opposed the project because they feared the competition with municipal power the aqueduct would generate, Huntington's Pacific Electric and Power Company endorsed the project. In addition, Huntington had recently extended a transit line into the San Fernando Valley, a sure sign that his development companies would soon follow. But this move would put Huntington at odds with the city water board for the meager water reserves available in the valley.[38] The revelation that a massive new water project was planned which would deliver water in great quantities for storage in the San Fernando Valley seemed an uncanny stroke of good luck for Mr. Huntington.

Almost as curious was the *Times'* support for the proposed aqueduct, for publisher Otis had at all other times opposed the principle of municipal ownership and had vigorously campaigned for an extension of the lease to the Los Angeles

Water Company between 1898 and 1901. Councilman Houghton's suggestion of corruption brought a violent denunciation from the *Times* for this "braying ass, a stench in the nostrils of decency" and his reform-minded friends Haynes and Irvine, "freaks and pests who see no good in the existing order." When Houghton rose to question Mulholland during his presentation to the Municipal League the night of August 15, he was hooted down by the distinguished business leaders gathered there, and the *Times* observed approvingly: "If councilman Howton [sic] had not been born by reason of a miscarriage (of justice) the city of Los Angeles would have escaped the annoyance and humiliation to which it had been subjected through his fool antics, his innumerable and disgusting monkeyshines, and his assinine [sic] performances in and out of the council chamber"[39]

Significantly, on August 22, the *San Francisco Chronicle* ran an editorial which pointed to the value of the proposed aqueduct to Los Angeles commerce and noted the recurrence of rumors in *Bradstreet's Financial Report* to the effect that the project was linked to a land development scheme for the San Fernando Valley. The *Examiner* waited two days to allow the *Times'* Otis to prepare his response; then, on the same day that the *Times* attacked the *Chronicle* in an editorial entitled "Baseless Rumors," the *Examiner* struck with the revelation of an organized land syndicate which had purchased 16,000 acres in the San Fernando Valley for $35 an acre, an investment which would return millions once water arrived from the Owens Valley. The *Examiner* named ten syndicate members, each of whom held 1000 shares in the San Fernando Mission Land Company at a par value of $100 a share. The list included: Henry Huntington, of course; E. H. Harriman, president of the Union Pacific and the man to whom Huntington had sold the Southern Pacific after the death of his father, Collis; W. G. Kerckhoff, president of the Pacific Light and Power Company; Joseph Sartori of the Security Trust and Savings Bank; L. C. Brand of the Title Guarantee and Trust Company; G. K. Porter, a San Fernando land speculator who owned the land bought by the syndicate; and, best of all from the *Examiner's* point of view, the owners of the three leading newspapers of the city, E. T. Earl of the *Express,* and Harrison Gray Otis himself, publisher of the *Times* and "its vermiform appendix," the *Herald.*

22. Main Street, Bishop, 1886. (Credit: C. E. Peterson photo, Eastern California Museum.)

The next morning, Otis lept to attack the Hearst "yellow atrocity" declaring, "The insane desire of the *Examiner* to discredit certain citizens of Los Angeles has at last led it into the open as a vicious enemy of the city's welfare." In subsequent days, Otis asserted that the company had been formed two years earlier, before the aqueduct was anything more than a gleam in Fred Eaton's eye, a claim which the *Examiner* promptly demonstrated to be false. According to the company charter issued December 3, 1904, the company was formed and its stock subscribed on November 28, 1904, after Mulholland had secured the approval of his superiors on the water board to go ahead with planning for the project. Also, on November 28, Otis had issued a check for $50,000 to secure an option on the ranch which was the core of the syndicate's holdings. Full purchase of the property, however, was not concluded until March 23, 1905, the day after Eaton made a down payment of $100 to secure his option on the Long Valley property.[40]

With less than two weeks to go until the city election, the high-pressure campaign for approval of the aqueduct bond issue was beginning to unravel. Otis' denials of guilt did not prevent the other newspapers of the state from picking up the *Examiner's* report on the syndicate. Huntington rushed back to the city and closeted himself with his advisors at the exclusive Jonathan Club. On August 30, 1905, the temperature fortuitously rose to 101 degrees, the highest in twenty years, and lent credence to Mulholland's claims of an impending water famine, but the incipient heat wave broke the very next day. Worst of all, business leaders outside the circle which stood to gain most from the construction of the aqueduct began to comment in public that there was no need for such haste.[41] In addition, on August 30, the *Examiner* observed editorially: "Of one thing the people of Los Angeles can be assured and that is that they will be in no danger of a water famine in the future even if the present scheme fails. No one else will acquire the water of the Owens Valley if the city needs it. And, maybe, if it is otherwise acquired there will be less suspicion of graft in the matter, and there will be competent engineers employed to devise a plan for impounding the water and bringing it here."

This, however, was as close as the *Examiner* would ever come to outright opposition to the aqueduct. There were, after all, larger interests at stake than those of Harrison Gray Otis and his partners in the land syndicate. Henry Huntington, for one, was then in the midst of negotiations to create a huge new seaport at San Pedro harbor to accommodate the traffic expected from the new canal in Panama. In addition, Huntington in July had initiated his latest land boom at Redondo. John M. Elliott, president of the Municipal League and himself a member of the water board, had spearheaded the consolidation of the First National Bank in August, the largest merger of financial institutions in the history of Los Angeles until that time. These and other new commercial ventures all depended for their success upon a growing metropolis with the water to serve a vast new population.

Accordingly, on September 2, the business leaders of Los Angeles invited Hearst to come to the city for private consultation. Hearst was by now a congressman and embarked at full sail upon his vain quest for the presidency. Political ambition had intruded upon the quality of his journalism by 1905, causing his editors across the country to be considerably more judicious in their exposure of graft, deception, and public scandal than had previously been the case.[42] On the morning after Hearst's meeting with the businessmen, the *Examiner* ran a front-page editorial, reportedly written by the Chief himself, endorsing the aqueduct and bond issue.

Although the editorial reiterated all the charges which the *Examiner* had already made against the project, it found an excuse for its apparent change of attitude in the recommendation made September 2 by representatives of the major business organizations in Los Angeles that funds to be derived from the municipal bonds not be spent until an independent panel of engineers approved Mulholland's plans at some point after the election. Considering its source, the city water board readily agreed to this condition. Therefore, the *Examiner* concluded, "The Board's promise not to embark deeply in the venture until the best expert advice is obtained, removes its most objectionable features."

The *Examiner's* justification for its change of position thus called upon city voters to approve the commitment of funds for a project which they did not understand; its dimensions, direction, and utility would all be revealed after they had agreed to buy this multi-million-dollar pig in a poke. Hearst's decision to endorse the project, however, was recommended by more than mere political gamesmanship. For all of the*Examiner's* revelations of double-dealing and deceit in the promotion of the bond issue, the fact remained unalterable that the entire community stood to benefit from the construction of the aqueduct. If the *Examiner* had sought to embarrass Otis for scooping the Hearst paper, that objective had been achieved. Personally, and as a matter of his public policy in Congress and the press, Hearst supported the principle of municipal ownership of utilities. But, by silencing his *Examiner,* he eliminated the last strong voice against the bond issue, which, four days later, passed by a margin of 14 to 1.

This battle won, Los Angeles next turned to the United States Congress to obtain a right of way for the aqueduct across federal lands. There, for the first time, they confronted the Owens Valley interests directly in the formidable presence on the House Public Lands Committee of Sylvester C. Smith, congressman from Inyo County. Smith proposed a compromise in the form of an amendment to the right-of-way bill introduced for the city by the Republican senator from Los Angeles, Frank P. Flint. By the terms of the proposed Smith compromise, the Reclamation Service would proceed with its irrigation project for the valley; any excess water would be available for transport to serve the domestic needs only of Los Angeles; and any water left over after Los Angeles' needs were met would revert to the Owens Valley.

Smith's proposal would protect the survival of the valley while at the same time allowing enough water for Los Angeles to meet those 'needs' which Mulholland had described in such desperate terms during the campaign for the bond election. But, by granting primacy to the claims of the Owens Valley upon the water, the Smith amendment was anathema to the as-yet-unspoken intentions of the city which looked ahead to the day when Los Angeles would tap the entire flow of the Owens River. Under the Smith amendment, as the city's need for water grew with her population, she would have to fight the valley in court for every additional drop she took from one year to the next. Alternatively, if agriculture in the valley blossomed, Los Angeles would perhaps wither.

The dilemma which the Smith amendment posed for the city as a whole was even more extreme in the case of the interests of the San Fernando syndicate. The success of the syndicate did not depend upon immediate settlement of the lands it held in the

San Fernando Valley. Instead, the syndicate looked forward to years of profitable agricultural production made possible by the new water to come to these otherwise useless lands until the tide of urbanization would eventually reach out and claim their property. But, if use of the water for agriculture were prohibited under the Smith amendment, the syndicate would lose both the promise of income in these intervening years and, more importantly, its claims upon the water once settlement did begin. Once again, the private interests of Huntington, Otis, and the rest joined with greater public interest served by Mulholland. As before, the need for water as perceived by both sides was founded in prospect rather than the existing conditions of the Los Angeles water supply. No conspiracy was necessary; their objectives were the same.

In Washington, Inyo Congressman Smith was joined by the Secretary of the Interior Ethan A. Hitchcock in opposition to the syndicate and support of the Owens Valley ranchers. Confronted with this alliance of authority, Mulholland agreed to accept the Smith amendment in a meeting with Smith and Flint on June 21, 1906.[43] Senator Flint, however, was not so ready to concede defeat, and he turned for assistance to President Roosevelt's close personal friend and chief of the Forest Service, Gifford Pinchot. On the night of June 23, Flint obtained an audience with Roosevelt, and, with Pinchot's help, he succeeded in convincing Roosevelt to oppose the Smith compromise. Hitchcock did not learn of this turn of events until June 25, when Roosevelt, despite the secretary's strenuous objections, sent a formal request to the House Public Lands Committee asking that the Smith amendment be removed. The committee reported Flint's bill out the next day drawn according to TR's instructions, and the House promptly approved it. On June 28, five days after Flint's first late night call, the bill went to the president's desk for signature.

Roosevelt's decision to side with Los Angeles and the special interests which stood to profit from the city's scheme to exploit the water of a small agricultural community would seem to mark a significant lapse in policy for a president who is remembered today as trustbuster, friend of the little man, and early champion of the modern conservation movement. As Henry Pringle notes in his biography of the president, "Roosevelt's passionate interest in the national forests, in reclamation of arid western lands by irrigation, in conservation of water power and other natural resources, may well be considered as part of his campaign against the malefactors of great wealth. . . . His opposition to exploitation of water power was based on the conception, novel in that day, that this was the property of the people and should redound to their benefit."[44]

But, as John Morton Blum observes in *The Republican Roosevelt*, TR's policy was informed not so much by love for the weak as by a vision of Spencerian progression, the principles of Social Darwinism, and an overriding desire to establish order in a period of rapidly changing social relationships. His objective in battling the moneyed interests while favoring the formation of labor unions and agricultural associations was not the destruction of corporate wealth but rather the creation of "an equilibrium of consolidated interests over which government would preside." While his vision encompassed the details of individual cases of hardship, his eye was fixed ultimately upon the greater benefits for the nation which would proceed from such a balance of competing interests. Thus, Blum argues, "Roosevelt sponsored conservation not so much to preserve a domain for agriculture as to preserve and enhance the strength of the whole nation."[45]

In the case of the Los Angeles Aqueduct, the locus of the national interest seemed clear to Roosevelt. While he acknowledged that the concerns of the Owens Valley were "genuine," he concluded that this interest "must unfortunately be disregarded in view of the infinitely greater interest to be served by putting the water in Los Angeles." In a formal letter to Interior Secretary Hitchcock, drafted June 25, 1906, in the secretary's presence as "a record of our attitude in the Los Angeles water supply question," Roosevelt argued, "It is a hundred or thousand fold more important to state that this [water] is more valuable to the people as a whole if used by the city than if used by the people of the Owens Valley."[46]

For his part, Hitchcock focused upon the evils of the San Fernando syndicate, warning that the passage of Flint's bill without the Smith amendment would enable the city "to use the surplus of water thus acquired beyond the amount actually used for drinking purposes for some irrigation scheme."[47] Flint responded with the conventional argument that Los Angeles had to possess the surplus in order to retain the city's rights to it in the future, and he added that Smith's amendment was so faultily drafted that it might prohibit use of the water for domestic gardens in the city itself.

Roosevelt resolved the problem of the syndicate's interest after a fashion by insisting upon an amendment to the Flint bill which prohibited Los Angeles from selling the surplus to any private interest for resale as irrigation water. But, as the congressman who carried Flint's bill in the House observed, it was clear to the Public Lands Committee that the Roosevelt amendment "could not prevent the Los Angeles City Council from doing what it chose with the water. This water will belong absolutely to Los Angeles and the city council can do as it pleases with it—sell directly to private individuals or corporations for irrigation purposes, or sell to Pasadena or other surrounding towns for the same purposes, or for a water supply, or use it in any other way the council chooses." Smith himself agreed that, "It did not make any difference what became of the water after it was taken to the Los Angeles neighborhood."[48]

Roosevelt found further cause for his support of Flint's bill in the fact that it was opposed by "certain private power companies whose object evidently is for their own pecuniary interest to prevent the municipality from furnishing its own water." The Southern California Edison Company and the Los Angeles Gas and Electric Corporation, seeing their interests threatened by the proposed aqueduct, had joined in the back-room lobbying against the Flint legislation. This unfortunate identity of interest with the power companies proved fatal for the future of the Owens Valley, for, as Roosevelt observed of the power companies, "Their opposition seems to me to afford one of the strongest arguments for passing the law."[49]

Although the local power companies might have hoped to share in the general prosperity which aqueduct water would bring to Los Angeles, they feared more the competition from the municipal power that the project would generate. The dilemma posed by the aqueduct was especially acute in the case of the Pacific Light and Power Company, which was owned by Henry Huntington and directed by William G. Kerckhoff. Both were members of the San Fernando syndicate, and their interests were consequently divided between a proprietary fear of public power and the private gain they stood to make through the syndicate upon the project's completion. They reasoned that their problem could be resolved if the private power companies retained control of the power distribution system within the city. After the Flint bill had passed, Kerckhoff accordingly approached Mulholland to discuss a long-term lease of the power facilities on the aqueduct. Mulholland's view of the aqueduct as a wholly municipal enterprise, however, did not allow for such a compromise. He viewed Kerckhoff's proposal in the same light as Eaton's earlier advocacy of private ownership of the water itself, and he rejected Kerckhoff's overture just as firmly.[50]

Mulholland's stand on behalf of both public power and public water left the companies with no other option than to throw their weight against the second municipal bond election, scheduled for June 12, 1907, to provide the estimated $23 million needed for actual construction of the aqueduct. The campaign, however, was doomed from the outset. Every other business institution in the city supported the bonds, and the opposition lacked a creditable issue on which to hang its case. The project had already been approved by the panel of engineers called for in the 1905 bond election. The companies could scarcely attack Otis, Huntington, and Kerckhoff on the issue of a syndicate conspiracy, and public arguments for their own self-interests predictably carried little weight with the electorate. From the perspective of the Los Angeles voters, it was one thing for a group of special interests like the San Fernando syndicate to profit from a project which would yield greater benefits for all and quite another for the special interests combined in the power companies to stop the project altogether.

The leaders of the resistance to the aqueduct bonds of 1907 ultimately resorted to specious charges that the Owens River was polluted by unnatural concentrations of alkali. This campaign issue, easily and promptly disproved by chemical analysis, was promoted through the pages of the *Los Angeles Evening News,* a new paper set up under the editorship of Samuel T. Clover. In debunking the charges of "Alkali Sammy," Otis at the *Times* was scarcely moved to retorical heights he had reached in promoting the intial bond election.[51] Otis made one misstep on May 24, however, when he published a declaration that he had sold his interest in the San Fernando syndicate in February, 1905, and defied the "alligators" to prove him wrong. It was stupid for Otis to make a claim that Clover could so easily disprove by checking the public records of the syndicate's incorporation, and the personal embarrassment that resulted was unnecessary in view of the ineffectuality of Clover's campaign.

When Clover turned to attacking the syndicate, however, Kerckhoff formally withdrew from the fight he could not truly have wished to win, and the other power companies soon gave up, too. Without the contributions from the power companies which had kept his paper afloat after the other elements of the business community withdrew their advertising, Clover went out of business.[52] By the end of May, the *Times* reported, the only corporate opposition to the bond issue came from one J. D. Hooker, owner of a steel pipe manufacturing firm who hoped to convince the city to use his product for constructing the aqueduct rather than concrete.[53] On election day, the bond issue passed in every one of the city's 143 precincts, and the *Times* wryly observed, "The antis were as rare as a ham sandwich at a picnic of the sons of Levi."[54]

The burden of responsibility now descended upon Mulholland, the self-educated engineer whose judgment and ability had been made an issue in both the campaign of 1905 and 1907. Opponents of the project had been quick to point out that he had never constructed a waterworks of any size and that for the sixteen years he served as superintendent of the Los Angeles Water Company, he had scrupulously hued to the company line that there was no need for a water project of the kind he now proposed to build. Beginning in September, 1907, Mulholland thus began to fulfill what had been in part a vote of confidence in himself.

The Los Angeles Aqueduct was one of the largest municipal projects ever undertaken in modern times. In its original form, it extended 233 miles, included 142 tunnels totaling 53 miles in length, and took six years to complete. To service the construction work, 120 miles of railroad track and more than 500 miles of highways and trails had to be laid. Mulholland insisted that municipal rather than private contractors be employed wherever possible and, toward that end, the Bureau of the Los Angeles Aqueduct built its own cement plant, developed a special mix of cement, and constructed two hydro-electric plants to provide power to the project.[55] For the construction work itself, Mulholland devised a system of quotas under which bonuses were paid to each man who surpassed his quota for the day. In this way, the work proceeded rapidly, with new records for drilling being set and reset while the project as a whole remained safely within its projected budgetary limits.[56]

23. Lone Pine Bridge over Owens River (circa 1900) near Lone Pine Station. (Credit: Eastern California Museum.)

While Mulholland's crews worked their way across the mountains and desert, great political changes were sweeping Los Angeles which threatened to alter distribution plans for the aqueduct water. The Southern Pacific's domination of local politics had been broken, and the Republican party had split into Progressive and regular factions. In the spring of 1909, the Progressives succeed in electing Mayor George Alexander in a recall campaign during which the incumbent resigned just before election day. The Progressives posed no direct threat to the aqueduct, and Mayor Alexander promised nothing more radical than "honest business government," but the tide of reform was rising fast, and in the same election which saw Alexander take office an unfunded and virtually unknown Socialist candidate came within 1700 votes of victory.[57]

The anti-union zeal of Harrison Gray Otis had kept Los Angeles locked in a battle with organized labor ever since the typographers' strike of 1890. Following the Pullman Strike of 1894, Otis had founded the Merchants and Manufacturers Association to fight the threat of unionism. Businessmen who refused to join the organization found their credit cut off at the banks, and members who weakened in the face of union demands had their products boycotted by the association.[58] In 1910, the American Federation of Labor responded by establishing a unified labor council in Los Angeles to fight against the open shop in what they called "the scabbiest town on earth." Mayor Alexander and his Progressive allies on the city council, all of whom scrupulously avoided any contact with labor, struck back against the AFL with an ordinance drawn up by the Merchants and Manufacturers Association which prohibited picketing of any kind. Mass arrests followed, and in the mayoralty campaign of 1911, the union forces drew behind the candidacy of Job Harriman, Socialist nominee for governor in 1898 and for vice-president in 1900 and an early critic of the aqueduct during the bond election of 1907. In the primary election November 1, Harriman led the field and looked to be an easy victor over the incumbent Alexander in the general election scheduled for December 5.

The threat which the anticipated election of Job Harriman posed to Mulholland's project was, at best, indirect. With less than fifty miles yet to be constructed, Harriman could scarcely have ordered a halt to the aqueduct so near to its completion. But he did raise numerous charges concerning the safety of its design and the financing of its operation. More important, in Harriman's rhetoric the aqueduct intertwined with the schemes of the San Fernando syndicate to become a symbol of all that was corrupt in the incumbent administration. All of the charges made against the aqueduct in 1905 and 1907 were brought out again, and Harriman warned from the stump that if the San Fernando syndicate ever secured the water from the Owens Valley, the city would lose its right to regain it for municipal use. Harriman accordingly promised that if he could not stop the project, as mayor he would make certain that the syndicate never received a drop of water from the aqueduct.[59]

The mayoralty campaign of 1911 was thus considerably more significant to the party of interests behind the aqueduct than either of the bond elections of 1905 and 1907 had been because it raised the prospect of a complete change in the administration of public policy under a political movement in no way allied with the business community and its objectives. From the point of view of the *Los Angeles Times,* the issues in the election were clearly drawn: "The forces of law and order against Socialism—peace and prosperity against misery and chaos—the Stars and Stripes against the red flag."[60]

In response, the business community drew together to meet the threat in full force. Otis dropped his customary line of vituperation against Progressivism, and the operations of Mayor Alexander's Good Government League were suspended after the primary and its Progressive leaders absorbed into the regular Republican organization. In its place, Bradner Wells Lee, chairman of the County Republican Committee, and William M. Garland, president of the Realty Board, agreed to lead "a great, strictly non-partisan general committee unshackled by any partisan ties, embracing Democrats, Republicans, and Independents into one great party—the People—to crush in defeat the Socialist movement that is declared to be threatening the city's progress."[61]

While Harrison Gray Otis patrolled the streets in his private limousine with a cannon mounted on the hood and held forth daily against the "anarchic scum" who challenged his "Campaign to Save Los Angeles," the other major papers in town imposed a virtually total blackout on any news of Harriman's campaign events. Harriman's name appeared only in conjunction with predictions of the dreadful cost for the city if he were elected.

24. Fifty-two mule team hauling steel pipe to construction camp at Jawbone Siphon. (*Credit: Los Angeles Department of Water and Power.*)

Newspaper editorials warned variously that eastern investors would withdraw their support from municipal projects if a socialist took office; that the American Home would be undermined by hordes of "aliens" poised to rush into the city at the moment of Harriman's victory; that the city under Harriman would be no better than San Francisco, which was just then undergoing the revelation of scandals by Abe Ruff and the Union Labor party; and, finally, that since Harriman had won the primary in the first election at which women in the city had been permitted to vote, his ultimate victory would mean the death of women's suffrage as other states saw how women abused their franchise.

Mayor Alexander, rather than try to answer every charge against his conduct in office, barricaded himself in city hall and explained that the press of public business left him no time for speechifying. Similarly, all other city officials declined repeated requests from the Harriman camp to debate the question of "political and financial manipulation for the private interests of a few capitalists" in the construction of the aqueduct.[62]

The aqueduct, however, was not the only issue in the campaign of 1911. Of equal importance on the local scene, and far greater significance nationally, was the simultaneous trial of two brothers, James B. and John Joseph McNamara, on charges of having dynamited the offices of the *Los Angeles Times* on the night of October 1, 1910. Harriman himself was a member of the team of defense attorneys headed by Clarence Darrow, and throughout the city workers bore campaign buttons reading "McNamara's Innocent! Vote for Harriman!" Mayday, 1911, was declared McNamara Day, and huge supportive parades were organized in every major city across the country. Small contributions to the McNamara Defense Fund poured in from laboring men and women throughout the nation, and thousands came for the trial itself.

Darrow's problem, though few could be sure of it at the time, was that his clients were guilty. With the *Times* charging that Harriman was a member of the dynamite conspiracy and that Darrow was financing the Harriman campaign from the McNamara Defense Fund, Darrow realized that the election and his case were fatally intertwined and that any negotiated plea for his clients would have to be approved by Otis' allies in the business community. Darrow sent as his agent in these negotiations the journalist Lincoln Steffens who personally favored a guilty plea because he hoped thereby to see Darrow extend his concept of justifiable homicide as a defense against capital punishment to what Steffens saw as a greater principle of "justifiable dynamiting." Steffens' offer of a guilty plea met with favor in the inner councils of the Merchants and Manufacturers Association, and Otis was convinced to forego the pleasure of seeing the brothers hang. But, the business leaders demanded as their price for this agreement the defeat of Job Harriman. And so, on December 1, four days before the election, Darrow rose in court to announce a change of plea to guilty.[63]

The shock of Darrow's action was immediate and devastating. Darrow walked out of court that day on streets littered with discarded Harriman campaign buttons. Harriman himself had not been consulted on the settlement, and he read the doom of his hopes of election in the press next morning.[64] In one stroke, the business community had turned back the Socialist challenge and emerged from the conflict stronger than before. The Progressives had been forced to fall back upon the regular party machinery in their hour of need, and neither they nor the Socialists would ever mount a significant electoral challenge again. But the charges against the aqueduct had not been answered in the campaign of 1911, and they would be raised again, first by the embittered socialists and their allies in the labor movement, and later from a quarter the city officials had all but ignored, the Owens Valley itself.

## NOTES

1. Undoubtedly the most influential of the histories which advocate a conspiracy theory for the aqueduct was Morrow Mayo's *Los Angeles* (New York, 1933) a sensationalist tract which included a chapter on the aqueduct controversy under the title "The Rape of the Owens Valley." Mayo's influence can be read most clearly in Carey McWilliams' treatment of the subject in *Southern California Country: An Island on the Land* (New York, 1946), in numerous articles, speeches, and essays which appeared after the destruction of the Owens Valley, and in *Billion Dollar Blackjack: the Story of Corruption* and the *Los Angeles Times* (Beverly Hills, 1954), an intemperate attack on Harrison Gray Otis and his successors written by a former member of the State Board of Equalization, William G. Bonelli, just before he fled the country to avoid indictment. By 1950, as Remi Nadeau observed in his *Water Seekers* (Garden City, N.Y., 1950) Mayo's "wild charges

and inaccurate history" had been "tacitly accepted as fact" (pp. 127-128).

The film *Chinatown* proceeds on the assumption of a conspiracy. The story of the film is set in the midst of a bond election for a new municipal water project. The project is opposed by the city water engineer on the basis that its design would repeat the mistakes made in the construction of an earlier project which collapsed, causing considerable loss of life. The project is backed by a powerful local industrialist who once owned the city water supply in partnership with the current city water engineer. In the course of the film, it is discovered that the city's water is being secretly diverted to the sewers in order to create the illusion of a water shortage and that the water from the new project would benefit not the city but the semi-arid farmlands of the San Fernando Valley, which the backers of the project have been purchasing through forced sales in connivance with city officials. Each of these elements of the plot has a basis in the history of the aqueduct, but the sequence of events has been rearranged in the film, characters have been compressed and simplified, incidents of murder and incest have been added, and the whole had been updated to the 1930's.

2.    In "Joseph Barlow Lippincott and the Owens Valley Controversy: Time for Revision," *Southern California Quarterly,* 54 (Fall, 1972), Abraham Hoffman ably reviews the historiography of the controversy and the interdependence of the various authors who have treated the subject. Hoffman has been searching for correspondence relevant to the controversy for many years. In this article he describes his difficulties in this enterprise and presents one of his more significant finds, a letter from J. B. Lippincott in which Lippincott attempts to justify his actions with regard to the Owens Valley.

3.    In 1887, the California legislature passed the Wright Act which permitted fifty or more landowners to petition their County Board of Supervisors for the formation of a public irrigation district to be financed by the issuance of bonds and the imposition of taxes on the landowners to be served by the district. Although fifty public districts were formed in the three years following enactment of the Wright Act, few succeeded, and private companies chartered by the state continued to dominate water development through the first two decades of the twentieth century. See Ralph J. Roske, *Everyman's Eden* (New York, 1968), p. 409.

4.    The Los Angeles City Council initially intended to surrender the city's entire interest in its own water supply and would have done so had not Mayor Christobal Aquilar vetoed the lease in its original form. See Vincent Ostrom, *Water and Politics: A Story of Water Policies and Administration in the Development of Los Angeles* (Los Angeles,

1953), pp. 42-47. The rates which the company paid on its lease were permanently set in 1868, and the company successfully resisted subsequent attempts by the city to establish a more equitable charge for the use of the water during the latter decades of the lease. By the time the lease expired in 1898, the company was declaring regular 6 per cent dividends and had earned an estimated 10-35 per cent return on its investment. See Robert M. Fogelson, *The Fragmented Metropolis: Los Angeles 1850-1939* (Cambridge, Mass., 1967), p. 95.

5.   Ostrom, *Water and Politics*, p. 46, reports on J. B. Lippincott's authority that under the company's rate structure, the average family in Los Angeles paid $5 a year for water and $10 for company profits.

6.   The 1903 amendment to Article XVIII of the Los Angeles City Charter specified that each of the five members of the board should serve four-year staggered terms, and that no more than three of the five should come from one political party. In addition, the board controlled its own fund into which all of the revenues from the water system were deposited. See Los Angeles City, *Charter as Adopted January 1889 and Amended January 1903* (Los Angeles, 1903), pp. 58-60.

7.   The city may have had little choice with regard to retaining Mulholland. The Los Angeles Water Company kept few records, and when the members of the new city water board asked to see a map of the distribution system they had acquired, Mulholland replied that there was no map but that he could tell them anything they wanted to know. According to this story, which may have improved in the retelling, Mulholland was able to recall from memory the age, diameter, and length of every section of pipe in the company's 325-mile system, and he was the only source the city had for such information. See J. B. Lippincott, "William Mulholland—Engineer, Pioneer, Raconteur" Part II, *Civil Engineering,* 11:161-64 (March, 1941).

8.   First settled in the early 1860's by prospectors and stockmen, the Owens Valley had no sooner overcome the resident Indians than hard times descended on the region. In the 1870's, the area became a refuge for bandits, and as late as 1875, the outlaw Tiburcio Vasques commanded the highways of southern Inyo. Although mail service and a telegraph line were established in 1875 and 1876 respectively, the Owens Valley did not truly begin to share in the prosperity of the more settled regions of Nevada and California until the turn of the century. See Willie Arthur Chalfant, *The Story of Inyo* (Published by the Author, Second Revised Edition, 1933). Hereinafter, Chalfant, 2nd.

9.   *Sacramento Union,* March 30, 1927.

10.  The initial surveys by the Reclamation Service were made in June, 1903. In July, 21,000 acres of Owens Valley land were removed from entry; in August, an additional 436,480 acres; in October, 58,000

acres; and in January, 1904, a final 50,000 acres, for a total of 564,480 acres. Chalfant, 2nd, p. 339.

11. Lippincott's apologium to a family friend, Fernando Lungren, is dated September 19, 1905, and is reprinted in full in Hoffman, "Lippincott and Owens Valley Controversy," fn. 2. Lippincott commented, "If I have done any wrong in connection with this matter, it was in the writing of this report [on Southern California water, for which he was paid by Los Angeles.]" Lippincott explained, "I wrote this report because I considered it a public duty, because I wanted to help the city that I lived in for fifteen years, and because I believe it is the real purpose of these records that they should be used in aiding the best development of the country at large."

12. *Los Angeles Times*, August 5, 1905. A Miner's Inch, a unit of measurement employed by Southern California hydrographers of this period, was equivalent to .02 of a cubic foot per second flow. Over the course of a year, this proposed $1.5 million sale would have yielded approximately 217,138 acre feet of water to Los Angeles.

13. *Los Angeles Examiner*, August 5, 1905.

14. Quotation attributed to Lippincott by Nadeau, *Water Seekers*, 25.

15. Eaton discusses his plans for a cattle empire in the *Los Angeles Examiner*, July 30, 1905. In addition to the cattle, which were his to keep regardless of whether the aqueduct was approved, Eaton received $10 a day plus expenses for his efforts in securing options on behalf of Los Angeles. Chalfant, 2nd, p. 343, reports that it was understood at the time that Eaton only invested $30,000 of his own money to secure the option on Long Valley.

16. Lippincott, in his letter to Lungren (see footnotes 2 and 11) denies supplying Eaton with credentials and comments, "The allegation that these options were entered into under the assumption that they were given for the Reclamation Service may or may not be true, but certainly the Reclamation Service or myself have never in any manner, directly or indirectly, given these people to understand that this was the case. It was a conclusion which they jumped at themselves." Lippincott does admit sending Eaton a letter, but declares that it simply asked Eaton to report on his progress. Lippincott could not produce a copy of this letter at the time he wrote to Lungren, and Chalfant, 2nd, p. 342, states that the letter Eaton produced established him as Lippincott's agent in examining right-of-way applications for a federal power project in the valley. If Lippincott did not provide Eaton with the credentials of a federal agent, he was certainly aware of what Eaton was doing, because Lippincott told Lungren he had to tell Eaton to stop representing himself as a federal agent "on more than one occasion."

17. Arthur P. Davis to F. H. Newell, undated correspondence, quoted in

Chalfant, 2nd, p. 343. Davis' concern was prompted by an investigation of the service's action on the Owens Valley project by Acting Secretary of the Interior Thomas Ryan. Ryan, in turn, was acting on complaints concerning Eaton's activities which had been made to the Department of Interior and to the president by the registrar of the land office in Independence.

18. Lippincott to Lungren in Hoffman, "Lippincott and Valley Controversy."

19. Clausen estimated the total cost of the Reclamation Service project for the Owens Valley at $2,293,398. This included a reservoir and 140-foot dam at Long Valley and irrigation canals skirting the Sierra and White Mountain ranges on the west sides of the valley. Chalfant, 2nd, pp. 340-341.

20. Nadeau, *Water Seekers,* p. 28.

21. *Los Angeles Times,* July 29, 1905.

22. Ibid.

23. The Newell resolution was not recorded, but portions of it are quoted in Chalfant 2nd, p. 345, and in the *San Francisco Call,* April 28, 1924. Chalfant reports (p. 348) that the Reclamation Service spent $26,000 on its plans for the valley, for which it was reimbursed $14,000 by the city. Also, in the first edition of *The Story of Inyo,* published in 1922 (hereinafter Chalfant 1st), he states that Lippincott and an aide received $1,000 from the city in direct payments (p. 324).

24. Remi Nadeau, *Los Angeles* (New York, 1960),p. 69. See also Roske, *Everyman's Eden,* p. 415.

25. The *Examiner* was the only agency to provide the citizens of Los Angeles with a detailed map of the Owens Valley itself, which the paper's staff pieced together from topographic studies and published on August 20, 1905.

26. See, for example, *Los Angeles Examiner,* August 16, 18, 1905.

27. See, for example, *Los Angeles Examiner,* August 17, 28, 1905.

28. Erwin Cooper, *Aqueduct Empire* (Glendale, 1968), p. 60. Cooper uses 1895 as the starting date for the drought; Roske and Nadeau use 1892. Mulholland used both without partiality.

29. United States, Department of Agriculture, Weather Bureau, *Climactic Summary of the United States* (Washington, D.C., 1930), section 18, Southern California and Owens Valley, pp. 3-5, 17, 18.

30. Nadeau, *Water Seekers,* 20-21.

31. Rainfall in August, 1904, totaled 0.17 inches as compared with the average rainfall for August in the period 1891-1930 of 0.03 inches; the next greatest August rainfall in this four-year period occurred in 1901, 0.09 inches. There was no August rainfall at all in thirty-one of the forty years included in this survey.

32. Calculations for the period 1958-1973 and 1950-1973 are made from

the precipitation tables which appear in the *California Statistical Abstract* in the volumes for 1971-1974 and the comprehensive edition of 1970. Precipitation data is prepared by the California Department of Water Resources in cooperation with the United States Department of Commerce, Environmental Science Services Administration.

33. Mulholland's calculations were based on a total water supply estimated at 33-34 million gallons per day at a peak consumption rate of 190 gallons per capita. See *Los Angeles Examiner*, July 31, 1905. Nadeau, *Water Seekers*, p. 34, notes that critics of the project later charged that Mulholland diverted water from the city reservoirs into the sewers in order to create the illusion of a water famine. No such allegation ever reached print during the campaign of 1905, although the *Examiner*, on September 1, 1905, carried a story in conjunction with Mulholland's claim of drought which noted that the city was losing 24,000 gallons a day from leaks in the municipal high service reservoirs.

34. *Los Angeles Examiner*, August 2, 1905.

35. *Los Angeles Examiner*, July 30, 1905.

36. *Los Angeles Examiner*, August 15, 1905.

37. *Los Angeles Examiner*, August 16, 1905.

38. At the same time that the city began acquiring property in the Owens Valley, it initiated suits to prevent 200 ranchers in the San Fernando Valley from tapping the underground storage waters of the Los Angeles River. See *Los Angles Examiner*, August 20, 1905.

39. *Los Angeles Times*, August 25, 1905.

40. See *Los Angeles Examiner*, August 24, 25, 28, 1905.

41. See, for example, the comments printed in the *Examiner*, September 2, 1905, by H. W. Hellman, president of the Merchants National Bank, and C. Seligman of the M. A. Newark and Company calling for the creation of a "committee of large taxpayers" to investigate the project.

42. Swanberg describes the situation of the Hearst chain in the summer of 1905 as follows: "Every Hearstman from Boston to Los Angeles knew how the Chief had been bitten by the Presidential bug, and it subtracted something from their already limited integrity in reporting the news. Most of all, it affected the Chief himself. Before politics seized him he had taken a fierce pride in his journalistic achievements, outlandish though they often were. Now, Politician Hearst subtracted something from Editor Hearst. While it would not be quite fair to say that he now considered his newspapers simply as a means to reach the White House, that would be an important part of their function." W. A. Swanberg, *Citizen Hearst* (New York, 1961), pp. 221-222.

43. *Los Angeles Times*, June 23, 1906.

44. Henry F. Pringle, *Theodore Roosevelt* (New York, 1931), Harvest Books Edition, p. 302.

45. John Morton Blum, *The Republican Roosevelt* (New York, 1966), pp. 106-113.
46. Roosevelt's letter to Hitchcock is reprinted in full in the *Los Angeles Times*, June 28, 1906.
47. Ibid.
48. *Los Angeles Times*, June 29, 1906.
49. Roosevelt to Hitchcock, *Los Angeles Times*, June 28, 1906.
50. In 1911, the local power companies attempted to promote this same proposal once again in the form of an unsuccessful charter amendment which would have allowed the companies to buy power from the aqueduct and market it within the city, thereby saving Los Angeles the cost of building its own distribution system (See Fogelson, *Fragmented Metropolis,* 230-233). Mulholland, by this time, was safely removed from any position which would bring him into direct confrontation with the private power interests. In 1907, he retained E. F. Scattergood as the aqueduct electrical engineer. On Mulholland's recommendation, Scattergood was subsequently placed at the head of a separate bureau exclusively responsible for the distribution of aqueduct power. This division of responsibilities made practical sense because Mulholland had no expertise in the field of power generation. But it also proved politically fortunate for Mulholland, whose water programs were generally popular, while Scattergood met with intense opposition from certain segments of the business community and became the focus of controversy for many years. Ostrom, *Water and Politics,* pp. 83-84, describes this political division as follows: "Mulholland and the water bureau usually had the political support of the more conservative commercial and business organizations of the community. The Chamber of Commerce always supported a water bond and the *Los Angeles Times* always gave Mulholland a favorable press. . . . On the other hand, the power bureau was consistently opposed by a substantial group of the business community identified with the private utility companies. . . . Beginning in 1914, the *Los Angeles Times* opposed power bond issues as consistently as it supported water bond issues."
51. See for example, *Los Angeles Times*, May 20, 21, and 24, 1907.
52. *Los Angeles Herald*, June 4, 1907.
53. *Los Angeles Times*, May 26, 1907.
54. *Los Angeles Times*, June 13, 1907. The election was novel in that it marked an early appearance of the automobile in the strategy of modern campaigning. For the first time, the wealthier members of the community donated their new horseless carriages to ferry voters to and from the polls. The resulting turnout was the largest yet recorded for a special election in Los Angeles: 24,051 as compared with only 11,542 ballots cast in the first bond election two years earlier.
55. Mulholland enjoyed an estimated 20 per cent savings on construction

costs by relying on municipal employees rather than private contractors. The Bureau of the Los Angeles Aqueduct itself built all but eleven miles of the canal and drilled all but 1485 feet of tunnel. See Ostrom, *Water and Politics*, 94.

56. In his haste to get construction under way, however, Mulholland failed to secure his financing. Instead of waiting to accumulate funds from the bond sales, Mulholland arranged for advanced sales of the aqueduct securities to New York City bond merchants. As a result, he operated with a cash reserve sufficient to cover only thirty days of continued construction. In May, 1910, the bond market collapsed, and Mulholland was forced to lay off more than 70 per cent of his work force. These massive layoffs, in turn, brought increases in the unit prices charged for food by Mulholland's concessionaires on the project. The resulting dissatisfaction among the work crews provided a long-awaited opening for the radical Industrial Workers of the World, which began organizing the laborers on the aqueduct through the Western Federation of Miners. By November, Mulholland faced a strike along the entire length of the project, and order was restored only when the bond market recovered in the middle of 1911.

57. For an overall review of the Alexander administration, see Martin J. Schiesl, "Progressive Reform in Los Angeles under Mayor Alexander, 1909-1913" *California Historical Quarterly,* 54 (Spring, 1975), pp. 37-56. The promise of "honest business government" is drawn from George Alexander, "What I am Going to Do" *Pacific Outlook*, April 3, 1909.

58. Roske, *Everyman's Eden*, 475.

59. The relatively mild Socialist platform on which Harriman campaigned was drafted by a New Haven clergyman, Alexander Irvine, who had been driven from his pulpit for preaching Christian Socialism. The platform is reprinted in Irvine's *Revolution in Los Angeles* (Los Angeles, 1911), p. 84.

60. *Los Angeles Times*, November 1, 1911.

61. *Los Angeles Herald*, November 4, 1911.

62. *Los Angeles Herald*, November 9, 1911.

63. The history of the trial has been told often and well from a wide range of perspectives. The way in which Darrow's negotiations were intertwined with the course of Harriman's campaign is brought out in particular detail in Irving Stone's biography, *Clarence Darrow for the Defense* (Garden City, N.Y., 1943), pp. 248-343.

64. Darrow expressed regret at this effect of his decision, but he explained, "The lives of my clients were at stake, and I had no right or inclination to consider anything but them. I could not tell Mr. Harriman; it would place him in the position of either deserting his party or letting one client go to almost certain death, which he could not do." Clarence Darrow, *The Story of My Life* (New York, 1932), p. 184.

In "The Politics of Exploitation", Part II of "The Politics of California Water: Owens Valley and the Los Angeles Aqueduct, 1900-1927" William Kahrl describes how the delivery of Owens Valley water to Los Angeles fueled the growth of Los Angeles: "the city's population increased twelvefold between 1900 and 1930 while its land area multiplied by ten." With this growth, and the continued expansion of its Owens Valley land holdings, Los Angeles faced conflict and controversy on several fronts.

"The Politics of California Water: Owens Valley and the Los Angeles Aqueduct, 1900-1927" by William L. Kahrl. *California Historical Quarterly.* Vol 55, No. 2 (Summer, 1976). Reprinted by permission of the California Historical Society.

# THE POLITICS OF CALIFORNIA WATER
## Owens Valley
## and the
## Los Angeles Aqueduct, 1900-1927
## Part II

by William L. Kahrl

## II. The Politics of Exploitation

Throughout the campaigns in Los Angeles that gave birth in 1913 to the Los Angeles Aqueduct, no voice was ever raised on behalf of the Owens Valley, the distant source of the prized water. As vigorous as the debate became, its terms were at all times limited to the interests of the City of Los Angeles. In 1906 the competing interests of the two communities clashed on the floor of the United States Congress, but the Owens Valley ranchers were outmaneuvered by the city water planners who successfully encouraged President Theodore Roosevelt to support the proposed project.[1] The story of the valley's destruction over the next twenty years is in part the story of the ranchers' continuing failure to find a forum in which to gain a fair hearing for their plight.

In 1907, the ranchers joined in protest once again at the meeting of the National Irrigation Congress in Sacramento. They could not have chosen a worse event for the presentation of their case, however, for the Irrigation Congress was one of several national organizations created at this time to back Roosevelt's conservationist policies described by the slogan, "Save the forests, store the floods, reclaim the deserts, make homes on the land."[2] In Sacramento as in Washington the year before, the hapless Owens Valley ranchers found themselves allied with the selfish interests of the private land and power

155

companies in opposition to "hysterical conservationism."[3] They were derided in the meeting and the press as "kickers" of a worthy principle, and as the *San Francisco Call* observed of the debates, "Anybody here who plays tennis at the White House can have anything he wants from these people and the kickers had no more chance than a snowball."[4]

In both instances, the ranchers were not seeking to stop the project but only to assure that their access to the Owens River streamflows would be protected. Unable to affect development of the aqueduct, however, the ranchers watched helplessly as Los Angeles gained virtually complete control over future settlement in the Owens Valley. When the Department of the Interior formally dropped its plans for a reclamation project on the Owens River immediately after Los Angeles passed the bond issue for aqueduct construction in 1907, the half-million acres of valley land withdrawn from settlement under the Homestead Act by the Reclamation Service were not returned to entry. Instead, along with all its maps and surveys, the Reclamation Service gave Los Angeles control of the storage rights which the Owens Valley ranchers had so willingly signed over to the federal government in 1903.[5]

Opportunities for settlement in the valley were further restricted in 1908, when Gifford Pinchot, head of the Forest Service, extended the borders of the Sierra National Forest Reserve over an additional 275,000 acres of valley land, despite the fact that no trees grew on this land. Henceforth all applications from the ranchers for settlement or water storage on the federally protected lands were referred to Los Angeles, where they met certain rejection.[6]

"This is not a government by legislation; it is a government by strangulation," complained the congressman from Inyo County, Sylvester Smith.[7]

Although President Taft did repeal Pinchot's order establishing a forest preserve in the treeless valley in February, 1911, the ranchers had determined by this time that they would have to bargain for their future with Los Angeles. In 1910, they had opened negotiations with the city officials for an equitable division of water within the valley.

25. Cascades where the Los Angeles Aqueduct empties into the north end of the San Fernando Valley. Dedication ceremony, 1913. (*Credit: Los Angeles Department of Water and Power.*)

The prospects for an accommodation between Los Angeles and the Owens Valley were better in 1910 than they would ever be again. Even though the aqueduct had been under construction for three years by this time, Los Angeles had still not developed a policy for disposing of the great surplus of water which the aqueduct would provide. From September 20 to October 7, the city council held public hearings twice a week on the question of what should be done with the excess water after the city's immediate needs had been met. Although there was general agreement that the city should not alienate its existing rights to the Owens River water without a two-thirds vote of approval by the electorate, opinions divided as to whether the city should sell the surplus water for the highest possible return or use the surplus as an instrument of a broader policy for the annexation and consolidation of outlying areas.

Mayor George Alexander, who favored the expansion of the city to include the entire county of Los Angeles, formed a special commission in November to study both the disposition of the surplus and the problem of consolidation. Early in 1911, the Public Service Commission, which had charge of the city's water program, established its own panel of consulting engineers to estimate the amount of the surplus and to formulate a program for its disposal.[8] In their report released a few months later, the engineers advised that the opening of the aqueduct would provide the city with four times as much water as it could consume, leaving an excess of at least 360 second-feet, enough to irrigate approximately 135,000 acres of land each year.[9] Although this was an amount sufficient to service the needs of the Owens Valley twice over, such an application of the surplus was never seriously entertained by the panel. Instead, their report—named for its principal signators the Quinton-Code-Hamlin Report—recommended a general policy for city expansion. Under this policy, any area outside the city limits that desired to share in the surplus would have to agree to be annexed to the city as a condition of receipt of the water. Water would not be supplied to those areas where there was not a "reasonable assurance" of ultimate annexation. In addition, any area receiving water from the aqueduct would be required to pay in advance the cost of constructing a distribution system according to city specifications and to assume as well a proportionate share of the tax burden for the costs of the aqueduct.

The appearance of the Quinton-Code-Hamlin Report stirred immediate controversy, not for the general policies it advocated, but for a specific recommendation within the report that the San Fernando Valley receive first consideration in the allocation of surplus waters. The engineers proposed that fully three-fourths of the surplus be devoted to irrigation in the San Fernando Valley and observed that since the valley drained into the Los Angeles River, the city would ultimately regain a portion of the water assigned to the valley for reuse.[10]

Ever since the first aqueduct bond election in 1905, the aqueduct and the San Fernando Valley had been linked by charges of municipal corruption involving a syndicate of speculators in San Fernando properties which had been actively preparing for the advent of aqueduct water. Formed in 1904 as the San Fernando Mission Land Company to purchase 16,000 acres in the northern part of the valley for $524,000, the syndicate included most prominently among its ten original members: Henry Huntington, by 1911 the largest individual landowner in Southern California; E. H. Harriman, owner of the Southern, Central, and Union Pacific railroads, among others; and Harrison Gray Otis, publisher of the *Los Angeles Times*. These ten were joined by Moses Sherman, a local street-railway magnate and member of the city water board, and Harry Chandler, Otis' son-in-law and heir apparent at the *Times*. Chandler brought with him an additional 2300 acres purchased for $200,000 which made the company's holdings predominant in the upper valley.[11]

In 1909, with Harriman dead and Huntington entering semi-retirement, Otis, Chandler, and Sherman extended their interests into the southern portion of the valley. In September, they acquired an option on 47,500 acres held by the Los Angeles Farm and Milling Company at a total purchase price of $2.5 million. For this enterprise, the three members of the northern syndicate formed the Los Angeles Suburban Homes Company in partnership with Otto Brant, vice-president and general manager of the Title Insurance and Trust Company, and H. J. Whitley, a local builder and leader in the effort to consolidate Hollywood, who served as general manager of the company. The company exercised its option in 1910 and on March 14, 1911, filed a subdivision map for Tract 1000, the largest single development undertaken in Los Angeles history until that time.[12]

As the increasing prices which the syndicate companies had to pay for their acquisitions indicate, land values were escalating rapidly in the semi-arid San Fernando region. Even though the aqueduct would not be completed for another two years, the Los Angeles Suburban Homes Company and its subsidiaries had already embarked upon a brisk and raucous landsales program by the time the Quinton-Code-Hamlin Report appeared.[13] In the context of these events, the water engineers' recommendation that the San Fernando Valley should receive more than twice as much water from the aqueduct as Los Angeles gave sudden new credence to the charge that the project had been intended to benefit the syndicate rather than the city from the very beginning.

In the hard-fought mayoralty election that fall, such charges figured prominently as an issue which very nearly swept the Socialist party into office.[14] Once the regular Republican organization had turned back the Socialist challenge, however, William Mulholland called for a thorough investigation of his project, either by a committee of the city council or by a panel of citizens. The chamber of commerce at first declined to participate, and the council, acting on a recommendation from Mayor Alexander, appointed a five-member investigating committee that included two Socialists, a number deemed proportionate to the number of votes cast for the Socialist candidate in the last election. Almost immediately, the council reconsidered this egalitarian gesture, removed the two Socialists, and attempted to force the resignation of a third, leftward-leaning appointee. The Socialists responded with an initiative ordinance, passed May 29, 1912, which established a new committee funded separately from the council's control. This panel included two Socialists as well as the apostate council appointee, plus two members approved by the council and the chamber of commerce.

By mid-July, the two original council appointees had resigned, declaring that they "could not retain their self-respect and remain of the body." To their minority report, which dealt largely with technical questions concerning the physical construction of the aqueduct, they added the conclusion that "there is not a single thing the matter with that aqueduct except the knockers who are attempting to bring discredit upon a magnificent undertaking and upon men who wrought even better than they know."[15]

26. Excavation for construction of the Los Angeles Aqueduct, Owens Valley. Russell Spainhower, top left. Others not identified. *(Credit: Eastern California Museum.)*

The three remaining investigators published their report at the end of August, a voluminous, free-swinging attack upon the aqueduct in every aspect of its conception and construction. The radicals displayed a catholic enthusiasm for charges of every kind, and in their report, relatively trivial complaints—about the quality of food served to the aqueduct construction crews, the consistency of the cement used, and the danger of pollution caused by cows falling into the open canals—jostled for attention with more serious charges involving Mulholland's alleged failure to develop the Los Angeles watershed fully before seeking an alternate water source. Although the report fastened upon the peculiarities of Mulholland's contract with Fred Eaton for the purchase of Long Valley and called for the indictment of both men if Eaton did not return his cattle and deed to the city the remainder of the Long Valley property, the report concluded on the most critical question: "No direct evidence of graft had been developed."[16]

The confusing outcome of the investigation satisfied none of the participants in the controversy. Although no action was taken on the charges contained in the majority report, neither the minority report's conclusions nor the radicals' exoneration of Mulholland and his staff succeeded in silencing the debate over syndicate corruption. Immediately after the release of the majority report in September, a member of Mayor Alexander's special committee on consolidation and the water surplus, S. C. Graham, offered an alternative to the policies advocated by Quinton, Code, and Hamlin. Rather than applying the surplus in a way that would directly benefit syndicate speculation in the San Fernando Valley, Graham proposed that the city simply sell the surplus for the highest rates it could get and turn a profit on the aqueduct as quickly as possible. The city council approved the Graham Plan two weeks later for submission on the November ballot as a referendum. With the support of Mayor Alexander's Progressives, the issue was approved by the electorate two to one.

In contrast to the Quinton-Code-Hamlin proposal, which would have required recipients of the surplus water to build their own distribution systems, implementation of the Graham Plan depended upon the approval of $8.4 million in municipal bonds to build conduits to the outlying regions that could afford the city's rates.[17] On January 8, 1913, the council approved the submission of the bond issues in a special election called for

February 25. Mulholland at this point declared his opposition to the Graham Plan and began to campaign publicly against passage of the bonds. This was a bold move for a public employee, because Mulholland was taking a stand against the policies of the Alexander administration and his employers on the Public Service Commission. Graham was himself a member of the commission, and the board had already rejected Mulholland's request that the Quinton-Code-Hamlin proposal be placed on the same ballot with the Graham bonds. By taking a role in the campaign, Mulholland adopted the Quinton-Code-Hamlin policies as his own and thereby opened himself to the charge that he was working to advance the interests of the San Fernando syndicate.

Graham, joined by the president of the Public Service Commission, F. G. Henderson, led the fight for the bonds, arguing that implementation of the plan offered the best means of defusing the charges of a syndicate plot behind the aqueduct. Moreover, the Graham Plan for turning a quick profit by devoting the surplus to its highest economic use sounded like good business practice, a point which appealed to both Alexander's Progressive supporters and the regular wing of the Republican party.[18]

Mulholland advocated a broader vision for the municipal enterprise he had begun with the construction of the aqueduct and argued that the surplus should go to support the sustained growth and expansion of the city. Annexation, which would require the granting of long-term rights for the use of the municipal water supply, was antithetical to the Graham Plan. Therefore, Mulholland charged, the implementation of the Graham Plan would both destroy the possibility for a consistent policy of municipal growth and work a "base deception" upon the recipients of the surplus.[19]

The genius of the Graham Plan lay in "an automatic process" by which any person who contracted to receive surplus water could be subsequently priced out of the water market "whenever the public service desired to receive the water." By forcing such "voluntary" withdrawals of service, Graham argued that the city could recover its water at any time "without controversy and without the payment of damages for improvements."[20] Mulholland opposed the cruelties involved in such a policy, contending that "water once put on the land should never be removed."[21]

As the campaign became more heated, the city council repeatedly delayed the date of the election. But when the votes were finally counted on April 15, 1913, Mulholland's gamble paid off, and the bonds on which the Graham Plan depended were turned down. In the mayoralty election two months later, the Progressives collapsed in disarray, and the new mayor, Henry Rose, who had argued against Mulholland's annexation proposals during the campaign, switched his position soon after taking office July 1. On August 29, 1913, the Public Service Commission formally adopted the policies of the Quinton-Code-Hamlin Report, thereby opening the way to a decade of massive annexations to the City of Los Angeles.

Throughout this extended struggle over city policy for the disposal of the surplus, Mulholland's negotiations with the Owens Valley ranchers continued. In May, 1913, a tentative agreement was reached which would have allowed the ranchers to draw enough water to continue operation of their existing irrigation systems.[22] But the conditions favoring a peaceful settlement that existed in 1910 had changed drastically by this time. The Graham bonds had been defeated, and the subsequent adoption of the Quinton-Code-Hamlin Report in the months following this tentative agreement meant that the needs of the San Fernando Valley would henceforth take precedence over those of the Owens Valley. Consequently, when one of the Socialist members of the aqueduct investigating committee filed suit to enjoin the city from formalizing its agreement with the ranchers on the grounds that the city would thereby be forfeiting a portion of its rights to the Owens Valley water, Mulholland did not bother to contest it. The agreement collapsed, and further negotiations were suspended while Mulholland began the lengthy process of obtaining exact measurements of the actual diversions the ranchers would require.

Thus, the opening of the aqueduct on November 5, 1913, effectively sealed the fate of the Owens Valley as it marked the start of Mulholland's negotiations with the San Fernando interests over the delivery of the surplus. Despite acrimonious resistance from the new towns of the San Fernando Valley, Mulholland insisted upon annexation as a condition for their receipt of the water. In support of his case, he cited not only city policy as adopted from the Quinton-Code-Hamlin Report but also the terms of the original federal grant of a right-of-way for the aqueduct, which specified that the surplus water from the project could be used for irrigation only within the boundaries of the city.[23] Mulholland's use of the federal statute to force the communities of the San Fernando Valley to join Los Angeles is ironic in view of the fact that these provisions of the act had been inserted at President Roosevelt's request for the express purpose of assuring that the aqueduct would not be used for the benefit of the San Fernando syndicate.[24] In exchange for the surrender of independence, however, the San Fernando Valley received favorable consideration in the setting of rates for the aqueduct water with the result that the valley paid substantially less for its water than any other area annexed by the city in this period.[25]

With the annexation of the first major sections of San Fernando and Palms in May, 1915, Los Angeles more than doubled in size from 108 to 285 square miles. Subsequent additions in 1916 and 1917 brought the city's total land area to more than 350 square miles, a rate of expansion supported entirely by the introduction of the aqueduct water.[26]

By 1920, when the city had expanded to 364 square miles, Mulholland had reason to worry that the pace of annexation had already over-reached the project's capacity of supply. With regard to supplying water for domestic use, the problem was more potential than real. The annexed areas were largely uninhabited, and the 266 square miles added to the city between 1915 and 1920 increased the city's population by only 12,701. But, with the opening of the Panama Canal in 1914, Los Angeles had already begun to emerge as the premier port and commercial center on the West Coast, and the end of World War I brought a flood of new immigrants to the city at the rate of 100,000 per year.[27]

With regard to water for irrigation, on the other hand, the problem was already acute and centered almost entirely on the changes in agricultural production that had occurred in the San Fernando Valley since the introduction of aqueduct water. The city water engineers had originally prepared their plans for supplying water to the San Fernando Valley on the assumption that the valley's agricultural economy would continue to be based upon tree crops, which required only intermittent irrigation over a long season. When the first aqueduct water was delivered at the end of May, 1915, the valley had only 10,000 acres under irrigation, a total which increased to 18,000 acres in the next year. In 1917 and 1918, however, wartime demand brought a rapid expansion in agricultural production, and the irrigated area in the valley extended to cover 45,000 and then 75,000 acres. In addition, the crops changed; instead of trees, large sections of the valley were given over to the more water-intensive production of beans, potatoes, and truck garden crops. As a result, during periods of peak irrigation demand, Los Angeles had to supply the valley with a third again as much water as the entire surplus from the aqueduct, an amount which exceeded at times the total mean flow of the Owens River.[28]

Mulholland's problems of supply were further complicated by the fact that in his original design of the aqueduct, he had failed to include sufficient reservoir capacity to store the winter flows from the High Sierra. Hence, in 1921, he proposed a $3 million bond issue for the improvement of the San Fernando irrigation system and the expansion of reservoirs at the lower end of the aqueduct. Intense opposition from the labor-oriented *Los Angeles Record*, which campaigned against the bonds on the issue of syndicate corruption, handed Mulholland his first defeat in a water bond election.

As a result of this setback, Mulholland was forced to turn back to the Owens Valley, where the city, under the terms of its original agreement with Fred Eaton, already possessed the right to construct a small reservoir at the headwaters of the Owens River. The calculation of the Owens Valley's needs for irrigation water, begun in 1913, was rapidly finalized in a form satisfactory to the ranchers, and the city once again offered to guarantee sufficient water, based on these calculations, to continue agricultural production in the valley at its existing level. Such a promise was essential because the construction of a dam on Eaton's property at Long Valley would have interfered with the right of all the downstream owners, including those in the Owens Valley, to the full use of the river flow. Such rights at this time were held inviolate by the California courts, and so, to avoid litigation, Los Angeles had to secure unanimous approval of its proposal from all the downstream owners.[29]

The possibility for such a uniform agreement, however, had been foreclosed by the events succeeding the collapse of Mulholland's friendship with Eaton several years earlier. Eaton's original agreement with the city allowed an easement sufficient for the construction of a 100-foot dam in Long Valley. While the aqueduct was still under construction, Eaton had offered to sell Los Angeles the remainder of his holdings at a price in excess of $1 million. Because the city had already paid the entire purchase price of Eaton's ranch for control of the water rights and only 20 per cent of the land, Mulholland considered this second proposal excessive, and he rebuffed his old friend declaring, "I'll buy Long Valley three years after Fred Eaton is dead."[30]

An arrangement whereby Mulholland would secure control of Long Valley only over his dead body was perfectly acceptable to Fred Eaton as well. Embittered, at dagger's point with the city, and a pariah in the valley he had betrayed, Eaton withdrew to his cattle ranch, refusing even to attend the dedication ceremonies for the aqueduct he had fathered. Instead, Eaton returned to his former dreams of private development of the Owens River and opened negotiations with a number of private power companies for the construction of a generating station below the Long Valley dam site. Although Eaton failed to profit from the deal, the Southern Sierra Power Company did succeed in obtaining a privately held site located at the point of the greatest power drop in the middle of the Owens Gorge. This acquisition blocked the completion of a power generating plant which Los Angeles had itself begun in the gorge in 1915.

Late in 1921, the city gained the support of the Bureau of Reclamation for a joint project at Haiwee Reservoir which would have enabled the city to develop its power project without going through the gorge by tunneling instead through the Mono Craters. But, this project demanded the diversion of two creeks behind a 150-foot dam at Long Valley while Eaton's original agreement with the city allowed for the construction of only a 100-foot dam.

The city thus found itself trapped in a multiple stalemate. The city could not proceed with its own public power development project without either gaining possession of the key site in the gorge owned by the Southern Sierra Power Company or making an arrangement with Eaton for a 150-foot dam at Long Valley. The development of a private power project by the southern Sierra Power Company, on the other hand, could not proceed unless the city constructed a dam at Long Valley to assure an adequate water flow. The development of a dam and reservoir at Long Valley, in turn, depended upon a resolution of the water rights problem. And, the competing water needs of the city, the ranchers, and the private power developers could not be met unless the city paid Fred Eaton's price, which Mulholland would not do.

Mulholland chose instead to begin construction on a 100-foot dam while at the same time instituting proceedings to condemn the water rights of the power company and to obtain a right-of-way across its property. A party of Owens Valley ranchers, later joined by Eaton, immediately filed suit to stop the small dam, which they feared would be insufficient to supply the water the city had promised them. When the United States Circuit Court of Appeals in 1922 turned down the city's action against the power company, Mulholland dropped the project altogether.[31]

With the failure of the Long Valley project and the advent of a prolonged period of drought beginning in the winter of 1921-22, Mulholland embarked upon a three-part program for the preservation of the city's continued growth and prosperity. For the long term, he looked toward the development of another new source of water on the Colorado River, where federal engineers were preparing preliminary surveys for a dam in Boulder Canyon. For the short term, he began to advocate a slowdown in the city's annexation policies; the annual report of the Public Service Commission in 1922, for example, for the first time warned against further expansion of the city limits, recommending instead that future annexations be confined to those territories which would "tend to make the city's outline more symmetrical."[32] These two policies complemented one another, for each area which was denied access to the aqueduct water by reason of Mulholland's new policy of symmetry became a ready candidate for enlistment in the Metropolitan Water District that Mulholland was forming to underwrite the costs of a connection to the Boulder Canyon project.

Meanwhile, in the Owens Valley, Mulholland moved to assure Los Angeles' total control of the valley water supply. The city initiated a new series of land acquisitions, focusing upon the key properties which controlled points of access to the river so that the less favorably situated ranchers inland could be cut off from their water supply. Further, the Reclamation Service was hired to return to the valley to make soundings for the drilling of pump wells in the Independence area.[33] When the ranchers discovered that their underground water supply was being drained off by pumps on adjacent properties owned by the city, they appealed first to the County Board of Supervisors and then to the courts. In each case where suit was brought, an injunction was issued which the city invariably vacated by the simple expedient of buying off the affected property.[34] Individual ranchers along the river who resisted the blandishments of the city agents and built their own irrigation ditches and storage dams had their ditches cut and dams blown up by city work crews.[35]

Residents of the Owens Valley recall that the Owens Valley was "still a beautiful agricultural area" as late as August, 1918.[36] But as Los Angeles grew and flourished in the early 1920's, hard times descended on the valley. Los Angeles' control over future settlement badly undermined the valley's credit. Local banks became over-extended, while the national and state banks that might have provided farm relief withdrew from the area altogether. Even the State Veterans Welfare Commission refused loans to qualified veterans who wished to locate in the valley.[37]

Some valley residents continued to dream of a brighter future. Between 1922 and 1925, for example, the town of Bishop constructed a new high school, American Legion Hall, and Masonic Temple, while a farmers' cooperative in Laws built a large new crop warehouse. A locally written history published in 1922 concluded on a hopeful note as it observed of the city officials: "We shall gladly list with them the professions of amity, whenever by meeting the just and reasonable demands of Owens Valley, the city shall show that any consideration it may extend arises from the sense of equity, and not merely as an incident in securing some further concession."[38]

With its people thus divided between hope and despair, the Owens Valley was ill-equipped to meet Mulholland's new policy of militancy in the early 1920's. The valley ranchers lacked the financial resources and singleness of purpose that the city officials could marshal. Leadership of the the valley's resistance to the city's onslaught fell to the brothers Wilfred and Mark Watterson, whose string of local banks united the principal farming communities of the Owens Valley.[39]

Under the leadership of the Wattersons, the ranchers served by the four major irrigation canals of the upper valley voted on December 26, 1922, to form a consolidated irrigation district

27. Hauling equipment for construction of Los Angeles Aqueduct. *(Credit: Eastern California Museum.)*

through which to deal with Los Angeles in united strength. Before the plan could be confirmed, the city struck back by buying out the owner of the oldest and largest upstream irrigation canal and by bringing suit to block the sale of bonds by the Wattersons' district. As Los Angeles pressed ahead with its purchases in the upper valley, the ranchers responded by increasing their diversions downstream. While armed guards kept watch over the ranchers' diversion canals, the city found itself confronted with steadily escalating demands for the cost of the properties it wished to buy.

In March, 1924, the residents of Bishop banded together to demand a total of $8 million for their collective holdings, land and water combined, plus $750,000 in "reparations" to the local merchants for the trade they would lose from the block sale of their community. The Bishop organization made its offer not to Mulholland but to a delegation from the San Fernando Valley where Mulholland had been restricting the use of aqueduct water needed for the summer season's crops. To make matters worse for Mulholland, the Hearst press on April 21 returned to the story it had once discarded and began a twelve-part series in the *San Francisco Call*  which detailed the plight of the Owens Valley at the hands of Los Angeles.[40]

Mulholland returned from negotiations in Washington over the Boulder Canyon project to deal severely with this multifold challenge to his authority.  He blocked the proposed deal between the residents of Bishop and the San Fernando Valley and continued in effect his prohibition on the use of aqueduct water for irrigation in the San Fernando Valley. He publicly declared his adamant opposition to the payment of reparations. And, on May 10, he filed suit to prevent the ranchers from continuing their diversions of Owens River water.

Mulholland's aggressively strong stand helped to bring forward the more violent elements within the Owens Valley communities. The anger of the local ranchers had proven a ripe field opportunity for the Klu Klux Klan, then resurgent across the nation and organizing on a wide range of populist and agrarian issues.  As relations with Los Angeles steadily worsened through the summer months of 1923 and spring of 1924, midnight visitations by large bands of armed men upon the homes of those who opposed the Wattersons' irrigation district became more frequent.[41] Finally, in the early morning hours of May 21, 1924, two weeks after the announcement of Mulholland's suit, a band of forty men planted three boxes of dynamite along the aqueduct and blew a hole in the city's concrete ditch.

The effect of this attack was electric. Hearst's series in the *Call* had helped to awaken the general public to what was happening in the Owens Valley; the first explosion on the aqueduct now brought a flood of reporters from all over the state to study the situation. In Los Angeles, although the *Times* did recall Hearst's infamous association with the war with Spain as it blamed the *Call* series for inciting the violence, Mulholland found support for his policies eroding. On June 24, the *Los Angeles Record,* long hostile to Mulholland and the aqueduct, began a series of editorials demanding the immediate construction of the Long Valley dam, fair settlements with the Owens Valley ranchers, and Mulholland's resignation.[42] In July, Los Angeles Mayor George E. Cryer returned from a personal tour of the Owens Valley recommending that the city buy up the entire valley either through direct negotiations or arbitration.

Mulholland and the Public Service Commission determined to buck the mayor while still giving the appearance of attempted accommodation with the valley ranchers. Not only did they reject the mayor's suggestion for arbitration, a proposal which the ranchers supported, but they also suspended all negotiations for land purchases in the valley. Instead, the commission on October 14 abruptly reversed its prior policies and offered an irrigation plan designed to keep 30,000 acres of the valley green. This proposal, based on a report by J. B. Lippincott, also offered the city's assistance in constructing a highway to the valley "to make the scenic region accessible to tourist travel which should be profitable to the valley and its citizens."[43]

This offer of an apparent compromise was totally unacceptable to the valley ranchers. Given its authorship by Lippincott, the valley's first betrayer, the proposal was suspect from the outset. The ranchers had heard such promises from the city before in 1913 and 1921, and this one came too late. Acceptance of the proposal would have meant the denial of reparations and the destruction of the Wattersons' irrigation district. The Wattersons' strategy, on the other hand, recognized that the city and valley were competitors for the

Owens River water in a contest the valley could not win. The strategy assumed that the valley would have to sell out and was geared, in consequence, at obtaining the best price possible. The ranchers were no longer fighting for their homes, only for money.

On November 16, 1924, one month after Los Angeles made its new offer, the ranchers seized the Alabama Gates which controlled the main flow of water into the aqueduct. In open rebellion, they shut the gates and sent the water spilling back into the river bed. For four days the ranchers held the gates, supported by the cheers of hundreds of valley residents. Meanwhile, in Los Angeles, pressures mounted upon Mulholland to reach an amicable settlement. On November 18, the *Los Angeles Times* deserted him, noting editorially that the ranchers were not anarchists but honest citizens of the hardy stock of pioneers who made California great: "They have put themselves hopelessly in the wrong by taking the law into their own hands, but that is not to say that there has not been a measure of justice on their side of this argument." The *Times* concluded by calling upon the Public Service Commission to pay for the suffering its policies had caused: "It is not a time to drive the hardest possible bargain. The city can afford to be liberal in its settlement with these pioneers whose work of half a century it will undo."

On November 20 the siege at the Alabama Gates ended when the Los Angeles bankers, through their Joint Clearing House Association, offered to intercede with the city to achieve a settlement. The Wattersons, speaking for the valley, proposed compulsory arbitration or a cash settlement including reparations.[44] The Public Service Commission refused to consider either course. On January 19, 1925, the commission rescinded its offer to keep 30,000 acres of the valley green and ordered a renewal of its purchasing program.

Despite the failure of the bankers' efforts at mediation, the so-called California Civil War of 1924 did help to focus public attention on the valley's plight. The valley ranchers no longer had to deal exclusively with Los Angeles but could instead carry their complaint to the larger forum of public opinion in an effort to obtain crucial relief from the state government. After the seizure of the Alabama Gates, Governor Friend W. Richardson dispatched the state engineer, Wilbur F. McClure, to study the situation. McClure's report submitted January 9, 1925, took the ranchers' side in the dispute over reparations. In May, the legislature followed through with the adoption of a bill specifically allowing the payment of reparations, thereby undercutting Mulholland's claim that he had no legal right to compensate valley merchants for their losses.[45]

The pressure of population growth in Los Angeles had worked to end any prospect of the valley's long-term survival, but, once the ranchers accepted this conclusion, these same pressures turned to their advantage and forced Mulholland toward acceptance of their terms of sale. By 1925, the oil boom in Long Beach and the growth of the motion picture industry combined to make it all the more imperative that the city settle quickly to remove any further threats to its embattled water supply. In May, 1925, the Public Service Commission offered to buy all lands tributary to the Owens River. The first to take the city up on this offer was Wilfred Watterson, an action which caused his allies in the valley to question why they should continue to hold out while he had not. Watterson explained that the money was needed to continue to fuel the resistance movement in the valley, and he thereby retained his leadership position. The city's attempts to obtain further purchases, however, quickly ran aground, and by the summer of 1925, the dynamiting of the aqueduct was renewed. The pressure on the city increased throughout 1926 as valley resistance hardened. Prices demanded of the city steadily increased, while the merchants busily filed their reparations claims under the new law.[46] All of this activity proceeded to the intermittent punctuation of explosions along the aqueduct.

With the arrival of 1927, events began to converge which again worked to the valley's advantage. In Washington, D.C., Mulholland's drive to tap the waters of the Colorado River was coming to a vote. Arrayed against him were the state's private water and power interests allied with the most ardent editorial defenders of the free enterprise system in a battle which proved to be the forerunner for the conflict over development of the Central Valley that dominated the 1930s. Meanwhile, in Sacramento, the presentation of a new state water plan and a series of court decisions unfavorable to orderly water development forced the issue of water to the fore. In the midst of both disputes stood the Owens Valley, a model of the dangers of Mulholland's policy and an example of the need for overhauling the state's outmoded water laws.

In March, the legislature began a series of public hearings on a proposed constitutional amendment which would require the owner of property adjacent to an existing streamflow to make reasonable use of his water.[47] The Wattersons, now at the head of a unified resistance group titled the Owens Valley Property Owners Protective Association, seized upon the occasion of these legislative hearings to present the valley's case directly to the people. On March 20 and again on March 22, the association bought full-page advertisements in each of California's major newspapers in which they detailed the plight of the Owens Valley, "a name writ in water. . . its characters salt with tears and stained in blood." This passionate appeal was immediately echoed in a series of articles printed in the *Sacramento Union* from March 29 through April 3.

Although extreme examples of the purple rhetoric popular in journalistic prose of the period, the association advertisements together with the *Union* articles marked a sophisticated departure from the appeals of old. Gone were the fatal associations with the interests of private power companies and the unpopular opposition to "hysterical conservationism" which had proved so detrimental to the valley's interest in 1906 and 1907. Instead, these articles found more common strains with which to sound the heart strings of their readers. They described an authentic American tragedy, rich with Biblical overtones, which touched one of America's fondest cultural themes: conflict between the city and the frontier, the strong, sophisticated society against the weaker primitive, the machine run rampant amidst the primeval garden.

In the advertisements in the *Sacramento Union,* the Owens Valley became a democratic Eden threatened by the aqueduct, "an evil serpent, bringing ruin as another serpent did to the earliest valley in human history." The advertisement further described how "the sturdy winners of the wilderness, whose fiber made America great,. . . pushed back the disputing sands and reared the homes of their families, the halls of their democracy, and the altars and thanks of their God—until happy, lovely Owens Valley was a fairyland of beauty surrounded by peaks and desert and dotted with monuments to human industry."

Through this frontier paradise the *Union* stories followed "the trail of the wreckers," presenting "a record of political ownership run rabid, the record of a great city which raised itself above the law." Here the *Union* watched the destruction of the fruit orchards by city tractors: "Shame-faced Los Angeles removing the traces of civilization in the hope that the future will not curse her." There the *Union* found an abandoned schoolhouse with flag still flying, "its blood-red stripes now twined and twisted with the halyard . . . tired of neglect . . . the last thing to yield to the decree of abandonment."

In the press, Mulholland emerges throughout as the cruelest of villains, architect of "a policy of ruthlessness, of 'sink without trace,' of brutality and sharp practice which leads crooks to jail or makes them fugitives from justice." When asked by the *Union* what justice he felt was due to the Owens Valley ranchers, Mulholland was quoted in reply, "Justice! Why there are not enough trees in the valley to give the _____ _____ _____ (sic) justice!"

The immediate impact of this appeal was felt even before the *Union* series had run its course. On March 25, the assembly committee on constitutional amendments held hearings on the proposed amendment which would have tended to restrict the rights of the valley ranchers as riparian owners. The committee stripped the bill of its enforcement powers, leaving a toothless statement of general policy, and passed it to the Floor without a recommendation for passage. Then, on March 31, Assemblyman Dan E. Williams of Chinese Camp announced that he would ask Governor Clement C. Young to allow the legislature to act as an arbiter in the controversy between Los Angeles and the Owens Valley. When this effort failed, Williams headed a special assembly investigating committee which set out on April 16 to visit the valley personally. As guests of the Property Owners Protective Association, the assembly delegation met with 200 ranchers in Bishop on the night of Saturday, March 17.

The following Monday, the committee convened again in Sacramento for hearings on a resolution introduced by Williams which damned Los Angeles and all its works in the Owens Valley. After seven hours of bickering, the Los Angeles officials refused to participate further in the committee hearings. Before the chief counsel for the city representatives left, he told the committee that, regardless of what had happened in the Owens Valley, Los Angeles would enter any other part of the state, including the San Joaquin Valley, if it needed the water. He concluded with the declaration that Los Angeles had the money to do what it pleased.[48]  On Friday, March 23, after a tumultuous debate highlighted by a fistfight on the floor of the assembly chamber, the Williams resolution criticizing Los Angeles passed by a vote of 43 to 34.[49]

Encouraged by their success in Sacramento, the ranchers of the Owens Valley resolved to stand firm against the city. At the beginning of the year, Los Angeles set a deadline of May 1, 1927, for the acceptance of the city's offer to buy riparian lands in the valley; after that date, Los Angeles declared with dubious legality, no reparations payments would be made. The ranchers ignored the deadline. On May 27, one of the largest siphons on the aqueduct was blown up. The next night, sixty more feet of pipe were destroyed. Los Angeles assembled 600 reservists at the city police headquarters and dispatched a contingent of private detectives to the valley armed with Winchesters and tommy guns with orders to shoot to kill anyone found loitering around the aqueduct.[50]  Undeterred, the ranchers blew up portions of the aqueduct again on the nights of June 4, 19 and 24. On June 10, Los Angeles sent an entire trainload of guards to the valley bearing sawed-off shotguns. No blood had been shed in the "Civil War" of 1924, but, in the super-heated atmosphere of the valley in the summer of 1927, the stage was set for a violent confrontation of major proportions.

Mulholland, however, had already prepared a killing blow by which he meant to end the conflict once and for all. In planning the destruction of the Owens Valley, he had throughout displayed a preference for attacking the valley economy rather than its residents directly. Accordingly, he turned once again to the Los Angeles business community, which had borne his project to completion, to save it now from further destruction.

Mulholland's line of attack was directed at the valley banks owned by the Watterson brothers. In October, 1926, Mulholland contacted the Bank of America to secure their assistance in establishing a branch in Bishop to compete with the Wattersons' banks. The application for a charter was made in the names of five valley residents who had already sold their holdings to the city for a combined total of $474,000.[51]

28. The first well drilled in the Owens Valley by the City of Los Angeles. Located east of Independence near the Los Angeles Aqueduct. (*Credit: Eastern California Museum.*)

Mulholland, however, had succeeded too well in undermining the economy of the Owens Valley, and the United States Comptroller of the Treasury refused to issue a charter for a national bank on the grounds that there was not sufficient business in the valley to justify another bank. Similarly, the state bank commissioner also refused the application after a hearing on March 31, 1927, at which the Owens Valley representatives warned that the new bank was a front for the city which intended to drive the Wattersons out of business and thereby secure all the mortgages outstanding in the valley.

During the process of application, however, Los Angeles officials had obtained detailed financial statements on the Wattersons' operations which suggested that some bank funds had been diverted to other Watterson enterprises. On August 2, 1927, Mulholland took this evidence to the state corporations commissioner, who dispatched a state bank investigator to the Owens Valley. Three days later, the Watterson banks closed while an audit was conducted, and on August 10, both brothers were jailed on charges of embezzlement. At their trial, the brothers did not deny the charge that they had channeled more than $2.3 million of the ranchers' savings into their own companies, and their explanation that they had acted only to preserve valley industries in the face of the city's onslaught was ruled inadmissible. Convicted on all counts, the brothers were sentenced to concurrent terms of one to ten years in San Quentin.[52]

For the Owens Valley, this was the cruelest in a long history of betrayals. Scarcely a rancher or merchant in the valley did not have a mortgage from the Watterson banks. With their lifesavings lost and their property forfeited, the ranchers' resistance was broken. The long war was over. Following the Wattersons' conviction on November 12, 1927, someone posted a sign on the north side of Bishop reading, "Los Angeles City Limits."[53]

The year 1927 marked the culmination of Mulholland's achievements on several fronts. In addition to securing the city's water supply in the Owens Valley, Mulholland succeeded, after three years of intensive lobbying in Sacramento, in obtaining the legislature's approval of a bill creating the Metropolitan Water District. With this victory, the Public

Service Commission called for the formal suspension of the city's annexation program until the new water from the Colorado River became available.[54]

Any joy Mulholland may have found in these events, however, was short-lived, for the failure of the Long Valley project which had accelerated the destruction of the Owens Valley had also set Mulholland on a course which proved his ultimate undoing. Desperate for the reservoir capacity that had been denied at Long Valley in 1922, Mulholland in 1924 began construction of a new dam in San Francisquito Canyon to store the water flowing into the ocean from the city's power plants upstream. The dynamite attacks upon the aqueduct that summer spurred Mulholland's rush to build a secure storage facility at the Los Angeles end of the project, far from the scene of battle in the Owens Valley.

Mulholland's haste in bringing the Saint Francis Dam into service only compounded the error he had made in not including a reservoir at Long Valley in his initial design of the aqueduct. Completed in May, 1926, the Saint Francis Dam was unfortunately located upon the San Andreas Fault, and within two years it began to show signs of leakage. On March 12, 1928, Mulholland himself inspected the structure and declared it safe. That same night the dam collapsed. A 100-foot wall of water bearing huge chunks of concrete on its crest swept down the Santa Clara Valley and obliterated three towns and more than 400 lives along its path.[55] Mulholland assumed full responsibility for this greatest unnatural disaster in California history.

Mulholland's shortcomings as an engineer thus worked to undermine all the skill he had displayed in retaining his position at the head of the city's water program through more than forty years of political transition. In Washington, the future of the Swing-Johnson Bill, which would open the way to construction of Boulder Dam, was still in doubt. The plight of the Owens Valley at the hands of Los Angeles combined with the Saint Francis Dam disaster to cause the city's supporters in Congress a degree of embarrassment they could ill afford in the midst of their negotiations over the Boulder Canyon project. As the architect of both the dam and the city's policies toward the Owens Valley ranchers, Mulholland had become a liability that could no longer be sustained. "I envy the dead," he told the coroner's inquest investigating the Saint Francis Dam disaster in the summer of 1928.[56] At the end of November, almost a year to the day after the Watterson brothers entered San Quentin and only a month before President Coolidge signed the Swing-Johnson Act, Mulholland resigned in disgrace.

With Mulholland gone, Los Angeles, beginning in February, 1929, moved swiftly to settle accounts in the Owens Valley by purchasing the remaining townships and privately held ranchlands. Throughout this last series of purchases, the city adhered strictly to Mulholland's original precepts that there be no arbitration and no payment of reparations. The city did agree to increase the 1929 market prices set by its own panel of appraisers according to a schedule of percentage adjustments which reflected the depreciation of market values since 1923. But no payments were made for estimated business losses or for the value of fixtures and equipment, and all sales were conditioned upon a release of the city from liability for any reparations claims.[57] On these terms, the city, by May, 1933, had expanded its holdings in the valley to include 95 per cent of all farmlands and 85 per cent of the town properties.[58]

By agreeing to purchase at artificially inflated prices, Los Angeles wound up paying taxes to Inyo County on assessments which in some cases exceeded the actual market value of the properties involved.[59] In the years of the Depression that followed, these generous settlements proved a boon to many valley refugees, as did the opportunity for short-term employment on the aqueduct. But for those who chose to remain and work their ranches, Los Angeles' policies were less kind. Although the city did agree to lease back the farms it had acquired at an annual rate of 6 per cent of the purchase price plus taxes, these leases were granted for no more than five years and were cancelable at any time on the city's option. Most important, the granting of a lease carried with it no promise of a continued water supply. Los Angeles promptly made the perils attendant to such an agreement abundantly clear to the ranchers in 1930 when the city abruptly canceled nearly all of its leases and diverted the entire flow of the Owens River to the San Fernando Valley during the peak of the irrigation season.[60]

Fred Eaton, meanwhile, did not escape the fate of his neighbors in the valley. His dreams of a cattle empire never came to fruition. In 1926, at a time when the Eaton Land and

Cattle Company was floundering, the other officers of the firm took out a $200,000 loan from the Watterson banks, offering Eaton's land at Long Valley as security. When the Watterson banks collapsed, the $200,000 went with them, and the note on Eaton's land was sold to a Los Angeles bank which promptly initiated foreclosure proceedings. Together, Eaton and Mulholland had conceived the aqueduct and labored to make it a reality. In the end, they both became its victims.[61]

As the ranchers left and the valley's economy shifted to tourism and agricultural activities such as cattle grazing and feed-crop production which had low water needs, tranquility was restored to the Owens Valley. In 1939, the city began to loosen its grip by offering to sell portions of its land while reserving to itself all water rights. Relations between the city and the valley have remained sensitive, however, and on those rare occasions when the valley residents have joined to protest some aspect of city policy, Los Angeles officials have sometimes responded with a display of gratuitous cruelty that recalls Mulholland at his worst.

In 1944, for example, the city reversed an earlier policy of giving preference to leaseholders in the sale of its properties and began instead to conduct its sales by sealed bids. When the valley leaseholders protested, Los Angeles retaliated by increasing the rents charged on all of its properties in the Owens Valley. This action was taken at a time when federally-enforced wartime rent controls were in effect across the country, and the notices of the increase, effective January 1, 1945, were mailed to arrive during Christmas week.[62]

Similarly, in the early 1970's the valley residents obtained a court order requiring the city to submit an environmental impact report before engaging in an increased pumping program which threatened to lower the valley's water table still further. When the city produced the required report within one month and the valley residents sought a court review of the report's adequacy, Los Angeles abruptly announced that it was cutting off all water to its agricultural and recreational lessees in the Owens Valley. On Friday, September 20, 1974, the city mailed notice of the cutoff which took place the following Monday, September 23. To shut off the water, city workers had to dynamite irrigation valves that had been rusted open since the aqueduct's completion sixty years before. In a public statement, Duane L. Georgeson, the city engineer responsible for the aqueduct, denied that the city's extreme action was a punitive measure and described it instead as "educational."[63]

Such incidents have helped to keep alive the memory of Los Angeles' actions in the Owens Valley from one generation of valley residents to the next. This residual bitterness, together with the high drama of the events themselves, has no doubt helped to fuel the continuing controversy over the old charge that the aqueduct was built to serve the interests of Henry Huntington and his associates in the San Fernando syndicate.[64]

The syndicate's interest in the aqueduct, while considerably more than coincidental, was something less than corruption. To say that the financial leaders of Los Angeles in the early part of this century exercised great influence over the conduct of municipal affairs, and that some consequently benefited from the exercises of this influence, is simply to state a characteristic which was obvious in many aspects of the city's administration during this era. Yet, for all the profits it derived from the project, the syndicate did not pervert the aqueduct's purpose. Rather, the aqueduct amply fulfilled the synthetic need for which it was created: the city's population increased twelvefold between 1900 and 1930 while its land area multiplied by ten.

The ethic of growth and not simply the greed of a few Los Angeles financiers laid waste to the Owens Valley. For all of the deception Mulholland practiced in promoting the project, the fact of the syndicate's interest was consistently a central, but never a sufficient argument in any of the elections affecting the aqueduct to block the project and the general prosperity it promised. Los Angeles approached the Owens Valley as an expanding enterprise seeking a resource for exploitation. The decision to sacrifice the future of the Owens Valley for the sake of development in the San Fernando Valley was made unilaterally by the city, but it involved a choice between competing public interests. All of the efforts of the Owens Valley ranchers in the 1920s came too late to reverse this policy. The ranchers' fate had been sealed at the moment President Roosevelt determined in 1906 that the greater public interest would be served by a greater Los Angeles.

In his last annual message to Congress, Roosevelt reflected upon the changes which were occurring in the nation as the result of the growth of giant corporations, national labor organizations, and the new urban metropolises: "The chief breakdown is in dealing with the new relations that arise from the mutualism, the interdependence of our time. Every new social relation begets a new type of wrong-doing—of sin, to use an old-fashioned word—and many years always elapse before society is able to turn this sin into crime which can be effectively punished."[65]

In the case of the Owens Valley, the evolution of the law that Roosevelt predicted began almost immediately. When the state senate sent an investigating committee to the Owens Valley in 1931, for example, it was acting not simply to berate the city but, more importantly, to prevent the repetition of a similar conflict as Los Angeles extended the aqueduct into the Mono Basin. Aided in part by the recommendations that grew out of this investigation, the legislature that same year adopted California's "County of Origin Law" which prohibits the exploitation of rural areas like the Owens Valley by establishing a means of mediating conflicts over future water needs.[66]

In addition, the example of the Owens Valley aided the resistance in the struggles that followed over the construction of new public water projects in California. In 1927, for example, the *Sacramento Union* did not forego drawing an obvious moral from its series of stories on the Owens Valley: "There is a warning to be heeded. Here is a case where political ownership of public utilities had full sway for demonstration. The city concerned reverted to ruthlessness, savage disregard for moral and economic equations, to chicanery and faith breaking . . . The municipality became a destroyer, deliberately, unconscionable, boastfully."[67]

More than any other individual, William Mulholland, through the building of the aqueduct and the formation of the Metropolitan Water District, established the principle of public ownership of water indelibly on California history. The growth of Los Angeles demonstrated the validity of the principle, just as the memory of the Owens Valley made its further advancement all the more difficult. The damage done by Mulholland to the principle he worked all his life to establish may provide the harshest judgment of his action, for, in the end, Mulholland's methods poisoned the legacy he left behind.

29. Stacking bales of hay at the Joseph L. Gish farm at Laws (circa 1910). *(Credit: Eastern California Museum.)*

## NOTES

1. For more detail on Roosevelt's action, see Part I of this article in *California Historical Quarterly,* 55 (Spring, 1976): 12-15.
2. George E. Mowry, *The Era of Theodore Roosevelt* (New York, 1958), pp. 214-216.
3. W. A. Chalfant, historian of Inyo County and a valley resident during these events, agreed with the desirability of preserving natural resources, but observed of Roosevelt's policies, "In the stages of novelty, it ran so far toward hysteria that there was danger of all being conserved for the future with little regard for necessities of the present . . . Pinchot [head of the Forest Service], who has stated that he did what he could to help Los Angeles, was able to read into his authority the power to assist the city by preventing settlement. He has since asserted that 'the end justifies the means.' So might the highwayman say as he blackjacks his victim into helplessness; the end itself is not justifiable." W. A. Chalfant, *The Story of Inyo* (published by the author, Second Revised Edition, 1933), pp. 363-364. (Hereinafter Chalfant, 2nd.)
4. *San Francisco Call,* September 4, 1907.
5. See Part I of this article, *California Historical Quarterly,* 55: 5-7.
6. The extension of the forest preserve apparently was one of several similar moves by which Roosevelt and Pinchot withdrew seventeen million acres of land in 1907 and 1908 before their actions in this regard could be brought under congressional review. Even so, Pinchot had to send three foresters to the Owens Valley before he found one who would sign a report recommending withdrawal of the land. Chalfant, 2nd, pp. 339-340 and 367. See also Mowry, *Era of Roosevelt,* pp. 214-216.
7. Chalfant, 2nd, p. 368. In the first edition of his history, *The Story of Inyo,* published in 1922 (hereinafter Chalfant, 1st), Chalfant commented, "the government held Owens Valley while Los Angeles skinned it." (p. 329)
8. The Board of Public Service Commissioners succeeded to the powers of the Board of Water Commissioners in March, 1911, pursuant to amendments to state statutes governing public works projects.
9. The engineers estimated that the watercrop from the aqueduct and the Los Angeles river combined would total 480 cubic feet per second or 24,000 miner's inches. One-fourth of this total would be needed to service the 45,000 acres of habitable land within the city, assuming an average daily consumption rate of one miner's inch for every 7.77 acres of developed urban land. See J. H. Quinton, W. H. Code, and Homer Hamlin, *Report Upon the Distribution of the Surplus Waters of the Los Angeles Aqueduct* (Los Angeles, 1911).
10. The engineers advised that "at least one-fourth of all the water used in

San Fernando Valley will eventually return to the Los Angeles River as underflow." *Ibid.,* p.11. Assuming that 275 second-feet were assigned to the San Fernando Valley, the engineers estimated that 80 second-feet (29 per cent) would return to Los Angeles.

11. Frank M. Keffer, *History of San Fernando Valley* (Glendale, 1934), pp. 73-74.

12. In 1911, the five principal directors of the Suburban Homes syndicate were joined by William Paul Whitsett, who purchased a half interest in the syndicate's Van Nuys townsite and proceeded with its development through the Janss Company. See W. W. Robinson, *The Story of San Fernando Valley* (Los Angeles, 1961), pp. 37-38.

13. In addition to the general profits of the company, individual members of the syndicate reaped subsidiary benefits through construction and the supply of support services to the new towns of the San Fernando Valley. Huntington's Pacific Light and Power Company doubled its earnings between 1905 and 1915 through extensions into the area. The first official act of the town of Burbank following its incorporation was to extend an exclusive contract for the supply of street and home lighting to L. C. Brand, another member of the northern syndicate. Keffer, *History of San Fernando,* p. 80. Each of the principal members of the southern syndicate selected choice tracts for themselves: Sherman took 1000 acres at the site of what is now Sherman Oaks; Otis took 550 acres which he later sold to Edgar Rice Burroughs who renamed it Tarzana; Brant secured 850 acres to form the Brant Rancho; and Chandler and Whitley received smaller tracts at Sherman Way and Van Nuys boulevards. Robinson, *Story of San Fernando,* p. 38.

14. For more details on this election, see Part I of this article, *California Historical Quarterly,* 55: 17-21.

15. *Los Angeles Times,* July 17, 1912. See also *Report on the Los Angeles Aqueduct After an Investigation Authorized by the City Council of Los Angeles* (Los Angeles, 1912).

16. *Report of the Aqueduct Investigation Board to the City Council* (Los Angeles, 1912) p. 14. A description of the details of Mulholland's agreement with Eaton appears in Part I of this article, *California Historical Quarterly,* 55: 5.

17. Under the proposed construction plan approved by the Public Service Commission, one conduit would extend through the Santa Monica Mountains at Franklin Canyon to service the Providencia, Cahuenga, Inglewood, and Glendale areas. A second major conduit would run to Pasadena and east to San Dimas. Three smaller conduits would supply 40,000 acres in the Mission, Fernando, and Chatsworth districts of the San Fernando Valley.

18. In the public views of successful politicians of the period, industry was seen not as an adversary of government but as its partner or teacher. The principles of one were considered applicable to the other. Meyer Lissner, a prominent Progressive ideologue, for example, promised in 1909 that the incoming Alexander administration would "do public business like great private business is done." *Pacific Outlook*, 7 (December 11, 1909): 4. Similarly, in 1915, after the regular Republicans had returned to power, charter revisions were drafted on the charge, "Can the city be administered as an efficient business corporation?" Robert M. Fogelson, *The Fragmented Metropolis: Los Angeles 1850-1930* (Cambridge, Mass., 1967), p. 221.

19. *Los Angeles Times*, April 15, 1913.

20. *Los Angeles Record*, September 12, 1912.

21. J. B. Lippincott, "William Mulholland—Engineer, Pioneer, Raconteur," *Civil Engineering* (March, 1941): 163.

22. The agreement specifically granted the ranchers storage rights on Big Pine Creek and north of Fish Springs as well as free use of all underground waters. The city also agreed to withdraw its opposition to settlement on public lands and to admit the water rights of the existing ditches. Chalfant, 2nd, p. 373.

23. Keffer, *History of San Fernando*, p. 86.

24. See Part I, of this article, *California Historical Quarterly*, 55: 14.

25. In the other areas annexed by the city, aqueduct water was supplied for domestic use only, and any farming activity was supported by the local underground water supply. Even where combined use of the water was permitted, the area paid a domestic-irrigation rate which, while lower than the domestic rate, was nonetheless appreciably higher than the irrigation rate charged to the San Fernando Valley. Ostrom, *Water and Politics*, p. 161, notes that the San Fernando Valley was the only area developed as an integral irrigation project. The Public Service Commission noted this inequity in its annual report for the fiscal year ending June 30, 1918, when it pointed out that irrigation revenues from the first full harvest year in the valley totaled only $200,000, "an amount hardly sufficient to justify the low rate at which the water was sold." See *Seventeenth Annual Report of the Board of Public Service Commissioners* (Los Angeles, 1918), p. 6.

26. Following the annexation of 170 square miles in San Fernando and seven square miles in the Palms district in 1915, Los Angeles added Owensmouth in 1917, West Lankershim in 1919, Chatsworth in 1920, and Lankershim in 1923. By the time Mulholland's annexation program formally closed in 1927, the only communities still outstanding in the San Fernando Valley were the cities of San Fernando, Burbank, Glendale, Tujunga, and Universal City.

27. Ralph J. Roske, *Everyman's Eden* (New York, 1968), p. 486.

28. Ostrom, *Water and Politics*, pp.161-162.

29. The water rights of the owners of riparian lands were supreme under pueblo law. In 1872, the California legislature adopted the model of the New York Civil Code permitting diversion and impoundment. As development of the state proceeded, a line was thus drawn between the interests of riparian owners and the irrigation projects which depended upon large-scale appropriations of water. In 1886, the California Supreme Court, in the case of Lux *vs.* Haggin (69 Cal, 255) decided the issue in favor of the riparian owners, and, in the years that followed, the court repeatedly struck down the legislature's attempts to limit the effect of its ruling. Erwin Cooper provides a useful summary of the evolution of California water law in the last chapter of his *Aqueduct Empire* (Glendale, 1968). The more serious student should consult Wells A. Hutchins, *The California Law of Water Rights* (Sacramento, 1956).

30. Quotation attributed to Mulholland by Remi Nadeau, *Water Seekers* (Garden City, New York, 1950), p. 64.

31. In later years, Mulholland's withdrawal from the Long Valley project came to be blamed for the violence that followed. It became the policy of the city water agency to explain Mulholland's action with the contention that the high dam (which the federal government approved) was not feasible due to the loose and porous soil in the area. See, for example, Don J. Kinsey, *The Water Trail* (Los Angeles, 1928), p. 21.

32. *Twenty-First annual Report of the Board of Public Service Commissioners* (Los Angeles, 1922) p. 11. The San Fernando Valley interests, through their representative on the commission, W. P. Whitsett (himself a member of the Suburban Home syndicate), vigorously supported this policy as a way of reducing competition for the water available. *Los Angeles Record,* November 21, 1925.

33. Chalfant, 2nd, p. 382, reports that the drilling engineers arrived even before the failure of the Long Valley project. The city ultimately sunk a total of 150 wells in the valley before the collapse of the valley's resistance in 1927. See "Report of the Senate Special Investigating Committee on Water Situation in Inyo and Mono Counties" *Journal of the Senate*, 49 Session, May 6, 1931, p. 2448.

34. Ostrom, *Water and Politics*, p. 132.

35. The destruction of storage dams was limited to the area of Lake Mary, Fishlake Creek, and Hot Springs Creek. In a letter to the Los Angeles Clearinghouse Association on January 6, 1925, the president of the Public Service Commission, R. F. del Valle, explained that the bombing was necessary to protect the water rights the city already possessed. See *Sacramento Union,* March 30, 1927.

36. R. Coke Wood, "Owens Valley as I Knew It" *Pacific Historian,* 16 (Summer, 1972): 2.

37. Chalfant, 2nd, pp. 387-388.

38. Chalfant, 1st, p. 330.

39. The Wattersons' ownership of the Inyo County Bank and extensive investments in local mining operations made the brothers the predominant figures in valley commerce. In addition to their leadership in the resistance to Los Angeles, R. Coke Wood recalls that Mark taught Sunday school at the Methodist Church in Bishop and Wilfred served as the local scoutmaster. Wood, "As I knew It," pp. 2-3.

40. The Hearst series, which appeared under the headline, "Valley of Broken Hearts" was written by a former Owens Valley resident, C. E. Kunze, and ran from April 21 to May 3, 1924.

41. Even before the arrival of the KKK, the Owens Valley had developed its own traditions of frontier justice. In the latter part of the nineteenth century, two vigilante organizations appeared in Bishop: the Committee of Public Safety and the "145", which was patterned after the famous "601" of Virginia City. See Chalfant, 1st, pp. 312-314.

42. See *Los Angeles Times,* May 22 and 23, 1924 and *Los Angeles Record,* November 19, 1924. See also Marian L. Ryan, "Los Angeles Newspapers Fight the Water War," *Southern California Quarterly,* 50 (June, 1968).

43. Ostrom, *Water and Politics,* p. 122.

44. Watterson proposed three alternative means of settlement: (1) the city would sustain irrigation to 30,000 acres of the valley but also pay damaged property owners $5.3 million in reparations; (2) the city would buy the entire Watterson irrigation district for $12 million; or (3) at a price to be set by an independent arbitration board. Nadeau, *Water Seekers,* p. 92.

45. See Chapter 109, *Statutes of 1925* (Senate Bill 757—Inman). Although the act provided for its own liberal construction, claims were recoverable under its provisions only for damages caused by the loss of the water itself and not for damages resulting directly or indirectly from the actual construction of the aqueduct.

46. Claims submitted ultimately totaled $2,813,355.42. See Ostrom, *Water and Politics,* p. 124, for a detailed breakdown of the reparations sought.

47. The proposed amendment had been prompted by a state supreme court decision the year before, Herminghaus *vs.* the Southern California Edison Company (200 Cal. 81) in which the court rendered its starkest reaffirmation yet of the principles of private property by granting the owner of such riparian rights full and unqualified control of all the water flowing past his land. See fn. 29, *supra.*

48. *Sacramento Union,* April 21, 1927.

49. Assembly Concurrent Resolution 34 (1927) declared that Los Angeles' policy of "ruthless destruction" constituted "a menace to the peace and welfare of the entire state" and called upon the city to restore the Owens Valley to its former agricultural status or to give the valley residents and businessmen proper compensation for their damages. In the vote on the assembly floor, the representatives from Los Angeles were joined in opposition to the Williams resolution by the San Francisco delegation, who were having similar problems of their own with the Hetch Hetchy water development. Once passed by the assembly, the measure went to the senate committee on conservation, chaired by Senator Herbert J. Evans of Los Angeles, where it died without a hearing.

50. *Los Angeles Times*, May 29, 1927.

51. Prominent among this group was George Watterson, uncle of Wilfred and Mark and a consistent partisan within the county on the city's behalf.

52. In the Wattersons' fall the *Los Angeles Times* found a defense for the city's policies toward the valley. Upon their conviction, the *Times* editorialized, "The propaganda which for years has been directed against the city is now shown not only to have been financed by stolen money but to have been motivated by the necessity the Wattersons had of covering up their own criminal acts. . . this poison spring is now dried up and the two communities will be the healthier for it." *Los Angeles Times*, November 12, 1927.

53. Wood, "As I Knew It," p. 5.

54. Ostrom, *Water and Politics*, p. 159.

55. It is no accident that the Saint Francis Dam disaster has never achieved the prominence in California history as the San Francisco Earthquake, despite the fact that the death tolls in both incidents were roughly equivalent. In the preparation of his history, *Man-Made Disaster: The Story of the Saint Francis Dam* (Glendale, 1963), Charles F. Outland discovered that many of the most important records of the event have been destroyed or otherwise withdrawn from public inspection, with the result that it is impossible to determine exactly how many people were killed or how much compensation Los Angeles actually paid. With regard to the death count Outland advises, "Any death figure over 450 or under 400 is unrealistic." (p. 222).

56. Mulholland's acceptance of responsibility for the disaster was not entirely a noble gesture of submission. On the morning after the disaster, rumors began to circulate that the dam had been blown up by Owens Valley ranchers. These rumors proved to be without foundation, but Mulholland subscribed to them nonetheless and as late as the coroner's inquest was still trying to suggest sabotage as the cause of the dam's failure. Outland, *Man-Made Disaster*, pp. 138 and 191.

57. An investigating committee of the state senate in 1931 particularly deplored this provision of the city's contracts of sale as well as the city's refusal to consider the claims of the town of Keeler on the shore of the Owens Lake. When the lake dried up due to the diversion of the Owens River to the aqueduct, Keeler was inundated with shifting deposits of alkali, soda, sand, and dust. The committee reported, however, that reparations were the focus of continued conflict, and the committee urged the city to compensate the valley merchants, estimating that $500,000 would be sufficient to satisfy the claims of Bishop and all the other towns. See *Journal of the Senate*, 49 Session, fn. 33 *supra*, pp. 2450-2452.

58. The city paid a total of $5,798,780 for the town properties: Bishop was bought for $2,975,833; Big Pine for $722,635; Independence for $730,306; Laws for $102,446; and Lone Pine for $1,217,560. The farm properties were purchased for an additional $1,120,087. The only major block of properties not purchased was a pool of thirty-one parcels held by a former state senator from Inyo who demanded twice the assessed value for his holdings. See Ostrom, *Water and Politics*, pp. 125-126.

59. In 1936, Los Angeles tried to reduce its assessments by forcing the residents of Bishop to disincorporate their community as a condition of the city's purchase of the remaining properties. The town rejected the proposal in a special election August 22. Ostrom, *Water and Politics*, pp. 135-136.

60. The harsh treatment accorded the ranchers contrasts vividly with the support and encouragement Los Angeles extended to others who had an interest in the valley. At the same time as the ranchers were paying 6 per cent on the value of their leases, for example, Los Angeles offered to lease 6400 acres of the valley for use as a businessman's duck hunting preserve at an annual rate of less than $1/2$ of 1 per cent of the property's worth. (Chalfant, 2nd, p.402.) Whereas ranchers were denied assurance of a continued water supply, Los Angeles in 1935 returned 1511 acres to the valley's original residents, the Paiute Indians, with a guarantee of at least 6046 acre-feet of water each year. Ostrom, *Water and Politics*, pp. 138-139.

61. After a quarter century of silence, Eaton and Mulholland were ultimately reconciled at Eaton's deathbed in 1934. When Fred Eaton died, Mulholland told his daughter, "For three nights in succession I dreamed of Fred. The two of us were walking along—young and virile like we used to be. Yet I knew we both were dead." Mulholland died the next year. The quotation is attributed to Mulholland by Nadeau, *Water Seekers*, p.131, apparently from the reminiscences of his daughter, Miss Rose Mulholland.

62. Ostrom, *Water and Politics*, pp. 136, 137.

63. *Los Angeles Times*, December 1, 1974.
64. Until the appearance of Remi Nadeau's *Water Seekers* in 1950, the formal histories of the Owens Valley conflict, except for those published by the city itself, accepted the existence of a syndicate plot underlying the city's "rape" of the valley. In attempting to balance this construction, Nadeau perhaps argued too vigorously in the city's behalf. Nadeau points, for example, to the building of a railroad line to the valley, the supply of electricity to the towns of Independence and Lone Pine, and the city's willingness to pay taxes on its holdings in the valley as "examples of good will which in other circumstances would have earned the friendship of the settlers." This argument fails to comprehend that those "other circumstances" were all-important in determining the way in which what Nadeau calls "neighborly deeds" by the city were received. The city did not build a railroad line, for example, to benefit the valley it intended to depopulate, but rather because the line was needed to transport materials for the aqueduct. In fact, there is evidence in Chalfant (pages 291-293 of the first edition and pages 360-361 of the second) that the Southern Pacific planned to build a line into the valley as early as 1900 until Henry Huntington scotched the plan when he struck upon the scheme for the aqueduct.
65. Quoted in John Morton Blum, *The Republican Roosevelt* (New York, 1966) p. 109.
66. Chapter 720, *Statutes of 1931* (Senate Bill 141—Crittenden). The act authorized the State Department of Finance to supervise the assignment of water rights as part of a general plan for the orderly development of the state. In cases of dispute, the Department of Finance would act as the final arbiter, a power since transferred to the State Department of Water Resources.
67. *Sacramento Union*, April 3, 1927.

Beyond the differing perspectives of the controversies surrounding the construction of the Los Angeles Aqueduct lies the story of an immense engineering project requiring money, logistics, and thousands of people. This article focuses on the stories of some of these people.

Margaret A. (Maggie) Kilgore is a communications consultant and writer with 20 years experience as a journalist with United Press International and the *Los Angeles Times,* where she spent a number of years as a correspondent in Vietnam during the Vietnam war. She has also headed the public relations departments for two corporations. Kilgore has degrees from Stephens College in Missouri and Syracuse University in New York, with an M.B.A. from Pepperdine University.

Kilgore has been under contract to the Los Angeles Department of Water and Power (DWP) for three years, and is working on a booklet for the 75th Anniversary of the First Los Angeles Aqueduct. This article was written for *Mountains to Desert* at the request of Duane Buchholtz, Northern District Engineer, Los Angeles DWP, as their contribution to the Eastern California Museum's 60th Anniversary project.

# TALES OF THE BUILDING OF THE FIRST LOS ANGELES AQUEDUCT

by Margaret A. Kilgore

## INTRODUCTION

In many parts of the United States, the year 1907 was merely a footnote in American history. Wall Street was coping with a recession. The Chicago Cubs shutout the Detroit Tigers in the World Series. Theodore Roosevelt was President.

In the West, however, 1907 has gone down in history as the year that construction began on the first Los Angeles Aqueduct, the first major water project in the West and one of the largest public works projects ever undertaken by a municipality. It was completed six years later in 1913 at a budgeted cost of $24.6 million. At peak periods, it employed a work force of about 5,000 men.

The building of the 233-mile aqueduct to carry water by gravity from the Owens Valley in the eastern Sierra Nevada to the City of Los Angeles is considered a brilliant engineering feat even today. It involved tunneling 53 miles in brutal mountain terrain, laying railroad tracks and constructing roads, telephone lines and electric transmission lines. Two hydroelectric plants and a cement plant also were built. Fifty-two mules organized in teams pulled pipe from the rail site to the pipeline. Steam shovels, dredges and more than six million pounds of dynamite also were used to excavate soils.

195

30.  Steam shovel excavating for open, lined section of first Los Angeles Aqueduct.
(Credit: Los Angeles Department of Water and Power.)

Los Angeles in the early 1900s was in the grip of one of its periodic droughts—and still growing. The population had climbed from 50,000 in the 1890s to more than 325,000 by 1905 as people flocked westward, encouraged by agricultural opportunities, rail transportation and word-of-mouth on the good climate and job opportunities.

The municipal water department enlarged the distribution system to meet demand, but, by 1904, the water supply was seriously depleted and it was clear that new water resources had to be found to supplement the Los Angeles River, which had served the city since it was established as a Spanish pueblo in 1781. At one point, it was estimated that the river only had three weeks supply of water left to accommodate the semi-arid city.

It was this dire water crisis which led William Mulholland, a bluff, humorous Irish immigrant with foresight and obvious administrative abilities to undertake the building of the first aqueduct, a project which brought him much honor in his lifetime and remains a dramatic story more than 50 years after his death. In the early stages, he was aided by his predecessor as superintendent of the water company and later Los Angeles mayor, Fred Eaton.

Eaton, labeled by some as a dreamer, and Mulholland, the designer, conceived a plan to bring Owens River water 240 miles south to Los Angeles via an aqueduct. (By 1941, the aqueduct had been extended 105 miles north to tap the waters of Mono Basin.) Angelenos were enthusiastic about the project and approved a $23 million bond issue for construction in 1907.

The city had acquired land and water rights in the Owens Valley during 1905. Property owners in the vicinity of the pipeline were compensated for their property, but some were not satisfied, and lawsuits and violence continued for years.

In more recent times, city and valley interests have banded together to form a productive partnership aimed at protecting and enhancing the valley's environment. Tourism has become a major industry.

In 1988, land ownership in Inyo County was 91 percent federal, 3 percent state and local, 4 percent City of Los Angeles and 2 percent private. The federal government owns 75 percent of the land in Mono County; the City of Los Angeles, 3 percent; state and local 1 percent; and 21 percent is in private hands.

As with any project of this size where divergent interests and views are involved, politics and second-guessing play a large part. In the case of Owens Valley residents versus the City of Los Angeles, the controversy involved charges that Los Angeles stole the valley's water rights and exploited both its pastoral economy and pristine environment.

In this article, we make no effort to say who was right or wrong in the disputes. Some two dozen books and numerous articles have been written on the water controversy. Instead, we would like to tell some of the stories that have been passed down as aqueduct lore, small vignettes to explain how the aqueduct was built, who built it, and the many problems surmounted.

Also, because this article is included in a commemorative book celebrating the 60th anniversary of the Eastern California Museum in Independence (coincidental with the 75th anniversary of the completion of the Los Angeles Aqueduct), many of the incidents will concentrate on the aqueduct building on its northern sections and the problems encountered and overcome. It is a tale rich in California history and important to the further understanding of how the West was developed.

## IT COSTS MONEY TO BUILD AN AQUEDUCT

Although construction on the aqueduct did not begin until 1907, a gigantic preparatory operation had been led by the chief architect and designer of the system, William Mulholland.

At the early period of design, Mulholland's major concern was whether city officials would leave him alone long enough to get the preliminary work done. His crews were involved in establishing a 240-mile telephone line, more than 500 miles of good roads and trails and some 2,300 buildings and tents to facilitate work along the desert route.

In December, 1908, the Los Angeles Chamber of Commerce invited Mulholland to attend a meeting. Its members, knowing little of the engineering preliminaries involved, wanted to know why the project seemed to be moving slowly. Remi Nadeau in his book *Water Seekers*, reported Mulholland's response:

*"Well, we have spent about $3,000,000 all told, guess,"* Mulholland answered solemnly, *"and there is perhaps nine hundred feet of aqueduct built. Figuring all our expenses, it has cost us about $3,300 per foot."*

*He paused while the startled Chamber members digested his words.*

*"But by this time next year,"* he concluded, *"I'll have 50 miles completed and at a cost of under $30 per foot, if you'll let me alone."*

*The tension in his audience resolved into cordiality.*

*"All right, Bill,"* laughed the chairman. *"Go ahead; we're not mad about it."*

## A CAN OF TOMATOES TO SOBER UP

As the project continued, word spread that there were heavy construction jobs available near Los Angeles. An itinerant army of transient labor descended, a tough, hard-drinking lot of mixed nationalities, including Greeks, Bulgarians, Serbs, Montenegrans and Mexicans. In slang terms, they were called "Blanket stiffs."

In the middle management ranks came hardy young engineers from Western colleges who gained their first field experience in the rigorous desert life on "Mulholland's ditch." The experience they gained would enhance their job resumes for the rest of their lives.

In his *Men, Medicine & Water*, a personal recollection of the building of the aqueduct by its medical director, Dr. Raymond C. Taylor recalled:

*In the winter it was just as windy and bitter cold as it was hot in the summer. However, we had practically no heat prostration, although I think I have seen places in some of the big ditches in the lower Owens Valley that were 15 feet deep and 30 feet across the top, where the temperature in the bottom of the ditch must have been close to 130 degrees. There was no humidity, however, which I suppose is the thing that saved us from heat prostration. At that time we did not know, what is now common knowledge, the importance of replacing salt loss due to excessive perspiration, so ingestion of salt was not used or tried.*

Dr. Taylor and his staff also treated numerous infected hand injuries and handled an outbreak of contagious impetigo. The doctor decided impetigo was being spread by the miners' passing pick and shovel handles among themselves. To curb the outbreak, the doctor ordered that any man with an open sore on his hand must come to the hospital to have it bandaged and that pick and shovel handles must be wiped with antiseptic once a day. The hard rock miners—an independent lot—resisted the orders, but, eventually, complied.

Dr. Taylor goes on: *The usual background of a new man, especially out in the desert, was that many of them had been busted and hadn't had a square meal for some time and they came on the job half starved to death or just recovering from a good big drunk and everything inside them all upset. They would sit down and eat tremendous meals. Also, where the change of drinking water was quite marked, it resulted very often in acute gastritis or acute diarrhea, some of them quite alarming.*

The cure was castor oil, salts, camphor, lead and opium pills to dry them out and restore their normal appetite.

*I made many good friends and also had many acquaintances among the men themsleves,* Dr. Taylor recalled. *They would work, many of them, until they got what they called 'a stake' and then go to town and blow it on a big drunk if somebody didn't get it away from them the first night. I frequently would be accosted by fellows in Saugus at the railroad station as I came through, or in Mojave more often, who wanted to get up the line and get back on the job again, or asked for a ride or for a half dollar so they could buy A CAN OF TOMATOES so they could sober up. A good big can of ordinary stewed tomatoes eaten just as they come out of the can with all of the juice was thought among the men to be one of the best things to sober up. None of us knew then just what the reason was but it certainly did work . . . .* perhaps the acids and vitamins in tomatoes.

Accident and death figures on the aqueduct project differ slightly, depending on which report is read or how the accidents are categorized. However, the most authoritative account appears to be contained in the *Complete Report on Construction of the Los Angeles Aqueduct,* published in 1916 by the City of Los Angeles after a judicial investigation.

The report stated the total number of accidents resulting in death were 43; the number resulting in permanent injury, one, and the total number of miscellaneous accidents, most of which were of a trivial character, 1,282, for a grand total of 1,326 accidents.

When Dr. Taylor met his counterpart who was handling medical treatment at the site of the New York Aqueduct, being built at the same time, the two men compared notes. Taylor said he lost about 10 men a year to fatalities. The New York doctor said he lost about one man a week.

KEEPING COOL WITHOUT ICE

There were no refrigeration facilities in the cookhouses and desert mess tents as construction on the Los Angeles Aqueduct proceeded. Blocks of ice were used when available, but they often proved unsatisfactory.

The cooling problem and the quality of the food created major problems for the commissary operator, D. J. Desmond, one of only two outside vendors on the aqueduct construction. It also created problems for Los Angeles, which was forced to subsidize Desmond's operation because he apparently had underestimated his costs and the enormity of the problems when he bid on the project. At one point, the quality of the food became so inferior that sporadic food strikes broke out among the miners.

In his book, Dr. Taylor explains the problems: *The [commissary] contractor, Joe Desmond, ran the thing without proper supervisory help and with a very poor system for the first two years. Of course, he was up against a pretty tough proposition. There was no ice to be had and, although I think he could have put in an ice plant and the aqueduct would have probably given him power to run it if he'd been really serious about it. Shipping ice from Mojave by train or trying to get it out by automobile was a pretty poor proposition. He couldn't haul enough to amount to anything and if he sent it on the train, he found in trying to do this that two-thirds would melt or be stolen before it got to its destination.*

31. Concreting open, lined section of First Los Angeles Aqueduct. (Credit: Los Angeles Department of Water and Power.)

Dr. Taylor said that to beat this cooling problem and provide red meat for the men, Desmond would have beef butchered in Mojave, loaded into his car and then head north, driving as far as he could in the cool of the night.

*After the roads got in some sort of shape and people got so they knew how to drive the desert roads with loads, this worked fairly well. Of course, the beef was new and unhung and desert beef at that and pretty tough, but it was fresh meat.*

Initially, the employees were charged 25 cents per meal, until Desmond nearly went broke and the quality of food deteriorated. The city intervened and raised the price to 30 cents per employee, which alleviated the problem.

Taylor also was instrumental in having pies, cakes and pastry—unlimited sugar and carbohydrates—served to the men as an alcoholic substitute and simply to fill their appetites. Taylor observed:

*I've seen a man pile four pieces of pie, one on top of another, on his coffee saucer, before anyone else could get to it, just because it was something that had been hard to get. When they could get all they wanted of it, there wasn't as much hoggishness.*

## THE FLIES AND THE MESS HALL

In his book, Dr. Taylor also explains in some detail how he solved the fly problem which was a constant irritant on the desert construction and dangerous to everyone. He explains:

*Another pain in the neck was flies. There wasn't any way of keeping down flies consistently around kitchens and mess houses except screening. . . However, it was absolutely impossible to keep a toilet or mess house screen door in operating condition unless somebody watched and repaired it every day, if necessary, because the men would prop it open with a rock to get air and light in the hot weather. These toilets, which were outside, were just plain privies or latrines and were hot and uncomfortable, so that I finally bumped into an idea . . . a fly will not go in or stay in a dark place.*

*I finally got the engineers in one or two camps to put some toilets with the door facing the north, away from the sun, and then an entrance which was a two-turn maze before you got into the toilet proper. There was enough light filtered in so that one could get around and do what they wished to do, but dark enough to keep the flies out, and that solved the fly business at the toilets. Thereafter, we had toilets that were fairly free of flies. They didn't breed there and then go down to the mess house, as undoubtedly they had been doing before.*

Taylor also had the mule corrals placed downwind of the mess house to keep the flies at bay.

## HEALTH CARE FOR ONE DOLLAR

The aqueduct was built before health and medical benefits or workmen's compensation were established. However, the workers were guaranteed medical care under a contributory program, which was a forerunner to health benefits as we know them today. Illnesses were not given much latitude under terms of the contract, but apparently no worker was turned away at the doctor's door.

Here is a synopsis of the contract establishing a health department with an indication of wage scales:

*The Department is supported by assessments from all aqueduct employees, including those of Contractors and Subcontractors. Assessments are $1.00 monthly from those receiving a wage of $40.00 or over per month, and 50 cents from those receiving less. Any employee is entitled to Medical, Hospital and Surgical service when needed, except for venereal disease, intemperance, vicious habits, injuries received in fights, or chronic diseases acquired before employment.*

*Hospitals are of two kinds: Field, erected by the city at suitable points, with accommodations for six patients, surgeon and nurse; and General, located in Los Angeles. The city is to provide wagon transportation for supplies from the railroad to suitable points of work, and wagon transportation for sick and injured at the worksite, to Field Hospital or railroad.*

*Meals, food, water, etc. are furnished by the city and its Contractors to the Medical Department at regular rates at the various camps. Gasoline is furnished by the city at cost, plus 10%. The city grants the use of the telephone and telegraph lines owned and controlled by it.*

*Contractors agree to furnish and equip Hospitals, provide
Physicians, Nurses and Stewards; to furnish drugs, nursing
and medical and surgical attention; to furnish board for patients
in the Field, and all the patients in the General Hospitals; to
furnish railroad transportation, where necessary, to the General
Hospital and return fare, provided patients re-enter Aqueduct
service within five days of their discharge from Hospital.*

*Contractors are empowered to make sanitary inspection and
establish quarantine, if necessary.*

## TARZAN AT THE AQUEDUCT

Dr. Taylor, incidentally, always was amused to tell people
that he hired the first Tarzan of the Apes to work for him as a
hospital steward at the aqueduct.

Taylor hired Otto Elmo Linkenheldt of Rochester, Indiana,
a six-foot, 230-pound man, to help him in the medical centers.
Linkenheldt stayed until the completion of the aqueduct and then
moved on to Hollywood, where the movie industry was
beginning its ascent.

Linkenheldt was hired by producer D. W. Griffith to play in
the silent *Tarzan of the Apes, The Romance of Tarzan and The
Adventures of Tarzan,* plus other productions. Griffith changed
Linkenheldt's name to Elmo Lincoln.

Lincoln and the doctor kept in touch over the years, but the
medic/actor couldn't make the transition to talking pictures, and
he left California. He died in 1952.

## MOJAVE WAS WIDE OPEN

The jumping-off point for workers heading for work on the
aqueduct was the then rough-and-ready town of Mojave.

Dr. Taylor recalled that about 1910, as more and more men
were employed on the upper divisions of the aqueduct, they had
to pass through Mojave to get their paychecks cashed, visit
saloons or brothels:

*It was a regular hangout for all kinds of thugs and it was a
slow night when somebody wasn't knocked over the head,*

*robbed, and thrown out in the back alley after he had been gotten good and drunk, either encouraged by the saloonkeeper or by some toughs.*

He and others who wrote about this period were critical of saloonkeepers who made a systematic effort to get the wages of employees who were quitting their jobs. Apparently it worked like this: the worker would arrive at a Mojave saloon, check in hand, anxious for a drink. He would ask to have his paycheck cashed, and the proprietor would say, "Haven't got quite that much cash, but I'll have it before train time. In the meantime, ask for whatever you want, and I'll charge you with it and deduct it from your check when I give you your money."

After this friendly gesture, the man was plied with liquor until he was so drunk he either would pass out or perhaps be hit over the head and ejected into the back alley. He would wake up penniless. If he protested to the bartender, he would be told that the bar bill had been deducted from his check and that he must have been robbed. The hapless man then would bum his way out of town or be forced to go back to work—where the cycle would start again.

Crime in Mojave reached such a peak about 1911 that the Southern Pacific Railroad police were called into town to maintain order and provide protection for the citizenry.

NEXT TIME LET'S WALK

Dr. Taylor goes on with his stories of the aqueduct which illustrated what life was like in that rugged country early in the 20th century:

*In those days, if you ran across a man walking with a bundle on his back anywhere, especially in the desert, you always picked him up and gave him a ride to the next camp, at least. Nobody ever thought of passing up a walking man if they had a seat or a place where he could hang on. I never heard of anybody getting into trouble picking up a bum of that sort. Those fellows were not vicious, and they weren't robbers. . . In those days, up on the desert, it was a matter of life and death sometimes for a man to be left walking too far. However, if he knew anything about the desert, he could generally make it to water if he stuck to the road. . . [The men] all carried a bundle of blankets over their back [thus the name blanket stiffs] and a beer bottle with a wire handle twisted around the neck, full of water; of course, exposed to the sun, it got good and hot, but it was wet.*

*I remember one time having driven up to the dredger camp above Independence which was about 12 or 15 miles north of the town. On coming back, near Black Rock Springs, which lies about 10 miles north of Independence, there's a good four or five mile stretch of plain soft sand which makes walking hard and traveling awful, I picked up a chap with a bundle. When I stopped and asked him if he wanted a ride, he said sure. In the conversation, it came out that he had never ridden in an automobile before. It took us about 20 minutes, I imagine, to make Independence. It was on the downhill end of the road, so we bowled right along. We got to the general store there where I was stopping for gasoline. He got out, threw his bundle up on the platform, looked at the car, and looked at me and said: 'There's a half day's walk gone to hell.'*

## WILLIAM MULHOLLAND

William Mulholland is still the primary figure in the dramatic story of water in Los Angeles. He built the aqueduct system that brings the city about 75 percent of its water from the eastern Sierra Nevada, and it was he who conceived of the Colorado River as another important source of water. His influence on the Department of Water and Power also was immense.

Mulholland, a self-educated man with a photographic memory, spent 50 years with the Department and its private-industry predecessor. Born in Belfast, Northern Ireland, in 1855, Mulholland came to the United States in 1874, landing in New York after working for four years as a sailor on Atlantic runs. After reading glowing accounts of California, the adventurous young man made his way to Los Angeles, then a town of 7,000 people.

In the summer of 1877, Mulholland dug artesian wells in Compton and helped to install the first water system for the village that became Long Beach. The work sparked his interest in engineering.

After an unsuccessful attempt at prospecting in Arizona, he returned to Los Angeles in the spring of 1878 and took a job as a zanjero, or ditch-tender, for the Los Angeles City Water Company. Thus began his lifelong fascination with the water supply problems of his adopted city.

Stories about Mulholland are legendary and entertaining.

THE MULHOLLAND LEGEND

His colleague, J. B. Lippincott, writing in the publication, *Civil Engineering*, in March, 1941, told this tale of Mulholland's amazing memory:

*As is frequently the case with people of fine memories, his [Mulholland's] business records were not perfect.*

*After the Board of Engineers had politely expressed the opinion that his records were not sufficient for a proper evaluation of (water company) property, Mulholland asked, 'What is it you want to know?'*

*One of the engineers told Mulholland that the Board needed a complete list showing the length of pipe, its size, character, and age. They also asked for the number of gate valves, fire hydrants and other structures connected with the water system as it spread across Los Angeles.*

*Mulholland called for a map of the city which he spread on a drafting table.*

*From memory, he then gave the size, kind and age of the pipe in every city street, including the fittings. He also designated the gate valves and hydrants.*

*The Board expressed amazement at his recall, but they still weren't satisfied because they needed a written inventory. He seemed reluctant to take the time to do this.*

*Therefore, the Board told Mulholland that the pipe should be exposed at some 200 places around the city so that they could inspect it.*

Lippincott concludes: *Mulholland was not in the least disturbed by this request; in fact, he seemed rather pleased. He had the pipe dug up at the points designated and the Board actually checked the type and condition of all pipe exposed. This inspection indicated that his memory was very accurate and the Board thereupon accepted the inventory of the pipe system of the city based on the memory of Mr. Mulholland.*

## CALL IT A CATERPILLAR

When the engineers were choosing machinery to be used at the aqueduct site, they realized that they needed the most durable, state-of-the-art equipment available to survive in the difficult terrain.

In 1909, Benjamin Holt had invented a type of traction engine which had a broad continuous track running over sprocket wheels to create a wide bearing surface and great tractive power.

The engineers, including Mulholland, asked to see the machine at a demonstration. After watching it operate, Mulholland commented, "That thing looks to me like a caterpillar crawling across the ground." Holt quickly replied, "From now on, it will be called a caterpillar"—and that's how the caterpillar tractor was born.

## GIVE HIM AN EGG AND CHARGE HIM BOARD

Another story involving Mulholland and his relations with his workers was related in *The Water Seekers* by Canadian Remi A. Nadeau (1950). It goes:

*Progress on the Jawbone [Canyon] was in full swing by the fall of 1908. A thousand men were driving more than eleven miles of tunnels while the Sierra foothills shook to the rumble of blasting powder. The brawny crew on the two-mile Red Rock Tunnel, longest in the division, set the world's record for soft-rock tunneling with the feverish advance of 1,061 feet in a single month.*

*Superintending the division was A. C. Hansen, who had come to the aqueduct from flood-control work on the lower Colorado. A tall, wiry and serious Scandinavian, Hansen believed in hard work and made himself an example for his crewmen.*

32.  Kitchen force—Mojave division camp during construction of first Los Angeles Aqueduct. (*Credit: Los Angeles Department of Water and Power.*)

Mulholland respected Hansen, but he liked to tease him. On one of his inspection trips, Hansen advised Mulholland that a miner had been cut off by a landslide in one of the excavations.

*"We have been talking to him," explained Hansen, "through a two-inch pipe driven through the muck."*

*"How long has he been in there?" Mulholland asked.*

*"Three days."*

*"Then he must be nearly starved to death."*

*"No," replied Hansen, "We've been rolling HARD-BOILED EGGS to him through the pipe."*

*The Chief [Mulholland] assessed the man's predicament in the light of this added service.*

*"Well," he asked abruptly, "have you been charging him board?"*

*It was Hansen's turn to consider the situation. "No," he answered. "Do you think I ought to?"*

A rescue party extricated the stranded miner the next day.

ROUTE OF THE AQUEDUCT

The Los Angeles Department of Public Works and its advisory committee on the aqueduct laid out this game plan for its route:

The water was to be taken from the Owens River 35 miles north of Owens Lake. It was to travel through an open canal for 60 miles to a large reservoir, the Haiwee, with a capacity of 20 million gallons. The water then would be carried another 128 miles through conduits, tunnels and siphons to a reservoir at Fairmont on the northern side of the proposed tunnel through the San Fernando Mountains. The tunnel was 26,870 feet in length, a pressure tunnel regulated by the reservoir at Fairmont.

From the southern portal of the tunnel, the water would drop from the rapidly descending San Francisquito canyon through another series of channels, tunnels, siphons and conduits for 15 miles to the San Fernando Reservoir. The total distance of the aqueduct from the intake to the reservoir would be 233 miles.

In his book, *Water and Power,* (Berkeley: University of California Press—1982), William L. Kahrl observes, however:

*It later became part of the personal legend of William Mulholland that he completed the aqueduct within the budget set for him, a remarkable achievement for any engineering enterprise of such magnitude.*

*The project Mulholland built for $24.5 million, however, lacked storage reservoirs, power plants, and a distribution system—in short, all the components of the aqueduct that would actually make it useful for the people of Los Angeles. These parts of the project had instead to be funded from other sources. And even so, Mulholland had to make further reductions in the scale of the project in order to stay within the funding available.*

Engineer J. B. Lippincott had these figures: The San Fernando Reservoir was designed to accept the aqueduct flow of 400 cubic feet per second, sufficient for a population of two million people. As a yardstick of comparison, the aggregate capacity of all the aqueducts of ancient Rome was 210 cubic feet per second.

In his booklet, *The Owens Valley and The Los Angeles Water Controversy,* Richard Coke Wood of the Pacific Center for Western Historical Studies at the University of the Pacific, Stockton, spells out in considerable detail the costs involved in building the aqueduct. Wood states:

*When the city began work on the aqueduct, there was no railroad into the valley from the south, although there was a narrow-gauge which came into the northern end of the valley from the main line of the Southern Pacific at Mina, Nevada. Consequently, they were faced with the problem of getting their equipment from the main railroad line at Mojave into the valley. They considered hauling the material by wagon, but the expense of constructing a road, maintaining equipment and caring for mule teams would be greater than the construction of a railroad. City officials approached several companies, but the Southern*

*Pacific was the only one interested in the contract. They agreed to construct a broad-gauge road into Olancha, on Owens Lake, if the city would guarantee them sufficient amount of freight to warrant the expense. The engineers estimated that there would be 14 million tons of freight shipped north of Mojave, which was a considerable inducement to the railroad.*

Bids were let, and the Southern Pacific Railroad signed a contract for construction of the road, which was completed in 1910, a little late for actual start of aqueduct construction, but time enough to ease the transportation burden.

Professor Wood goes on: *For many miles across the Mojave Desert there was no water available for use in the construction. A pipeline virtually paralleling the aqueduct was laid from the intake to San Fernando. Branch lines were laid up the canyons to camps for water supply, the total mileage of pipe laid being 260 miles at a cost of $229,000.*

*Two power plants were constructed in Owens Valley, the Cottonwood plant and the Division Creek No. 2, [these two plants have been operating since 1908 and continue to generate power for the Owens Valley today], also 218 miles of transmission lines.*

*Telephone and telegraph lines had to be laid from the main offices in Los Angeles to the intake in Owens Valley, a distance of 240 miles. For the telephone lines, two Number Two copper wire lines were erected.*

*The roads into the valley were very inadequate, many of them only trails. The Gray Ridge road into the Jawbone camps, a distance of about nine miles, cost $44,000 to construct. A total of 505 miles of roads and trails were constructed at a cost of $279,300, with maintenance totaling $33,140.*

*Fifty-seven camps had to be established with suitable housing for protection from summer heat and winter storms on the desert. The cost of housing amounted to $341,544.*

*Provisions had to be made for a vast quantity of cement needed for the lining of conduits and tunnels. For this purpose, the city bought thousands of acres of land in the Tehachapi mountains covering the necessary deposits of limestone and* *clay. A cement mill costing $550,000 was built on the Cuddeback Ranch, five miles east of Tehachapi, on the main lines of the Southern Pacific. This plant is known as the Monolith Mill, and had a capacity of one thousand barrels a day. The output of this mill for use in construction of the aqueduct was not adequate, and an additional 200,000 barrels were obtained from other sources, a total of over a million barrels of cement being used.*

In its final report, the city said it operated one cement mill and three tufa cement mills. Tufa rock is a porous limestone indigenous to the area.

One hundred thirty-five thousand acres of land had to be purchased for protection of water rights and sites for reservoirs, a difficult task which exacerbated the feelings of Owens Valley residents against Los Angeles.

And this was only the preliminary work.

Here, briefly, is the task faced by the engineers as explained by Professor Wood and others:

*The tunnels required the greatest amount of time; there were 142, which totaled 53 miles in length. Twelve miles of steel siphon, from 7 $1/2$ to $11^1/2$ feet in diameter and $1^1/8$ to $1^1/4$ inches in thickness had to be laid; 34 miles of open unlined conduit had to be laid and 39 miles of open concrete-lined conduit had to be constructed. 97 miles of covered conduit at a cost of $10,000 a mile had to be completed and three large reservoirs, Haiwee, Fairmont, and San Fernando, had to be constructed. Tinnemaha reservoir, just south of Big Pine, has been constructed in the last few years [1935]. . .*

In the first 11 months of construction, 22 miles of tunnel were driven, 16 miles of concrete conduit completed, four miles of open canal in Owens Valley dug. A rate of progress was established that would have brought the water into San Fernando Reservoir in the fall of 1912 had the project not been hit with budgetary problems.

Construction ceased for several months in 1910, reducing the work force from about 4,000 men to 1,000.

33.  Siphon construction for first Los Angeles Aqueduct.
     (Credit:  Los Angeles Department of Water and Power.)

Other crises occurred. The first head of water which was turned into the aqueduct, in May, 1913, blew out the tunnel in Sand Canyon. It had to be replaced with steel siphon. However, the grand opening finally did occur on November 5, 1913, when the gates were opened at San Fernando Reservoir.

A crowd of 30,000 was on hand to hear William Mulholland's pronouncement, probably one of the shortest speeches on record:

"There it is. Take it."

PERSPECTIVE

As we stated in the beginning, this article is not designed to take sides in the long Los Angeles—Owens Valley water disputes. However, perhaps one of the best summaries of the modern day result was contained in William Kahrl's *Water and Power*. Kahrl wrote:

*If the development of the aqueduct and the city's subsequent treatment of the Owens Valley are to be judged as bad in some sense, it is necessary to specify on what score. There is no question that the city's water officials have consistently exaggerated the need for the projects they propose, and that the local newspapers have just as consistently abetted this deception. But the only cost the taxpayers of Los Angeles have paid for their victimization has been sustained economic growth and abundant water at low prices. With respect to the Owens Valley, the city's land and water management policies certainly compare favorably with those of any state or federal agency exercising jurisdiction over a similar expanse of property. Current residents of Los Angeles may regret the congestion, the smog, and the loss of many of the region's principal natural assets that have come with the economic growth water development made possible. But these afflictions are the consequences of failures for which the Department of Water and Power cannot be blamed. Within its own sphere of authority, the department has effectively preserved and, for the city's purposes, enhanced, the productivity of the valley's water resources. And in this sense, its policies are in the best traditions of the movement for scientific conservation . . .*

BIBLIOGRAPHY

City of Los Angeles, Department of Public Works, *Complete Report on the Construction of the Aqueduct,* 1916.

Kahrl, William L., *Water and Power,* Berkeley, 1982.

Lippincott, Joseph B., "William Mulholland: Engineer, Pioneer, Raconteur", *Civil Engineering,* Vol. II, No. 3 (March 1941).

Nadeau, Remi A., *The Water Seekers,* Bishop, 1974.

Taylor, Raymond G., *Men, Medicine & Water,* Los Angeles, 1982.

Wood, Richard Coke, *The Owens Valley and the Los Angeles Water Controversy: Owens Valley As I Knew It,* Stockton, 1973.

In this discussion of the events leading to the occupation of the Alabama Gates by Owens Valley citizens in 1924, John Walton illustrates how Owens Valley resistance to Los Angeles grew from a farmers' movement into a broad-based resistance consisting of farmers, merchants and professionals.

John Walton is a Professor of Sociology at the University of California, Davis, where he is continuing his research on the social history of the Owens Valley.

"Picnic at Alabama Gates: The Owens Valley Rebellion, 1904-1927" by John Walton. *California History,* Vol 65, No. 3 (September, 1986). Reprinted by permission of the California Historical Society.

# PICNIC
# AT
# ALABAMA GATES
## The Owens Valley Rebellion
## 1904-1927

by John Walton

Early on the Sunday morning of November 16, 1924, seventy men from Bishop, California, drove south in a caravan of Model T Fords through the narrow Owens Valley and took possession of the Los Angeles Aqueduct at the Alabama Gates spillway. By midmorning a crowd of several hundred valley residents had gathered at the site five miles north of Lone Pine to watch most of the Los Angeles water supply flow out of its concrete channel into the dry bed of the Owens River. A rebellion was under way. A rebellion whose social composition and local meaning remain obscure in histories preoccupied with the morals and motives of expansionary politics in Los Angeles.

The scene at the spillway soon transformed into a celebration of civic solidarity and feisty yet good-humored resistance to the metropolitan Goliath. The county sheriff, a friend and sympathizer of the trespassers, appeared with the obligatory appeal to desist and began recording names for future summonses. The insurgents declined his request, explaining that they would occupy the gates "until we gain our point," while insisting that the sheriff "put my name down" on his list to affirm their participation.[1] When the Inyo County judge at Independence was pressed by Los Angeles officials to issue arrest warrants, he disqualified himself in the case, citing a personal interest. No arrests were made. Local law was with the rebels.

219

34. This photo was captioned: "Army of Occupation, L. A. Aqueduct" by a Bishop photographer. The caption illustrates the rebellious attitude of Owens Valley citizens leading to the occupation of the Alabama Gates. Pictured here is the empty aqueduct on the south side of the gate. *(Credit: Derrick photo, Eastern California Museum.)*

By November 18, seven hundred people gathered at the Alabama Gates during the daylight hours—all enjoying the excitement, some drawn by rumors of coming retaliation by the city ("civil war feared" said one Los Angeles newspaper). The majority demonstrated the concerned mood of the agricultural and commercial communities in the Bishop area. In that town fifty miles to the north a professionally painted billboard mounted at the principal intersection read, "If I am not on the Job you can find me at the Aqueduct." Recruits spelled each other in night-long vigils, training searchlights on the highway approach from Los Angeles and the Mojave Desert. Elderly residents today remember delivering five-gallon cans of milk and homemade cakes. On November 19 a grand barbecue was provisioned by Bishop grocers, butchers, and bakers. A rancher in adjacent Mono County cabled a friend "aboard the aqueduct" indicating that some "cattle are just north of you across the ditch. Tell Jim to collect the fat ones for your barbecue. You are welcome as long as they last." Western movie star Tom Mix, who was filming in the nearby Alabama Hills, brought his crew and a Mariachi band. The *Los Angeles Daily Times*, perhaps downplaying the crowd with an estimate of 350, observed nevertheless that "Owens Valley Ranchers Picnic as Water is Wasted," "Camp at Aqueduct is Center of Family Life—Some Women Cook for Watchers While Others Care for Tots; Girls Form Orchestra."[2]

Behind these festive scenes, however, was cold fear and a desperate political gamble. The Owens Valley rebels rationally feared for their property, income, independence, community, and their way of life—all endangered by the city's steady appropriation of land, water rights, and power to decide the valley's fate. A prescient few, such as the novelist Mary Austin, had already mourned the valley and moved on. By 1924 the growing resistance movement had lived with the aqueduct for eleven years; during the last five water shortages had become more frequent, economic insecurity had increased, and negotiations with the city had bogged down in frustration.

The seizure of the Alabama Gates marked the culminating failure of a process of political negotiation between valley representatives and the Los Angeles Department of Water and Power (DWP), which managed the aqueduct as a city public utility. At issue was the allocation of water for use in the valley. The city required that the aqueduct be kept full and allowed water to be diverted to the valley only after selected and court-ordered allotments had been met.[3] Years of negotiation and, now, open rebellion sought to reverse these terms or to arrange collective land and water rights sales with reparations for financial loss.

The occupation was carefully planned. The rebels timed their move to coincide with the visit of one of their number to a group of Los Angeles bankers who were asked to serve as mediators in the escalated struggle with the city. An engineer and former DWP employee was recruited to open the hydraulically operated spillgates and then remove all the handles and levers with which normal operation could be restored. The plan—which almost succeeded—was to create an event of such notoriety that the governor, at the request of the county sheriff and district attorney, would send the state militia to "oust" the trespassers (who were ready to be arrested for the cause), restore order, and thereby affirm the extremity of local conditions.[4] The valley story would finally be told beyond its ten-by-one-hundred-mile compass along the Eastern Sierra. State intervention, public opinion, and fair play, the rebels were persuaded, would produce a just settlement in which the city and the valley could prosper together. Indeed, California's "little Civil War" was reported in supportively picaresque tones from Los Angeles to Paris. The Inyo County district attorney personally carried his request to the governor in Sacramento, and the sheriff sent two urgent telegrams. Only Governor Friend Richardson departed from the plan. Instead of sending state troops to enter a dispute between state jurisdictions, he sent an investigator. After four full days on the small hill above the Reno-Los Angeles highway, the rebels received word from their emissary to the bankers: the bankers would use their good offices in new negotiations. On that promise, the rebels closed the Alabama Gates. Celebration of the small victory featured another picnic with 1,500 supporters, songs, moist eyes and encouraging speeches.

With the first sign of good will—a flattering nod from the powerful received self-effacingly—the rebels gave up the strongest position they would ever hold against the city. They soon paid the wages of their naive optimism. Yet since 1904 they had carried on a resistance movement distinguished by a rare degree of town-farm political solidarity and inventive forms of collective organization. They left a legacy of struggle for local and environmental rights which is still recalled, but the record of who they were, how they fought and what they wanted remains largely unexplored.

Popular theories sprang up to explain the rebellion, and, as the years passed, some found their way into authoritative accounts. Powerful groups in Los Angeles and the DWP averred that lawless elements or a radical fringe had taken charge in the troubled community. Contemporary newspapers and subsequent local and academic histories reasoned that "the ranchers" were the perpetrators since it was their water and livelihood which were at stake.[5] Cynics countered that although the rebels were landowners threatened by dispossession, their motives were speculative—to drive up the prices Los Angeles would eventually pay for their water rights. The Los Angeles Board of Public Service Commissioners patronizingly characterized the rebellion as "the mental reactions of a pioneer community . . . uninformed and unaccustomed to the ways of the outside world."[6] The truth was deeper than any of these theories: it lay beneath a social structure and pattern of civic participation which was never analyzed.

Appreciation of the society of the Owens Valley begins with the pioneer experience. From the early 1860s until the turn of the century a frontier community settled the valley, joined the U.S. Cavalry in suppressing and exiling the indigenous Paiute Indians, wrestled homesteads from the desert, and built a network of farms and commercial towns whose economy relied on supplying provisions and services to an outer ring of mining centers.[7] Agriculture thrived on the abundance of water and suitable land, although the pioneers had little knowledge of scientific farming and flooded their fields in a profligate and unsound agronomy.[8] They excelled, however, in the development of an irrigation system borrowed from the Indians. According to one local history:

*There was much swamp land around Big Pine . . . Drain ditches were finally dug which carried much of the water away. . . North of town was the Big Pine Ditch, a canal built in the eighties by ranchers along its course. During its construction, after the crops were harvested in the Fall, the men would take their horses and mules, their dredges and shovels, and spend as much time as possible working on this waterway. Most of the canals in the valley were built by donated labor. Water for this*

*ditch was taken from the river a few miles south of Bishop and*
*water gates were put in for all the ranches it crossed.* [9]

In partnership and cooperative endeavors, the settlers built an intricate system of stream-diverting canals which coursed over 110 miles and irrigated 60,000 acres by the early 1900s.[10] More than a dozen cooperatively organized "ditch companies" levied construction fees and demanded labor commitments, even-handedly allotted water to members, and governed the material conditions of agricultural production in a rustic democracy.

The canal companies operated mainly in the northern reaches of the valley where harvests were copious and diversified. Because the temperate climate, water, and soil quality diminish toward the southern end of the valley, stock ranching and orchards predominated there. The value of agricultural production increased four-fold from 1910 to 1920, led by livestock, alfalfa and hay, cereals, wool, dairy and products, grapes, honey, potatoes, and fruit. Town businesses flourished: banks, groceries, hardware stores, liveries and garages, clothing and home furnishings, builders and real estate brokers, hotels, drugstores, ice plants, and a myriad of others. Between 1900 and 1920 the total value of property assessed for county taxes rose from $1.8 million to $5.9 million.[11]

The valley prospered, but never boomed. For one thing, the separate mining centers (Kearsarge, Cerro Gordo, Tonopah and Goldfield) did boom for brief periods and then collapsed, creating wide fluctuations in demand. For another, communication with outside markets was always poor. A narrow-gauge railroad arrived from Carson City in 1883, but it was designed primarily to serve the mines, running along the eastern edge of the valley and providing very indirect service to San Francisco. Rail connections with Los Angeles via Mojave came only in 1910, when a road was built in support of the aqueduct construction. The initiative for most trips by road and twenty-mule-team wagon between the valley and the southern metropolis came from the valley end. Los Angeles enjoyed closer links to other agricultural areas and, with the availability of Owens Valley water, began developing its own San Fernando Valley.

In the late nineteenth and early twentieth centuries the valley grew slowly, ruled by the egalitarian constraints of its modest physical endowments and pioneer ethos. Social and economic differences were marked, but not extreme. Between 1900 and 1920 the Inyo County population increased from 4,337 to 7,031 and the number of farms rose from 424 to 521. A reversal in the amount of farm acreage occurred between 1900 and 1910 when the federal government withdrew lands from public use for a water project—the Los Angeles project as it turned out. In the same years, however, irrigated land increased from 41,026 to 65,163 acres. In 1920 the farms were of middling size, near the state average of 250 acres and smaller yet on the better, irrigated land around Bishop, where the average holding was 102 acres. Most (80 percent) of these farms were owner-operated, and 56 percent were mortgage-free; 70 percent had been mortgage-free in 1910.

Socially the community was far from homogeneous. The *Great Register of Inyo County* in 1894 showed that 32 percent of the 1,078 voters were foreign born, mostly from Great Britain and northern Europe (72 percent of all foreign born were in these two categories). Among the 68 percent U.S. born, however, a decided minority (just 22 percent) came from California and Nevada; the rest came from a wide selection of other states, including New York, Missouri, Illinois, Ohio, Pennsylvania, Tennessee, Maine, and Iowa. There is no particular pattern to the migration, such as a predominant flow from the economically troubled southern and border states where the Populist movement thrived. Among the registered voters, of course, certain national and ethnic categories were under-represented. The 1920 census shows that the percentage of foreign born in the county had dropped to 13 (down from 21 percent in 1910) but that Mexicans were the third largest foreign born group after Canadians and English. Indians comprised 9 percent of the population and Asians almost 2 percent. Ethnic diversity declined over these years, yet in 1920 at least one-quarter of the population still comprised the combined minority of Indian, Mexican, Asian, or non-Anglo Saxon foreign-born.

Any tendency to romanticize these frugal pioneers should be balanced with candor about their provinciality. A rare progressive and feminist such as Mary Austin learned the ways of Paiute Indian culture, but "[T]he habit Mary had of making friends with the Spanish-speaking population was frowned upon by the conservative inhabitants of Lone Pine . . . those things were just not done, and they evidently felt that she was lacking in an understanding of the proper social distinctions."[12] Valley newspapers echoed California nativism by denigrating the achievements of Asians in agriculture as the result of inferior racial standards which enforced slave labor under subhuman living conditions.

The structure of social classes was reasonably diverse. In addition to the prototypical farmers and shopkeepers, the valley included a significant number of professionals, teachers and physicians, for example, and a district working class of farm and construction laborers, teamsters, miners, packers, and so forth. The clerical and supervisorial middle sectors were well represented in the towns. Table 1 provides a longitudinal comparison of the valley's occupational structure in 1908 and 1922 drawn from the *Great Register of Inyo County*. [13] Farming, ranching, and related agricultural occupations—for example, beekeeping and "orchardist"—comprise the largest category, about 40 percent of the population in both periods. Similarly, town services (clerks, for example) and labor are important categories whose proportionate sizes remain nearly constant. The relative numbers engaged in the professions, commerce, and managerial positions, however, increased significantly in these years from 9 percent to 15 percent in these two categories combined. The number of miners declined, although they and the tradespersons still constitute about one-fifth of the working population. In the aggregate, the occupational structure is stable, with a moderate shift toward professional and commercial activities.

There were a few large landowners, bankers, and wealthy merchants. Indeed, some of the leading local families had turned agricultural prosperity into commercial preeminence. Coming to the valley in the 1880s from the Isle of Man, the Watterson family successfully took up sheep ranching. The Leece and Watterson general merchandise store was opened in the 1890s and, as a local publicist noted in 1912, "its position of leadership in the commercial life of eastern California is scarcely disputed."[14] In 1902, Wilfred and Mark Watterson founded the first local bank, which came to play the leading institutional role in the valley's development and in the resistance movement. Several other merchants also maintained farms or ranches, but the great majority were dependent for their livelihood on small businesses.

## TABLE 1
### Occupational Structure of the Owens Valley and Protest Participants in Selected Years (percent)

| Occupational Categories[a] | Valley 1908 | Petition Signers 1904 | Citizens' Committee 1905 | Valley 1922 | Petition Signers (Irrigation Dist.1922) | Activists 1922-24 & Participants in Aqueduct Seizure 1924 |
|---|---|---|---|---|---|---|
| Professional | 4 | 4 | 20 | 7 | 10 | 0 |
| Merchant, Managerial | 5 | 5 | 0 | 8 | 14 | 28 |
| Clerk, Services | 11 | 6 | 20 | 12 | 11 | 13 |
| Farm, Ranch | 41 | 80 | 60 | 39 | 48 | 38 |
| Trades, Mining | 25 | 4 | 0 | 19 | 12 | 4 |
| Labor | 14 | 1 | 0 | 15 | 5 | 2 |
| Total (%) | 100% | 100% | 100% | 100% | 100% | 100% |
| Number | 1250 | 333 | 10 | 1954 | 299 | 60 |
| Housewife | — | — | 1 | 1027[c] | 52 | 10 |
| Retired | — | — | 0 | 38 | 10 | 1 |
| Total | 1250[b] | 333 | 11 | 3019 | 361 | 71 |

Sources: Index to the *Great Register of Inyo County California,* 1908, 1922; Petition "To the Right Honorable Secretary of the Interior of the United States," 1905; McClure (1925); Petition for formation of Irrigation District, The *Inyo Register,* August 22, 1922; *Los Angeles Daily Times,* November 17—22, 1924; Interviews, Owens Valley, 1980—1984.

Notes:

(a)  Categories include, for example: professional: physician, dentist, teacher, engineer, minister; merchant and managerial: storekeeper, small business person, sales agent; clerks and services: bookkeeper, bank clerk, civil service; trades and mining: carpenter, mechanic, electrician, blacksmith, miner; labor: teamster, laborer, packer.

(b)  In 1908 women did not have the vote; their exclusion from this enumeration produces some bias in the occupational structure. The numerical total of male occupations underestimates the economically active by approximately 150 due to missing data.

(c)  The occupational distribution for 1922 is computed without self-described "house-wives." No doubt many were responsible for household production and played key roles in the agricultural economy. Some also held professional and clerical positions. With no better guide to the types of work housewives performed, it is reasonable to assume that they are distributed as the occupa-tions are generally.

35. Sheep played an important part in Inyo County's early economy. Basque and French herders trailed flocks from the Bakersfield and Lancaster areas in the spring to summer ranges in the mountains north of Bishop. A 1902 *Inyo Independent* article noted 150,000 sheep tallied that season. Here, Alfred R. Giraud leads his band up Main Street of Bishop in the winter of 1924. (*Credit: Eastern California Museum.*)

During the first two decades of this century, in the reflective words of elderly residents interviewed in the 1980s, a social elite existed in the valley: the families of the two bankers, a prosperous rancher and owner of the popular hot springs resort, a physician couple, a dentist whose party list helped define "the elite," and a half dozen other families of Bishop businesspersons. They were the burghers whose status rested less on wealth than on a combination of professional or commercial position and participation in the Methodist church, the Chamber of Commerce, and the Masonic lodge. Below, and sometimes beside, these members of the social elite were clerks, the providers of small-town services, yeomen, and persons in all manner of trades, together comprising well over half the citizenry. In sharp contrast were the ethnic and working-class communities: Mexicans (half the population of Lone Pine around 1900), Paiutes, hardrock miners, and manual laborers (the two latter categories included ethnic and Anglo-Saxon workers). In 1920 these groups still comprised one-third of the valley's population, judged from the voter rolls—and doubtless a bit more since fewer were eligible and some chose not to vote. Although there were clear social boundaries between the burghers and workers, however, they mingled with familiarity and economic differences between them were modest. How did this industriously conservative community arrive at open rebellion in a few years? Why did it revolt in 1924 rather than earlier when to some observers its fate appeared sealed? The answers to these questions reveal the character and aims of the resistance movement.

The struggle was determined in a triangular relationship between the looming growth of Los Angeles, the national Progressive movement as it articulated with the political strategy of Theodore Roosevelt's administration, and the reception of those forces by local society in the Owens Valley. The first and, to some extent, the second of these causes have preoccupied most historical interpretation and require only brief mention.

The population of Los Angeles doubled in the last decade of the nineteenth century and increased from 102,000 to 577,000 between 1900 and 1920. The growth projected by local planners in 1900 would soon outrun the exiguous water supply, and growth was the business of the city's promoters organized in the powerful Merchants and Manufacturers Association. Lacking industry or a major harbor, Los Angeles thrived on land development and, as Carey McWilliams put it, "taking in one another's laundry."[15]  As early as 1890, former Los Angeles Mayor Fred Eaton had envisioned a gravity-fed aqueduct dropping 4,000 feet and 240 miles from the Owens to the San Fernando Valley.  Eaton's aqueduct plan was realized, in part, through the intrigues of Los Angeles moguls and land developers.[16]  Only to that extent, however, does the aqueduct history resemble the conspiratorial version popularized in the motion picture *Chinatown*..  The project was no secret foisted on unknowing Angelenos.  The land syndicate enlisted a willing DWP to assume public leadership of the undertaking, and open appeals were made to southland voters in referenda and bond issues.

After the 1902 passage of the Reclamation Act, two projects for the development of the Owens River as a source of southern California water were under consideration.  The proposal to be undertaken by the Bureau of Reclamation would have combined the supply of water to Los Angeles with a reservoir in the valley; the other, to be administered by the DWP, would simply move water to the city.  The political victory of the second plan shaped everything that followed.  Much was made of the duplicity of J.B. Lippincott, who served simultaneously as chief of Southwest Operations for the Reclamation Service and as a private consultant to the city.  Effectively, however, the decision favoring the city was made in Washington by President Theodore Roosevelt with the counsel of the senior senator from California and the head of the U.S. Forest Service. Progressives all, they reasoned that the greater good was served by a project benefitting the millions in southern California rather than the tiny population of the valley.  Moreover, the Reclamation Service plan to generate electric power in the valley involved private utilities—the bugbear of Progressives—and federal authorities considered this a further justification for an all-or-none choice that ignored the possibility of protecting local interests within a project designed to serve Los Angeles.  In brief, exploitation of the Owens Valley water supply was given over to the city, and the DWP never felt the need to compromise its own advantage for the sake of mutual development—save, perhaps, in the fleeting days of the rebellion.

Prior to the announcement of the city's project (published without authorization in the *Los Angeles Times* on July 20, 1905) and Roosevelt's fateful decision on June 25, 1906, citizens of the Owens Valley had already penetrated the city's scheme by watching Lippincott's moves. The resistance began mobilizing in 1904 with a petition drive in support of the Reclamation Service project. Concern mounted over the continuing appearance of city agents conducting surveys and placing options on land and water rights in the valley. In the late summer of 1905, after the Los Angeles announcement, an emergency was afoot.

A meeting in Bishop on August 1, was "attended by a large and enthusiastic assemblage" which determined to appoint a Citizen's Committee to plead their case in Washington.[17] On August 4, Stafford W. Austin, Mary's husband and the Register of the U. S. Land Office in the valley, wrote to President Roosevelt "to protest against the proposed abandonment of the Owens River project by the Reclamation Service. . . (and to expose) the whole outrageous scheme. . . to betray the Government by turning this important project over to the city of Los Angeles."[18] Inyo County District Attorney William Dehy suggested in a letter to President Roosevelt that the aims of the valley were close to "the policy of the administration to do its utmost toward enabling the plain everyday American citizen to provide a home for himself and his family. . . for the peopling of the valleys and the conversions of the deserts into well watered valleys rather than for the overcrowding of the large cities."[19] Mary Austin published an elegant essay in the *San Francisco Chronicle* defining the question as "how far it is well to destroy the agricultural interests of the commonwealth to the advantage of the vast aggregations of cities."[20] But the people spoke more vividly to the president through a farm woman from Poleta.

*There never has been any capitolist or rich people come here until lately and all the farms of the Owens Valley show the hard labor and toil of people who came here with out much more than their clothes. . . [S]ome rich men got the government or "Uncle Sam" to hire a man named J. B. Lippancott to represent to the people that he was going to put in a large damn in what is known as Long Valley . . . But—Lo! and Behold! Imagine the shock the people felt when they learned when Uncle Sam was paying Mr. Lippancott he was a traitor to the people and was working for a millionare company. . . Now as the President of the U.S. do you think that is right?. . . Is there no way to keep the capitolist from forcing people to give up their water right and*

36. A December 1913 skating party on the newly completed Los Angeles Aqueduct (near Manzanar). (*Credit: Eastern California Museum.*)

*letting the now beautiful alfalfa fields dry up and return to a barren desert waist? Is there no way to stop this thievering? As you have proven to be the president for the people and not the rich I, an old resident, who was raised here, appeal to you for help and Advice. My husband and I with in the last year have bought us a home and are paying for it in hard labor and economy. So I can tell you it will be hard to have those rich men say "stay there and starve" or "Go." Where if we keep the water in the valley it won't be any 3 years until the place will pay for its self. So Help The People of Owens Valley! Yours Unto Eternity, Lesta V. Parker.*[21]

These early protests went virtually unnoticed outside the valley. The November 1904 petition "To the Right Honorable Secretary of the Interior of the United States" signed by 380 citizens controlling 104,242 acres (some signers owned additional town lots which brought the average landholding to 301 acres) and urging continuation of the Reclamation Service project[22] drew no response. Although Lesta Parker was "advised" by an acting Secretary of the Interior "that the matter will be carefully considered by this Department" the decision which issued from the president's inner council proved that the citizens "lost without ever having had the opportunity to have their representative present."[23]

The 1904-1905 protest movement was largely agrarian. The issues revolved around security of land and water rights, the alternative advantages of an agriculturally oriented Reclamation Service project, and the western populist ideology inspired by the Roosevelt administration. Convincing evidence for this claim comes from analysis of the occupations and economic circumstances of the 1904 petition signers. These were uncovered by matching names on the petition to the *Great Register* of voters and the *Inyo County Assessment Roll*. Among 380 petition signers, 333 reported their occupations, and of this number fully 80 percent designated themselves as "farmer," "rancher," "stockman," and so forth. The remainder included small numbers of town professionals, merchants, clerks, and tradespersons. The small Citizens' Committee that led the resistance at this time had a similar social profile. That the protestors did not represent the whole population of the valley is indicated by comparison with the occupational data in Table 1. Among the 1904 petitioners, for example, agriculturalists comprise twice their relative proportion of the working population, while the trades and labor are only about one-eighth their number. With respect to social standing, none of the local elite was among the Citizens' Committee leadership. The narrow social base of the early protest movement may have contributed to its failure to draw a response from Washington. At this stage influential town business persons did not energetically support what was still a farmers' movement.

The valley protestors did not resign themselves to defeat when the aqueduct construction began in 1908, nor at the opening in 1913. By contrast to 1904-1905, however, a period of quiescence set in during which hope was widespread in the valley that mutual benefit might come with the aqueduct. Negotiations proceeded between the city of Los Angeles and successive local representative bodies, including the Owens Valley Water Protective Association—each of them representing agrarian interests and comprised predominantly of farmers and ranchers. The issue was always the extent to which the valley might share in the city's wealth: would the city build a storage reservoir from which valley irrigation water could be drawn in amounts consistent with continuing local growth?; would the city guarantee continued irrigation of the present 60,000 acres or some lesser, but assured, amount such as 30,000?; would the city deal with popularly chosen associations, rather than individual property owners?

Intricate maneuvers surrounded each point, but it suffices that valley representatives won no tangible concessions in the years leading up to 1920. Indeed, not everyone in the valley supported these negotiations. Town businesses considered themselves unaffected and an incipient faction of property owners believed their interest lay with the city, although they had no occasion to choose sides. While the city joined in desultory negotiations, it reaped benefits from the new water supply that only a philanthropist would bargain away. In the southland, speculative land development thrived, and irrigated acreage in the San Fernando Valley increased from 10,000 acres in 1915 to 75,000 in 1918.[24]

Decisive troubles and a second stage of resistance movement began in the summer of 1919. The worst drought in decades had begun. Los Angeles sank new artesian wells to fccd the aqueduct (dropping everyone's water table) and husbanded its storage reserves. In a seldom noted precursor to the Alabama Gates, on June 11, "Citizens [Took] Action to Save Their Crops. . . A delegation of probably fifty men went to Hillside Reservoir. . . and raised the gate enough to permit the flow of 2500 inches of additional water into Bishop Creek."[25] Editorial opinion discovered a new purpose in the unrest: "The interests of every person, *business or profession* are those of the farmers. The sympathy of the community is solidly with the farmers," asserted the *Inyo Register*.[26] The connection between water shortage, city control, a decline in local production, and the commercial prosperity of the towns forcibly entered the public consciousness. This was a turning point.

With the worsening drought and controversy over ground water, both sides steeled themselves for a struggle. The city, now appreciating its vulnerability to local risings and inevitable dry years, began wholesale purchases of land, water rights, and ditch companies. Buyouts soared from a half dozen per year to 104 in 1923 and about 250 in 1924. Residents alleged a "checkerboarding" pattern to the purchases which left working farms and canal sections cut off by city-owned abandoned plots that quickly returned to desert sage.

As city and valley interests became polarized, a fissure opened in local society. On the surface it appeared to divide stalwarts and sellers; those who chose a fight to "save the valley" and those who welcomed the opportunity to sell out at the generally attractive prices the city was willing to pay for secure water rights. As the struggle intensified, the large majority in the first group referred to the second as "traitors."

The split was more complicated. It involved, first, a division mainly among land-owning agriculturalists. One list for the Bishop vicinity of ninety-four persons or families who sold to the city between early 1923 and mid-December, 1924, shows that they were overwhelmingly farmers with average sized holdings.[27] Second, family and social antipathies helped precipitate the split, or at least to divide the leaders of the seller faction from the majority community. George Watterson, uncle to the banker brothers, participated in the pro-city faction largely, it seems, because of conflicts over family business interests which his elder nephew Wilfred dominated. George married the sister of a large land-owner named William Symons and together they pledged their lands to uses favoring the city. Their attorney was L. C. Hall, reportedly the spurned suitor of

37. Water draining down the spillway at the Alabama Gates during the November 16, 1924, occupation. (Credit: Ramsey photo, Eastern California Museum.)

one of the Watterson sisters. These men and their families, moreover, were outsiders to the social elite which was probably a source of resentment all round. Third, some unfairly labeled "traitors" had pressed for alternative solutions with the city, particularly a storage reservoir with guaranteed drawing rights for local farmers; they sold out only when that hope collapsed. Finally, some of the dissenters stood purely for the independent right to use or dispose of their property as they saw fit. Some of the majority tried to intimidate potential sellers by issuing vague threats and conducting latenight meetings with hooded men (hence the erroneous impression that the Ku Klux Klan operated in the valley),[28] and this latter group may have felt strongly about resisting such tactics. In sum, the seller faction was small (fewer than the ninety-four seller families listed in December 1924 since many of them had sold involuntarly), and its speculative interests should not be underestimated; some profited remarkably by selling. But neither did pecuniary motives fully explain the social division.

Despite the adverse conditions, the valley's best hour of mobilization came with the creation of an irrigation district based on an innovative application of state law. The idea was to unite all property owners and canal companies in a single association which would bargain exclusively with the DWP, the city, or any mediator. The Farm Bureau's annual picnic of 1922 at Keough's Hot Springs featured speeches on "the movement in this county" and Wilfred Watterson's plea for the irrigation district as "protection against encroachment by Los Angeles".[29] Experts were brought from the San Joaquin Valley to discuss details with "a large and representative audience" at the high school auditorium.[30] The novelty—and the organizational genius—behind the plan was the proposal that the district would include the owners of *town* lots and their water rights along with the farmers and ranchers.

In the spring of 1922 a petition began circulating that would mandate a referendum on creating the irrigation district. After an inadvertent misfiling in late May, the petition with 430 signatures was delivered to the county clerk on August 17 and published in the *Inyo Register* the same day. Since the proposed irrigation district would provide a legal and organizational vehicle for confronting the city, the petition itself provides one of the best, and certainly the largest, sample of supporters of the resistance. It also allows comparison with the

1904 petition and the social bases of the resistance in its two stages. Table 1 demonstrates some striking facts.[31] Farmers and ranchers are still the largest category of supporters, but they are represented in a proportion much closer to their numbers in the population (48 percent of the signers and 39 percent of the labor force). Professionals, merchants, and managers are even more heavily represented in the same sense, just as the trades, mining, and labor are underrepresented. The social composition of the resistance has shifted, and shifted in ways that are not explained by changes in the economy alone. For example, from 1904 to 1922 the percentage of persons in the combined categories of professional and merchant-managerial valleywide almost doubled (9 percent to 15 percent), but the number supporting the resistance nearly tripled (9 percent to 24 percent). Agriculturalists came closer to their proportionate share and the working class, although still more numerous in the population than in the resistance movement, had substantially increased its participation in the latter. In a word, the farmers' movement of 1904 had become a coalition of all social classes in 1922.

Heeding the *Inyo Register's* appeal that "The irrigation district, and apparently no other power, can put an end to this period of destructiveness which the city will inaugurate unless checked,"[32] citizens voted in January 1923 for the district itself and in August to authorize it to issue bonds; the respective votes were 599 to 27 and 702 to 80. The dissenting vote probably came from the pro-Los Angeles faction and provides the best estimate of how small the minority was.

By August 1923 town and farm interests were united as never before behind a strategy which demanded that the city either guarantee agricultural production and commercial life or accept mediated negotiations on business indemnities and purchase of all offered land and water rights in a collective agreement. Although the latter provision is sometimes interpreted as an intention to speculate in one large land sale,[33] other evidence supports the idea that the resistance movement was using unity—its strongest card—to force a settlement that would preserve private ownership and the community. When they could look beyond daily strife, spokespersons invariably repeated the hope that they might prosper along with the city.

As the resolve of both sides stiffened, the shoots of desperation appeared. Continuing city purchases fostered fear among stalwarts and intimidation of sellers; neighbors were bitterly divided, and some were uncertain whether to accept or cultivate an attractive offer. Litigation over water rights and pumping increased as the resistance sought a needed ally in the courts. Perennial negotiations were stalled with citizens emboldened by their demonstrated organizational unity and the city unwilling to announce a definitive policy. The economy and town life were suspended on a wire of doubt: investment was withheld, lending stopped, real estate trading stagnated save for the city's bidding, farm production dropped precipitously, schools began to close,[34] and doleful encounters on the street dwelled only on "which way is it going?" Then the bombs started exploding.

The dynamite blast that tore a hole in the aqueduct at the Alabama Gates on May 21, 1924 signaled open revolt. The valley's best organizational strategies had won no ameliorating results. On the contrary, the indecisive standoff made conditions worse. By June it is likely that the plan to seize the Alabama Gates was being hatched. The city had introduced dynamite and strongarm methods to break irrigation ditches and recover aqueduct water. According to statements sworn before a subsequent investigation, "In the summer of 1923 representatives of the city of Los Angeles dynamited the dam at Convict Lake . . . in order to get more water for their impoverished aqueduct . . . Other deeds of similar kind were resorted to by the city's agents, so it was the city of Los Angeles, and not the people here, who first used dynamite in this water controversy."[35] Beside this claim, it was also widely known in the resistance movement that one Major Watson, a colleague from Big Pine with military experience, was the uncelebrated hero of the May 21 sabotage. By fall, no new negotiating moves were seen or imagined. Something was up, as revealed in retrospective interview reports that late-night meetings at the Wattersons' were frequent that summer. When the rebels occupied the Alabama Gates, it was clear that they were the redoubtable citizens who had carried the resistance movement through so many years of legal and political struggle—neither outlaws nor yokels.

Analysis of social participation in the aqueduct occupation of November 1924 presents a special problem because there were no arrests and there is no other documentation. Although the sheriff issued summonses to the trespassers, no record of recipients survives, and the sympathetic county law enforcement agencies never attempted to punish the rebels. Accordingly, two methods were used to develop a list of participants. First, from local newspaper files and archival documents, a list of "activists" was constructed comprising people and members of sundry ad hoc committees who either sponsored mobilizing events or signed letters of protest to the city and federal government. Second, those who actually took over the aqueduct were identified in two ways. Los Angeles newspapers sent reporters to the Alabama Gates who filed stories identifying people whom they interviewed. Subsequent published narratives name some of the same people, although the number is small in both cases. The event was also photographed by the Los Angeles newspapers and local enthusiasts who caught representative crowd scenes. Enlarged copies of some of these photographs enabled elderly persons interviewed in the early 1980s to identify parents, relatives, and community figures. In this fashion it was possible to recover the names, occupations, and economic circumstances of seventy-one persons active in the events of 1924. By virtue of their identification by eye witnesses or their public record of active involvement, it is reasonable to assume that these people were among the seventy men who first seized the Alabama Gates, and certainly among the several hundred who gathered in support during the first day.

The results of this analysis complement the larger sample of irrigation district supporters from two years earlier (Table 1). Now agriculturalists are present in numbers (38 percent) virtually identical to their representation in the valleywide occupational structure. The trades and labor are rare. The difference is made up by the heavy participation of town professionals and merchants (a combined 43 percent) and clerical and service personnel. By the manner of their identification, we may assume that these people were the active leaders of the resistance. That is, they left a record of spearheading committees and letter-writing campaigns (activists) and were sought out by reporters at the aqueduct or remembered in photographs sixty years later (participants). Accordingly, this last sample is best compared with the small 1905 Citizens' Committee. When that is done, the results parallel the interpretation derived from the comparison of 1904 and 1922 petition signers: what began as a farmers' movement broadened into a coalition of town and agricultural interests in which

38. A 1916 rally in Bishop in support of prohibition. Citizens of the Owens Valley were sober but active participants in the politics of their day. (*Credit: Eastern California Museum.*)

merchants and professionals played key leadership roles. In short, the 1924 rebels formed a class alliance based on a new understanding that continued exploitation of the valley would ruin both agricultural production and town commerce.

The vast majority (85-90 percent) of irrigation district supporters and of activists and participants in the 1924 insurgency came from Bishop and its immediate environs. These districts were agriculturally and commercially more prosperous than the rest of the valley. A socio-economic profile of the activists and participants shows that their land-holdings were above valleywide averages in acreage and assessed valuation. For example, they owned property assessed at an average of $9,053 by contrast to the valley mean of $5,280 and Bishop's $5,868. Among those who owned land, the mean holding was 228 acres compared to the averages of 119 acres valleywide and 102 acres in the Bishop area. The larger sample of irrigation district supporters resembles very closely the averages for the Bishop area. These data, particularly in combination with the material on occupations, firmly support the proposition that the resistance movement represented the more prosperous farm and town groups in the irrigated areas of the valley, united and led by a bucolic bourgeoisie.

Three essential characteristics of the protest movement summarize this analysis. *First*, the resistance began in 1904 primarily as an agrarian movement. Four-fifths of the petition signers were agriculturalists by occupation, twice the valleywide proportion. *Second*, around 1919 the movement began to broaden its base dramaticaly to include professionals, merchants, and those in service occupations. In 1924 agricultural occupations represented less than half the insurgents, while middle class townspeople contributed an equal or greater number, particularly to the leadership. Only a small part of the shift is attributable to structural change, such as the labor force composition, in this short period. (Small differences favoring town occupations in 1922, moreover, are partly due to the inclusion of newly enfranchised women voters, some of whom were employed in town professions and services.) *Third*, by 1924 the movement had consolidated a distinctive alliance of middle-class townfolk and medium-sized agriculturalists.

The question returns: why were these classes rebelling? Undeniably, they were trying to protect their property or, later, salvage some of its value. The social bases of participants and nonparticipants suggest they acted on class interest. The rebels were medium-sized agriculturalists and the employees and owners of town businesses whose livelihoods were being destroyed by the city invasion. The same forces did not directly threaten the working class miners and laborers (some of whom found jobs with city agencies). Valley agriculture had never employed a large and steady labor force that might have made common cause with the typical owner-operator. The allied class base of the movement is reliably defined and clearly motivated by material interest.

Yet interpretation only in terms of class captures but a segment of the action and meaning. The struggle, in the first place, was a regional one between rural and urban interests. In that sense it was an intra-class struggle between urban developers, businesspersons, and their public servants in Los Angeles and small town agribusiness and services in the valley—the Bishop Chamber of Commerce badly mismatched with the Merchants and Manufacturers Association. From the standpoint of Owens Valley citizens, moreover, it was a fight to preserve their community and way of life.

Second, it was a struggle prompted by a reorganization of the state. The Roosevelt administration began the century with new aims "to elevate the executive as the dominant force in national government and to make the government the most important single influence in national affairs."[36] Roosevelt sought to incorporate a western constituency through the Reclamation Act and to attract urban reformers, especially in the eastern machine-cities, with such appeals as the development of public utilities. In 1906 he cited progressive tenets when he decided in favor of the DWP exploitation of Owens Valley water rather than the Reclamation Service project. Yet, as "an avid aggrandizer, the president understood and encouraged those aggrandizing executive officials who sought to construct small empires out of the growing demand for public management."[37]

Both sides of the Owens Valley battle built their aims and strategies on the presumption of state involvement. The Los Angeles Merchants and Manufacturers Association rallied to Progressivism and the brand of "good government" that ensured economic growth through the powerful DWP. Yet the protestors also called on progressive ideology to legitimate their struggle against a new species of monopoly and to support their ambitions to enhance properties and businesses on the rising tide of Los Angeles prosperity. They wanted economic growth, ideally within the city's ambit and regional market. A 1912 publication by the *Inyo Register* noted, "Bishop's people are alive to the importance of progressive things. . . This is a modern up-to-date community, with improvement as its object, and steady growth as a consequent certainty."[38] When they were denied a modest share by the uncompromising city-builders, the middle-class rebels used the state apparatus, the irrigation district and courts, in their defense. Ironically, their last act of protest was a dramatic appeal to put the case before the governor and a broader court of public opinion. To the extent that they ever had a chance to coexist with the city, their Progressive faith was their downfall.

Following the rebellion more negotiation sputtered and there was talk of reparations, but the city soon showed its intention to buy out the entire valley. DWP land purchases jumped again from approximately 240 in 1925 to 450 during the following year. Aqueduct bombings rose even faster as a sign of desperation and anger. In 1927 the local bank which had led and financed the resistance movement failed. The Watterson brothers misused depositor funds in an effort to keep the resistance alive. Their conviction on charges of embezzlement was an effect rather than a cause of the movement's collapse in the face of city determination to make no exception for individuals or the irrigation district in the fight for control of the valley. The resistance was simply worn down. Between 1920 and 1930, Bishop's population dropped from 1,304 to 850, the number of farms fell from 521 to 218, and the annual value of agricultural production slumped from over four million dollars to less than one. The valley of redolent alfalfa and community picnics died, although a few towns lived on as a redoubt for Los Angeles vacationers and an outpost of public agencies that manage the metropolitan hinterland.

Understood from below, the historical fight between Los Angeles and the Owens Valley evolved from a tradition of agrarian democracy to a militant town-farm class alliance animated by local culture. Citizens, far from "unaccustomed to the ways of the outside world," imaginatively developed their struggle for community survival in tandem with the changing incursions of the metropolitan economy and the means of protest

39. Owens Valley communities have always exhibited a great deal of civic pride. Pictured here is the Independence Silver Cornet Band, with mascot "Little Johnny Maroney".
(Credit: Eastern California Museum.)

available in the state. Over-matched and without the state support bestowed on Los Angeles, the valley rebels were finally defeated. Yet they did not go down gently. Their struggle was bolder and more resourceful than others in rural societies confronted by a centralizing urban world.

*This article is based on a study supported by a Faculty Research Grant from the University of California, Davis. For providing access to public records and granting me other assistance, I am grateful to Charles N. Irwin (former director of the Eastern California Museum), Bill Michael (director of the Eastern California Museum), Jane Fisher (Chalfant Press), Richard Crawford (Librarian, National Archives), Ann Crilly (Inyo County Free Library), Alice Boothe (Laws Museum), Mary Gorman, Enid Larson, Elma Crosby, and Gus Cashbaugh. I received helpful comments on an earlier version of this article from William Friedland, Gary Hamilton, William Kahrl, Norbert Wiley, and the editors of California History Magazine. Mainly, I am indebted to a great many residents of the Owens Valley who generously provided me with their time, memories, cooperation, and concern in this effort to recover part of their history.*

## NOTES

Interviews with Owens Valley residents have not been individually cited but are the source of much of my information on events and moods within the valley. In total, I conducted approximately fifty interviews over a period of four years.

1. Remi A. Nadeau, *The Water Seekers* (Santa Barbara: Peregrine Smith, 1974), p. 70.
2. *Los Angeles Daily Times*, November 20, 1924.
3. William L. Kahrl, *Water and Power: The Conflict Over Los Angeles' Water Supply in the Owens Valley* (Berkeley: University of California Press, 1982).
4. Nadeau, p. 77.
5. This claim appears in all of the histories including the recent and best by Kahrl, *op. cit.,* and Abraham Hoffman, *Vision or Villainry: Origins of the Owens Valley—Los Angeles Water Controversy* (College Station: Texas A & M Press, 1981).
6. Quoted in Kahrl, p. 298.
7. W. A. Chalfant, *The Story of Inyo*, Revised Edition (Bishop, CA: Chalfant Press, 1933).
8. Kahrl, p. 51.

9.  *Saga of Inyo County*,  Published by the Southern Inyo American Association of Retired Persons (Covina, CA: Taylor Publishing, 1977), p. 97.

10. Ruth E. Baugh, "Land Use in the Bishop Area of Owens Valley, California," *Economic Geography*, Vol. 13 (1937), pp. 17-43; W. F. McClure, *Owens Valley-Los Angeles Controversy*, Letter of Transmittal and Report to Governor Friend Wm. Richardson (Sacramento: California State Printing Office, 1925); Kahrl.

11. *Inyo County Assessment Roll*, 1900, 1920. Eastern California Museum, Independence, California.

12. Helen McKnight Doyle, *Mary Austin: Woman of Genius* (New York: Gotham House, 1939), pp. 164 and 195.

13. Voter registration data must be used here since the U.S. Census did not report occupational breakdowns for small rural counties. The particular (election) years selected are the closest to other years important in this narrative for which evidence (i.e. surviving copies of the *Great Register)* is available.

14. *Inyo County Anno Domini* (Bishop, CA: The Inyo Register, 1912), p. 24.

15. Carey McWilliams, *Southern California Country: An Island on the Land* (New York: Duell, Sloan and Pearce, 1946).

16. William L. Kahrl, "The Politics of California Water: Owens Valley and the Los Angeles Aqueduct, 1900-1927," Part I, *California Historical Quarterly*, Volume 55, Number 2 (1976), p. 11.

17. *Inyo Register*, August 11, 1905.

18. S. W. Austin, Letter to Theodore Roosevelt, August 5, 1905 (Record Group 115, Owens Valley Project 527, Department of Interior, National Archives, Washington, D.C.).

19. William D. Dehy, Letter to Theodore Roosevelt, August 18, 1905 (Record Group 115, Owens Valley Project 527, Department of Interior, National Archives, Washington, D.C.).

20. *San Francisco Chronicle*, September 3, 1905.

21. Lesta V. Parker, Letter to Theodore Roosevelt, August 15, 1905 (Record Group 115, Owens Valley Project 527, Department of Interior, National Archives, Washington, D.C.). Irregular spellings are contained in the original.

22. *To the Right Honorable Secretary of the Interior of the United States*, no date (Record Group 115, Owens Valley Project 527, Department of Interior, National Archives, Washington, D.C.). Some confusion surrounds the exact date and contents of this petition. I found only one document fitting its description in the National Archives. Kahrl, 1982, pp. 54 and 465, describes a petition dated November 1904 signed by "more than 400 individuals owning a total of 102,433 acres." Hoffman, p. 61, describes a petition from "several hundred

Owens Valley residents . . . received November 30, 1904." The document I found in the same record group they cite has no date and is signed by 380 persons holding 104,242 acres. It appears that we are referring to the same petition. In any case, the 380 signatories analyzed here most certainly represent the emergent resistance movement.

23. Kahrl, 1982, p. 142.
24. William L. Kahrl, "The Politics of California Water: Owens Valley and the Los Angeles Aqueduct, 1900-1927," Part II, *California Historical Quarterly*, Volume 55, Number 2 (1976), pp. 98-120.
25. *Inyo Register*, June 12, 1919. Italics added.
26. *Ibid.*, June 19, 1919.
27. McClure, p. 14.
28. No evidence of Klan organization in the Owens Valley has ever been produced. The allegation originated in Los Angeles newspapers hostile to the aqueduct occupation. Several historians subsequently repeated the claim without documentation. Nadeau, for example, simply asserts, "During the summer of 1923, while a revival of the Ku Klux Klan was raging throughout the nation, an organizer was brought into Owens Valley to help form its own band of Klansmen. An inner group of this faction took as its main purpose an underground opposition to the Los Angeles water board and its agents" (p. 63). The account is anecdotal and raises puzzling questions such as who was involved, how a radical faction could appear in the demonstrably unified opposition movement, what interest any valley residents might have in the Klan, and why such an organization, if it did exist, would want to oppose Los Angeles. Hoffman (p. 181) merely repeats the claim, citing Nadeau. According to Kahrl (p. 293), however, "The Los Angeles papers at first denounced the Wattersons as mobsters and printed false stories linking them with the Ku Klux Klan which even their own correspondents denounced." There is, of course, no way to disprove the existence of the Klan or of Martians in the resistance movement. Conversely, there is no reason to accept such claims without evidence and plausible argument. We do know that hooded men intimidated potential sellers in the small minority partial to Los Angeles (the ritual may have come from the Masonic Lodge, some of whose members were active in the resistance). One elderly person interviewed described such an encounter to me, but interpreted it as plain harassment with no Klan overtones. In lieu of any evidence, it is reasonable to suppose that Klan activity is a myth generated by sensationalist and slanted reporting of different known events and perpetuated by uncritical repetition.
29. *Inyo Register*, June 8, 1922.
30. *Ibid.*, April 26, 1923.

31. The figure of approximately 430 signers is reduced in the table owing to some duplicated names on the petition and many names that are not found on the voter registration rolls.
32. *Inyo Register*, May 25, 1922.
33. Especially in Nadeau, and sometimes in Hoffman.
34. McClure, Baugh.
35. McClure, p. 22.
36. Robert H. Wiebe, *The Search for Order, 1877-1920* (New York: Hill and Wang, 1967), p. 190.
37. *Ibid.*, pp. 190-191.
38. *Inyo County Anno Domini*, p. 22.